'Fourteen bouquets from the garden of real life, these pungent testimonies convey the unmistakable scents of authenticity'

Quentin Crisp

WALKING AFTER MIDNIGHT

Project Co-ordinators: Margot Farnham
and Paul Marshall

The group:
Glen Evans
William Pierce
Paul Marshall
Margot Farnham

Photographs:
Sunil Gupta
William Pierce

WALKING AFTER MIDNIGHT

Gay Men's Life Stories

HALL CARPENTER ARCHIVES
GAY MEN'S ORAL HISTORY GROUP

ROUTLEDGE
London and New York

First published 1989 by Routledge
11 New Fetter Lane, London EC4P 4EE
29 West 35th Street, New York, NY 10001

© 1989 Hall Carpenter Archives

Filmset by Mayhew Typesetting, Bristol, England
Printed and bound in Great Britain by
Biddles Ltd, Guildford and King's Lynn

British Library Cataloguing in Publication Data

Walking after midnight: gay men's life stories.
1. Male homosexuals. Biographies. Collections
I. Hall carpenter archives, Gay men's oral history
group
II. Farnham, Margot III. Marshall, Paul
306.7′660922

Library of Congress Cataloging in Publication Data

Walking after midnight : gay men's life stories / Hall Carpenter
Archives gay men's oral history group.
p.   cm.
1. Gay men – Great Britain – Biography.   I. Hall-Carpenter
Archives.   II. Title: Gay men's oral history group.
HQ75.7.W35 1989
306.7′662′0922–dc19   89–6020 CIP
ISBN 0-415-02956-2
ISBN 0-415-02957-0 (pbk.)

To all the men who told their stories
and in memory of Julian Salmon

CONTENTS

CONTENTS

NOTE ON THE TITLE

The title for this book, *Walking After Midnight*, refers to John Alcock's interview. He was involved in the campaign which led to the passing of the Sexual Offences Act of 1967, which decriminalized male homosexual activities in private for adults over twenty-one:

It was two in the morning, and I came out of the House of Commons with Antony Grey and all the crowd and we all said goodnight to one another. I walked down to the Embankment and I stood and lit a cigarette and was looking down at the water and I was very aware that I'd been part of making history. Part of something that people will be very glad about.

PREFACE

The life stories presented in this book come from interviews made by the Gay Men's Oral History Group and myself as part of our archival oral history project.

The Hall Carpenter Archives itself was formed in 1982, inspired by the success of similar North American collections, and became a registered charity a year later. The archives contain a huge collection of press clippings, periodicals, books, the published materials of lesbian and gay groups and ephemera.

The GLC provided funding for me to set up and co-ordinate an Oral History Project in 1985. Very soon two groups of volunteers formed to create a collection of tape-recorded life stories and memories. Because the sources for a lesbian and gay history have largely been the writings of experts, writers and stars, we focused on the spoken words of a cross-range of 'ordinary' – how we've grown to hate that word – lesbians and gay men. We wanted to emphasize the life stories of those of us who had been most marginalized within the historical accounts so far. We wanted to make sure that the foundations for a growing oral history archive contained a diverse range of voices and lives.

In all, the two groups interviewed over sixty people. With those interviews we created a large photographic and life story exhibition, two tape–slide shows and now two anthologies, this one from a gay men's group. We evolved our approach to oral history as a consequence of working on practical projects which forced us to engage with the realities of research and interpretation. As the co-ordinator of both groups, some of my work was with the gay men's group. I wanted to use my time as a paid worker to assist the group in whatever way they found helpful and I remained involved with the group for three years. During that time I learned a lot about a history of which I had known little.

In 1987 the London Boroughs Grant Unit cut all funding to the archives and we are still struggling to find a home for the collection. But what a unique couple of years we had. We aim to continue developing our oral history work and to uncover more and more stories, taking our part in releasing this wonderful clamour of the past.

Margot Farnham

ACKNOWLEDGEMENTS

Thanks to: Dee Bourne; London History Workshop Sound and Video Archives; Jeffrey Weeks; Hall Carpenter Archives Management Committee; Imperial War Museum; Will Todd; Sjors Van Vulpen; and Liz Fidlon.

INTRODUCTION

This book is a beginning of a search for our past as gay men. We wanted to explore the meaning of being a gay man, if and how it has changed over a period of decades, what it is that we share and also what our differences may be, and to question the extent to which 'being gay' affects and interacts with other social factors. Above all, we wanted to discover our history by having gay men tell their life stories in their own words.

Oral history, which is found in memory and not in documents, can uncover much which is hidden, neglected or dismissed by the traditional focus of history. By recording the personal and political events which have shaped the lives of the majority of people whose experiences are not normally recorded by 'official' history, we become the active participants of our own history and can have more control over its interpretation. A richer, more intimate picture of the past can be revealed, not only for ourselves, but to share with others.

Oral history is not new. Its practice today began by investigating the histories of working-class men's and women's lives, and of their communities. Such community-based oral history inevitably concentrates on the social relations of the family and the workplace. Sexuality, when it is explored within this context, remains almost exclusively heterosexual. Gay men and lesbians, of course, have families and are part of the community, but because our sexuality is other than heterosexual, our particular histories and those of any perceived gay community have been, for the most part, excluded.

Gay sexuality is continually measured against heterosexuality and it is that deep-rooted sense of 'difference' which we experience and have to try to make sense of in our lives. It is a reality which

1

is always with us and we each take different paths, negotiate our lives in different ways and experience different struggles in coming to terms with our own perceptions of ourselves and the way in which others perceive us. Our history reflects this diversity and complexity.

This book contains the oral histories of fourteen gay men. Their stories span the last seventy years and they are wide-ranging accounts, covering home and family life, parents' backgrounds, education and work, memories of friends and lovers, being gay in different countries and different cultures, sexual experience and desire. The men speak of being gay in the twenties and thirties and of historical events such as the Second World War; of the language used, books read, and the pubs and clubs where gay men met; of the fifties and the years leading up to the passing of the Sexual Offences Act of 1967; of the advent of the gay liberation movement and the gay commercial scene; of the impact of AIDS and the fight against the growing anti-gay backlash.

We interviewed many more gay men than those who tell their stories here. Wanting to present as great a cross-section as possible, however, we made our choices for the book on the basis of diversity in terms of age, class and cultural background. Those who shared their past with us did so with honesty and enthusiasm, recalling painful memories as well as happier ones, and often revealing incidents and feelings which had lain hidden for years.

The interviews were structured chronologically, usually based on an outline supplied by the speaker. They were long, some three or four hours, and when transcribed they ran to as many as 200 pages. We had the sad and somewhat daunting task of editing them down to some sixteen pages or so. We then had another difficult task of selection, of what to leave in and what to exclude, without losing the personality of the speaker. This was done in full consultation with the story-teller.

We did not want the book to be a series of case studies of gay men, nor did we want to make sociological comments; this has been done elsewhere. The men talk for themselves about themselves. Obviously, shared experiences and common themes emerge but we felt that by drawing conclusions and taking such themes out of context, the rich, multilayered texture of a person's life can so easily be distorted. The interviews stand on their own as testaments of a unique and timely history.

We see this book as a beginning – something on which to build and expand. Experiences which have not been recorded and areas which have only been mentioned or touched upon can be more fully explored in later oral history work. One obvious example is the urgent need to record the experiences of people with AIDS.

History can be a cohesive force. By looking back and seeing how other gay men have lived their lives, struggled and survived, we develop a shared sense of the past, a clearer understanding of the present, and an indication of the possibilities of the future. This is particularly pertinent now, given the increasingly virulent anti-gay hysteria and bigotry that are becoming a characteristic of Britain in the late eighties.

Above all, a study of gay history is essential in ensuring that we, as individuals and as part of the community, will not be hidden, neglected or dismissed. As one of the younger interviewees said,

Twenty years after the partial decriminalization of homosexuality, a whole generation of us are around who know what it is like to be ourselves and not to feel bad or guilty about it. They will not be able to take that away . . . In the short run things may get tougher; but in the long run I'm not pessimistic. How can we lose? That means not only them, but we ourselves have to deny our existence – and we can't do that.

THE STORIES

FRANK OLIVER

INTERVIEWED IN JANUARY 1986 BY PAUL MARSHALL

My mother was one of a family of ten and was born in Birkenhead, where her father was an alderman. My father's parentage was on the tragic side. His father had gone to New York in the late nineteenth century as some kind of representative and was knocked down and killed by a horse tram. My paternal grandmother, poor soul, took to drink and died of it. My father had been at sea and worked his way up to being a junior ship's engineer when I was born, in Kingston-upon-Hull, Yorkshire, in August 1907.

I had a ghastly childhood. My mother adored me but she was one of those people who clung like a leech. I never remember my father playing any game with me and I was beaten for even the slightest misdemeanour. I was so frightened of him that I would literally wet myself when he glared at me in anger. From the earliest possible age I had no love for him at all, but going back over my life I've realized that I badly wanted to be loved by a man. Some of my father's friends were really wonderful; they used to give me so much enjoyment – play games with me and hug and kiss me – and it made up, to some extent, for what I didn't get from my father.

My father would never allow me to have birthday parties. My mother begged and pleaded with him but there was never even another child in the house. I can remember quite vividly that I spent most of my time dressing up. I would drape myself in an old pair of my mother's Nottingham lace curtains and swish down the stairs, pretending that I was a bride. Of course, I must have known that there would have been terrible trouble if my father had ever found out, but my mother encouraged me. She would say,

7

'Oh, well, now try that on,' or, 'I've got a hat, maybe you'd like to wear that.' It was an extraordinary thing; having on one side a delicate, rather beautiful mother who just worshipped me, and on the other side a father who had no time for me at all. It was pretty evident from the word go that he thought his son was a namby-pamby and that something would have to be done to make a man out of me.

We had moved to Barry, in South Wales, because my father was working in Cardiff and I went to prep school, where I was happy. I used to act there, which I loved. I used to do little scenes like 'Where Are You Going To, My Pretty?' with another pupil, a little girl, and I got on wonderfully well with the son of the owner.

When I was seven, my father, who was being sent to Canada to do war work in the First World War, decided that I should be sent away from home. He sent me to a boarding school in Penarth, South Wales, run by a woman who had a reputation as a disciplinarian. She was a Quaker. It's always been said how good and kind the Quakers were, but she was a devil. Most of the boys were scared stiff of her and those who weren't were bullies, and I was bullied unmercifully for about four years. After two years I ran away but I was taken back and thrashed and given the most terrible tasks to do. Those years were absolute horror.

I remember Armistice Day quite well [1918]. It seemed rather strange. We were taken for a walk up through the town – *en crocodile*, as the French used to say, a long line of boys – and the thing that struck me more than anything else was the awful still-ness of the place. There didn't seem to be any rejoicing.

My father came back from Canada and we moved to Bristol. He cottoned on to the fact that I had a gentle nature and cast around for a really tough public school to send me to. He found one, West Buckland in North Devon, way up on the edge of Exmoor. The conditions were terrible. It was icy cold with no elec-tricity and when we got up in the morning to wash we had to break the ice in our basins. But in spite of that, I spent three wonderful years being loved by a man or boy, as the case might be.

I never really believed such a thing could happen, but of course, underneath everything, it was what I'd been yearning for. I was so thrilled and delighted and the first boy who made these advances to me was such a dish that I went willingly into his arms and I was treated wonderfully. I suppose I was with him for about a term and then he left and he had a successor and then another successor. I was platinum blond, cherubic and, I suppose, just the type of boy most of them wanted. Nearly every one of them had a flutter in one way or another and, because conditions were so spartan, we kept each other warm of course. I thought to myself that it served my father jolly well right. He wanted to make a man out of me and that's what happened!

We had a marvellous headmaster. He had his favourites with the boys and, being musical, I was one of them because he was very musical himself. He loved Gilbert and Sullivan and I used to play all the leading parts in the operas. He sent for me one day towards the end of '24 when I was about sixteen and said, 'I'm sorry to have to tell you this, but your father insists that you be taken away from school.' I was very upset and howled my eyes out. I got home to Bristol and found out exactly why I'd been taken away from school. My father had packed his bags and gone off to live with his fancy woman and left my mother and me to our own devices. I'd known by the age of fifteen that my father had been philandering left, right and centre. He was an extremely sexual, physical man and could be one of the most charming men imaginable.

My father sent for me to go and see him at his office and I went, this time full of hate and no more full of fear. He told me that he'd got me a job in London at a shipbroker's office, saying, 'The sooner you get away up there and try to be a man, the better for you.' I told him I didn't want to go. But he said, 'You'll do as you're damn well told and that's the end of it.' So I was just torn away from my mother, who was absolutely heartbroken.

He found me digs in Lewisham, 25s. a week, full board, which he paid for. I didn't have anything in common with the rest of the people in the house and I was miserable not knowing anyone in London, but the landlady was kind, and there were two men who used to visit her who both sang. Since I played the piano we spent a lot of time making music – mostly ballads; I never played jazz in those days.

I got 15s. a week from my job and, come Thursday, I usually didn't have enough bus fare, so I had to walk from Bishopsgate to Lewisham. The buses in those days had open tops so the journey was absolute purgatory. When the bus was full I would go upstairs, often with the rain pelting down. In front of each seat was a canvas apron, which you could lift up over your knees, and you'd sit huddled there with your umbrella up.

One day I saw an advertisement for an apprentice at the British American Tobacco Company. I decided to rid myself of my father once and for all, so I wrote, got the job and was sent to Liverpool. My mother packed up and came with me. That was happy enough. There were at least three other boys there who were gay. We didn't use the word 'gay' in those days. I remember that if you were talking about somebody to a friend, he would say very quietly to you, 'Is he "so"?' And I would say, 'Well, I don't think so, but he's probably "TBH": To Be Had.' But you didn't dare give any sign whatsoever in those days, not so much as a flicker of the eyelash, so the only time we were able to giggle and have a bit of fun together was when we visited each other's homes and digs. But it was nice none the less, and I had two years of that and then they sent me to Antwerp on a management course and that was pretty much like hell because I didn't meet anyone who was gay. After about eighteen months my health broke down; it was all the tobacco dust and everything else and I got bronchitis. They sent me home and said that there would be nothing further for me, so we parted company.

I was ill for some time and then, through a friend of my mother's, I was offered a job in London with Lionel Powell, one of the great impresarios of the day, so my mother and I moved to London and found a flat in South Norwood. The job was in the box office in Bond Street, which was entirely run by rather tough women. The most interesting part about it was that all the most famous names of that particular year, '29, would visit Lionel Powell. It was nothing to see people like Rachmaninov and Dame Nelly Melba. Lionel Powell also promoted Yehudi Menuhin's concerts. He would have been about ten years old and I remember delivering a cheque to his father of £1,000 for two concerts, which was a lot of money in those days.

One day a very handsome young American came into the office. He wanted tickets for the first Toscanini concert. I said, 'My goodness, you have left it late. I don't even know if I can scratch you a corner.' I managed to get him a seat and I saw him in the distance at the concert. He was so gorgeous. He saw me and waited at the end and said, 'I think I've got a little job for you. How would you like to be in a film?' He said he'd be in it too. He was an actor and he'd come over to get experience in British theatre and films.

The film was called *Dark Red Roses* and had some very famous names in it – Stewart Rome, Frances Doble – and three dancers – Balanchine, Lopokova and Anton Dolin. We went down by coach to the old studio at Wembley, long since gone, and were in a night-club scene. We finished shooting at two in the morning so he said, 'Don't you think you'd better come home with me?' He took me to a lovely flat in Ebury Street and that was literally my first love affair and also the night of my twenty-first birthday. It was painful, though [laughs], because he was a very well-made young man. The next day he met my mother, who thought he was absolutely entrancing. He only had one more week in England and he begged me to go back to New York with him. He said he'd look after me, find me a job and my mother would be taken care of. But I couldn't leave her, she was too vulnerable. She relied on me too much, you see. I was terribly upset and on the night before he left I was in floods of tears. We both cried when I saw him off at the station.

I left the agency after Lionel Powell died and got a job with a very big cinema chain as an assistant manager. It was terribly tough-going. The hours were very long and you could never have a friend into the studio to see you. Everything was suspicion for someone like me, because I suppose I was on the gentle side and the owner of this chain of cinemas was a terrible bully and he always used to pick on me. I stuck it for two years, though, and was sent to one of the biggest cinemas in London as house manager.

After a while I thought it was time I had an increase in salary, so I asked for a raise of 10s. a week [laughs] but they refused. I thought, 'Right, I'll show you.' I saw a marvellous job advertised – a general manager wanted for two cinemas almost side by side, the Rialto and the Albany in Upper Norwood. So I became the youngest general manager in London, at £6 a week – absolute riches.

We moved to Upper Norwood. Flats in those days were very easy to get and very inexpensive. The weekly rent was 22s. 6d. a week, unfurnished. I stayed in that job for two years and I eventually ended up at the State cinema in Thornton Heath, where I was in charge of variety acts. We always had a second feature, a stage show, then the organ and then the main feature, all for 9d. This was in the mid-thirties. It was absolute pandemonium if you had a film people wanted to see. There would be queues round the block and they'd nearly push the walls down. It was difficult work and I'd often have to deal with very aggressive people who would threaten me if they had to wait too long.

The thirties were the bad old days for cinema managers – very long hours – so I rarely had time to see anyone socially, but I used to go to a few pubs and clubs. There was a café in Wardour Street called the Rendezvous, and it was always full of gay people trying very hard to pretend they weren't gay. It was run, terribly discreetly, by two gay men and before you went in you would look round to make sure nobody saw you. A tremendous lot of affairs started at the Rendezvous and also at the Hong Kong club in Shaftesbury Avenue, which was mostly show business. Some of the people were gay, some weren't; it was a good mixture. The other famous place was the lily pond at Lyons Corner House in Coventry Street, up on the first floor. You'd go up there at about four o'clock and you'd look around the tables and you could spot them one after the other. It was pretty entirely gay and there was some discreet picking-up there. The management had a beady eye on everybody, so you had to be careful; but you could always ask for a light or something. I met one or two people and they were rather nice; but there was never an awful lot of getting together in those days.

Q: *Were you interested in politics?*

I was never greatly concerned, but I remember the time when the Prince of Wales made his journey down to Wales and saw the terrible deprivation of the miners and the poverty there. And he said, 'Something must be done.' But of course nothing very much was done. But I'm not a political animal; I never have been. All my forebears were Tories and I suppose I was a Tory because they were. Later, I was greatly attached to 'Supermac' and then of course we had 'Winnie', who fortunately brought us through to victory.

When war was declared in '39, I tried to enlist in the RAF but

At the Marigny Theatre, Paris, October 1944

Photo taken by Frank of his American friends, Paris 1943

Working with Americans, in
American uniform, the Opera,
Paris, 1945

Blackpool, 1941

14

was turned down because of a heart condition. So I was driving ambulances in Teddington, in South London, and because I'd met so many people when I was putting on variety shows in the cinemas, I could call on them to give free shows for the First Aid ambulance crews. I got people like 'Hutch' and Terry-Thomas.

It was one of the worst winters I ever remember, with the Thames frozen over. I was out doing an exercise, a pretty grim one, and I got pneumonia and nearly died from it. My poor dear mother, who was nursing me, was in despair. When I got better, I had a phone call from Hutch, telling me to go to Drury Lane. So I went, and got a job with ENSA [Entertainments National Service Association] and in February '40 I took a company of twelve entertainers to the British forces who were scattered around France.

Before I left for France I'd met a young officer at Drury Lane and the minute we looked at each other we fell in love! It was like a flash of lightning between us. The situation was impossible because we couldn't show any kind of affection for each other. At that particular time, the outbreak of war, everything was about as severe as it possibly could be. It was always 'Slap on the back, old chap,' and all the rest of it. But Andy and I knew instantly what had happened and as we shook hands in a very manly way, he said, 'You'll be coming to Reims, so I shall be seeing you because I've asked for your show.'

So we went over and we did little villages and big towns like Arras and Amiens. Some of the places were awful, but we gave a show. We got to Reims eventually. Andy was waiting at the hotel for us and I was worried to death because I was afraid my feelings for Andy would show. And he was afraid, too, but we managed to show in our eyes what we thought. One person in the company twigged what was going on. He was a ventriloquist, an awfully nice boy who wasn't gay but he could see what had happened. We did a wonderful show at the Paramount theatre and the officers arranged a party for us back at the hotel and you could almost have bathed in the champagne. I managed by guile to get Andy sitting beside me and we were able to press our knees against each other without anyone seeing. It was the first contact we'd ever had apart from shaking hands. The party ended rather rowdily, with everyone a bit sloshed. I managed to pack them off to bed and then said goodnight to Andy.

15

At about half-past two there was a tremendous knocking on my bedroom door and Andy was standing there as white as a sheet. I just looked at him and said, 'It's happened, hasn't it?' Because it suddenly came to me that the Germans had broken through. He said, 'Yes,' and quickly looked around and came into my room, put his arms around me and held me tight. It must have been for a whole minute and that was the first time in my life that I'd ever really been kissed. We were both in tears by this time and he just said, 'I'll try and keep in touch.'

I managed to get the company out of their beds, all in various stages of undress. Some of them were almost too drunk to walk but we set off and arrived at the port to find a tatty old ferry boat waiting for us. We got home safely and the company broke up into various units.

I was given a small concert party to take up to Scotland. During rehearsals the welfare officer came in and said how lucky we were to be alive. She told us that after we left Reims, Andy's unit was moved to Arras where we had been performing, to the same hotel, and the Germans came over and blasted if off the face of the earth. I didn't say a word. The ventriloquist was there and he took one look at me and his eyes flashed sympathy. I went and sat in the back of the theatre and I really thought that some part of me had died with Andy.

We went off on tour and played at various isolated RAF stations – this must have been '41 – and at the end of the first week we ended up in Lancashire. One night I went into Blackpool to a club called the Clifton, which was known to be very gay. I hadn't been there for more than a few minutes when I realized I was being picked up by a man much younger than myself. He was one of those sultry-looking people I used to describe as having 'come-to-bed eyes' and he was enjoying himself quite lavishly because he had gins lined up in front of him. He was quite obviously determined to grab me if he could, and after a while – since by that time you didn't have to ask for a light or ask somebody what the time was – he came over and asked me if I wanted a drink. In the end I took him home to my digs and we spent the night together – a quite disastrous night, as it happened. He later told one of his RAF mates, 'It serves me right. I was out looking to find myself a rich husband, and what do I get? An impoverished wife.' But the curious part about it was, although I decided he was the sort of person I most disliked – he was a drinker, used awful language and had no finesse whatsoever – in spite of all that, Jimmy and I were together for the next twenty-five years.

He was sent out to Burma in the jungle campaign against the Japanese and I went on with my own war work. Then, in '44, I was asked to go to France and take over one of the most beautiful theatres in Paris for the Allied forces. It was pretty tough-going because the Germans had stripped the stage of everything – lights, curtains, the lot. This was about eight weeks after the liberation of Paris and it was bitterly cold. Half the time the poor wretched French had no electricity and no heat, but we managed eventually to put on a show with a cast that couldn't possibly be paid for by anybody, headed by Noël Coward with Nervo and Knox, Will Hay, Bobby Howes, Josephine Baker, Frances Day and Geraldo and his full orchestra. It was an enormous success.

One day I was in the theatre alone and I was playing the piano and quietly singing to myself, when one of the French electricians came in and heard me. He said, 'You ought to do something with that talent.' He had a friend who worked at the French radio station and he said he would arrange an audition. I rather pooh-poohed the idea, but I got a call, gave an audition, and they gave six programmes called *Sweet Music in the Quiet Manner*, which were broadcast on short wave to America. It seems that they made quite an impact. We heard from some GIs whose people in the States had been listening and they enjoyed them enormously.

Having got the Marigny theatre well and truly opened and flourishing, I was asked if I would care to be transferred to the American army as their theatre administrator. I nearly did the Highland fling because the idea was delightful. I came back to England, where all hell was let loose because doodle bugs were dropping all over the place, got out of khaki, and was rigged out with a peaked cap, a golden eagle and they made special shoulder flashes for me with royal blue and silver. I felt very grand. Who wouldn't? The British uniform was so drab compared to this.

The first night back in Paris I went to a gay bar that had become quite famous, called Le Boeuf sur le Toit, and as I went in there were shrieks and whoops of delight from my GI friends, and they carried me from the door and all round the bar.

That started off a really mad caper. I did a very long day, start-ing at eight-thirty in the morning until five in the afternoon, then

17

back to the hotel to change out of battle dress to more formal uniform. I was given a car by command and that would call for me at seven and I would go round the theatres each night – four in Paris and two in Versailles. The nice little Frenchman who drove me was also gay, and he would drop me at the Boeuf at about one in the morning and we continued there till about four and I'd get to bed at five and up again at seven. It was a hectic life and continued for quite a while.

I didn't have many amorous adventures in Paris, although I had a great many invitations [laughing], but I've never been a promiscuous person. I had a lot of very affectionate friendships. I worked with Josephine Baker – because on one occasion we couldn't find a dresser for her and I had to do it – and we became great friends. She was very romantic and she adored gay boys. She had a godson called Mario Lembo who was a sweet, gentle and adorable young man and terribly timid, and all Josephine wanted to do was, as she described it, 'put us together'. Both of us had a little giggle because we both knew it would be absolutely impossible. I mean, we were just bread and bread! But we put on an act for Josephine and whenever we went round to see her we always held hands and kissed in corners and this sort of thing, and it made her happy.

All sorts of people kept arriving to entertain the Allied troops – Bob Hope, Marlene Dietrich, Mickey Rooney, Ingrid Bergman and Glen Miller. Life in the gay bars got madder and madder. But eventually the theatre days came to an end and, in '47, I returned to England. I managed to get a job as a film buyer at the BFI and then worked on the Marshall Plan as audio-visual aids officer, touring the Benelux countries, with an office in Paris. That job finished after two years and I came back to England and started work at the Academy cinema in Oxford Street.

I was still with Jimmy. I got him a job in Paris when he came back from Burma and, back in England, we moved into a flat in Streatham. My mother lived in the same block. She couldn't bear Jimmy and the first time they met you could almost see the sparks flying. She couldn't deal with him at all, and he didn't trust her. Once she said to me with scorn, 'How could you? Your grandfather would turn in his grave. A fishmonger's son!' I told her not to be so silly. There wasn't any shame in being a fishmonger's son. I never discovered to the day she died whether my mother knew

I was gay or not. She must have known but, being a Victorian, it was never discussed. As the years went on she clung more and more and, much as I loved her, it became a tremendous burden. She was prying all the time. She used to say, 'I'm sorry, darling, I didn't have my glasses and I thought this letter was for me but it's for you'! She died about eighteen months after we moved down to Byfleet in Surrey.

I was working for a film distribution company and one Christmas Eve I came home and had a massive coronary. I fell in the hallway but managed to reach the telephone and get the operator to call an ambulance. Jimmy told me that they expected me to die that night, but by six o'clock the next morning I was ringing for a cup of tea and a cigarette! It took me ages to get on my feet again. I lost my job but, luckily, I was left £3,000 by an aunt.

I decided to visit my old GI friends in America. I stayed in New York and one day I took a boat trip around the waterways of the city and as I went up the gangplank, I looked up and saw a most attractive face looking down at me and I thought, 'You're a bold one. In full daylight!' He was the courier and later he pushed a piece of paper into my hand with his name and address on it. He'd given me his phone number and for the rest of my stay he never left my side. My GI friends were enchanted by this unexpected romance. I had a wonderful time. This was in the late fifties and I never saw anything like the parading and cruising that went on at night on Third Avenue. It was outrageous, and the amount of Kleenex that had been stuffed into tight trousers was nobody's business!

I had to find a job when I returned to England. I was over fifty but I managed to get a job as a film and television buyer for the government. Then I became first secretary of the National Panel for Film Festivals and I spent seventeen years travelling all over the Continent. One year I went to Northern France and amongst the thousands and thousands of white crosses, I found Andy's grave. I stayed by the grave for a while, said goodbye and went off down to Greece. Shortly after, I retired.

I put my name down for two flats in Streatham. I thought it was about time Jimmy stood on his own two feet, took responsibility and paid his own bills. He lived above me for ten years.

Five years ago I went to a Sunday tea party at a dear old queen's flat. I was sitting in the corner of this packed room and the doorbell rang and in walked Michael. I looked towards him and exactly the same thing happened as it did with Andy. It was absolutely instantaneous and we could hardly take our eyes off each other. It has lasted now for five years. I'm afraid we're going to be separated because he's going to work in North Wales, although he says that, come July, he'll be back down here again. It can't be soon enough for me.

DUDLEY CAVE

INTERVIEWED IN MAY 1987 BY PAUL MARSHALL

My mother married my father really as a second choice. She'd fallen in love with a Canadian who went back to Canada in the First World War. My father persisted in wishing to marry her and she eventually did so. I was born in Golders Green in the house where I still live, in 1921. I was the only child. The marriage lasted about ten or eleven years and then they divorced. I remained with my father, which was one of the good things that happened to me in my life. He was my favourite parent; a rather old-fashioned, honourable gentleman.

I went to a little private school in Golders Green until I was about nine. I then passed the entrance exam to Haberdashers' Aske's, Hampstead, which was a selective grammar school, fee-paying, about 3 guineas a term, and continued there. I did not go to university. I was a good little boy, smartly dressed; I called people 'sir' appropriately; I was well brought up. I had plenty of good times at school. I mean, I got on well with my fellow-pupils. In those days being gay was OK. Nearly all the boys had sexual experiences with each other over the years.

I was constantly in love with various people and had sex with most of them in varying sorts of ways. There was an element of mutual masturbation in class, although I, being a religious boy, felt it was inappropriate to wank in divinity, so didn't [laughs]. And in the baths we had a small flooded room as was usual for people who played football with the right shaped ball. The master could see the boys on the left-hand wall but not the boys on the other, so the people we regarded as cissies sat on the wall under the master's eye and washed themselves and came out. The remainder of us played with each other and wriggled around;

21

Dudley Cave (left) and his lover, Bernard Williams, 1988.
Portrait by Sunil Gupta

you'd go into clean water and emerge from a soup of mud and semen and go on your way. The funny thing was that it was the more effeminate boys who I regarded as cissies and who didn't join in the sex.

When I left school at seventeen, I went into cinemas, to become a cinema manager. I couldn't be a manager until I was twenty and so I went into the projection room for two years. That was quite a culture shock. I'd come from Golders Green – private school – and suddenly moved into Burnt Oak where most of the people had moved up in the world from the Brick Lane slum clearance of the Watling estate. We barely spoke each other's language and it was very good for me.

I got on well with the other projectionists and had some sort of sexual fun with them from time to time. Becoming a cinema manager seemed an ideal job for me. In those days, they weren't too badly paid and it was a job which required things I'd got, which were a degree of organizing ability and superficial charm and a pleasant smile and wavy hair, I suppose. I started in '38. The boom really came with the war but business was good. Odeon were opening about two cinemas a month at that time, so it was really quite a growing industry.

Q: *Can you remember anything about the politics of the day?*

Yes, indeed, because going back just a little bit, it was the days of Mosley's marches on the East End. Now, Golders Green was, even then, a Jewish district and I felt very strongly about this, and I was wildly anti-Fascist. In fact, my first unpleasant encounter with the police was at a Fascist meeting on Hampstead Heath. It was an open-air Hyde Park-style meeting and the British Union of Fascists were speaking – black shirts and jack boots, the whole thing – and the speaker said that the Jews introduced venereal disease to Europe. And I quite correctly said, 'Nonsense!' As soon as I spoke, a heavy hand landed on my shoulder and the policeman standing behind me said, 'Shut up or shove off.' Now, it was really as if my faithful collie dog had turned round and bitten me. The police who I'd always regarded as the people who'd helped little Dudley across the road in his neat little school cap, and addressed my father as 'sir', had suddenly turned into this monster. It was really quite a bad shock. But I was certainly left wing – like most people in those days. My father put his foot down when he thought I was going to join the Communist Party – the only thing he ever stopped me doing. My father was a Conservative who read the *Daily Telegraph*.

I read the *Daily Mirror*, believe it or not, which was then quite a respectable, left-wing paper. I particularly followed Cassandra's column in the *Daily Mirror* and his views reflected mine pretty well on this anti-Fascist feeling, anti-Nazi feeling. But the general world went on perfectly happy with it, and I mean the stupid thing that Mussolini had made trains run on time in Italy was a real thing that people said. You know, that Mussolini was OK because of that.

The Fascists didn't march in Golders Green. The police wouldn't have permitted that. After all, Golders Green was a prosperous suburb. That sort of stuff was confined to the East End, Ridley Street. It was generally thought that the police were on the side of the Fascist marchers, and I have little doubt that they were.

Once I got in the cinema, I had no social life. I started work at ten o'clock in the morning, and finished about ten-past eleven at night. In the early days I had Sunday as my day off and I had a half-day from six o'clock on Friday. The rest of the time I was working, and very happy with it, too. I liked the comradeship and I got on well with the others, once we'd established that talking posh didn't mean that I was totally incompetent.

Q: *What about the events leading up to the Second World War? Can you remember the atmosphere?*

Yes, indeed, I can – I can well remember Munich. Mr Chamberlain and his bit of paper. I thought Mr Chamberlain was pretty good, actually, at the time. I thought he had saved peace and I felt peace was worth fighting for and very important.

Just before war broke out, I was on holiday in Chichester with two friends and we picked up the newspapers and realized that things were fairly serious, because London was being evacuated, so we packed up our tent and turned the car round and headed towards London. Unfortunately, because of the evacuation, a very large number of the roads out of London became one-way and we had to get in by rather a difficult journey. I clearly remember

24

coming over Hammersmith Bridge and for the first time seeing barrage balloons up in the sky. It was quite exciting, but a little bit frightening.

I got back home and found my call for the ARP service [Air Raid Precautions] on the doormat, so I went up the town hall and got on with it. On the Sunday of war breaking out, there was an announcement that something particular was happening at eleven o'clock, and we then heard the speech that 'A state of war between ourselves and Germany now exists,' the air-raid sirens went and we made our way towards the air-raid shelter fairly quietly, and then it was on. We had been led to believe that there was going to be mass destruction. There'd been a very powerful play and film on, called *Idiot's Delight*, which ended with the skies being black with aircraft and London being flattened by bombs. We were also aware of H.G. Wells's *Things to Come*, which had shown London flattened, and I was quite prepared for a flattened London. But the phoney war proceeded, where nothing much happened.

The cinemas were closed for the first week of the war, and so I was given leave to continue with the ARP services. Once we opened again, I went back to work.

Then the blitz happened and I transferred from Burnt Oak to Golders Green to be nearer home. The Regal, Golders Green, had a largely glass roof which was really quite fun in air raids because bits of shrapnel would fall and make cracks above your head. Audiences would be down to about thirty or forty in 2,000 seats and if they felt the noise was coming on them, people would get up and move seats to what they felt was a safer place. It was quite extraordinary. You had a system where you had to put a slide on the screen saying, 'The air-raid warning has sounded,' so people could do what they liked about it. Because of the raids, a large number of staff stayed in the cinema and the chief projectionist slept with the junior projectionist, wrapped up in a velvet curtain which was really rather smart. I became an air-raid warden and worked alternate nights on a night-shift and then back to work in the daytime.

During the war one tends to think – perhaps from literature – that everybody was worried sick about being bombed. In fact, they were very keen to have their sex life and everything else was going on. I certainly can't remember trolling or cruising, but there were so many people you met socially. There was a friend of mine whose girlfriend had, for good reasons, turned him down temporarily on her parents' advice. She was a Spanish Roman Catholic and his parents were East End Jews. They married subsequently, but she had agreed not to see him for two months and so he, frustrated, turned to me. My father was on Home Guard duty at the town hall one night a week and my friend would come over and keep me company as the blitz was on, and we would sleep together and have sex. When I became an air-raid warden, he signed on as a messenger, being a year younger than I was, and we had sex on the camp-bed in the warden's post and went right though it – which took a bit of explaining in the morning.

You got very quickly accustomed to bombs falling. At first, perhaps, you took shelter and were frightened. Very rapidly you didn't pay much attention unless you heard one coming fairly close, when you might duck down. I didn't go into shelters; I despised them. I also looked down my snooty nose at people who slept in the Underground. I thought they were really rather cowardly and I would go home and sleep in my bed or, at worst, under the dining-room table. I was not a aware that they'd been bombed out of their homes in the East End and I was sitting smugly in Golders Green, feeling all brave and looking down my nose at them.

I was called up in June '41, when I was twenty and three months, and I joined the army at Pembroke Dock in Wales for basic training. I was in the Ordnance Corps, which was relatively civilized, and we were treated more or less as human beings and I quite enjoyed it. I was mildly homesick, but not badly so. I was then sent to technical training at Twycross and was posted to a unit near Faversham, Kent. Then I got posted to Eighteenth Division, got tropical kit and was sent overseas.

We got on a boat at Bristol and went up to Gurrock, where we met our convoy, and set out in the October gales to cross the Atlantic. This was October '41 – before America had come into the war.

We were half-way across the Atlantic and suddenly there was smoke on the horizon and I thought, 'Oh, we're going to have a battle.' Again, not much fear, really; it was a sort of abstract thing. But it turned out it was an American convoy which was picking us up and we were marched off our troopships in Halifax,

Nova Scotia, and up a gangplank on to an American ship, the *Joseph T. Dickman*.

We travelled on that to Trinidad, but we weren't allowed off, down the South American coast into cold water and were across towards Cape Town when Pearl Harbor happened and the Americans were running up and down, talking about being stabbed in the back when they were neutral. It didn't strike them that they were not particularly neutral carrying us, and it only took a dolphin to stick its nose out of the water and they'd be hurling depth charges.

We got into Cape Town just before Christmas. The American escort left us, and we had just one troopship and we were carried on to Bombay, where we went up into the hills and were given toughening-up training. It had turned out we were intended to go to Iraq and Iran, I forget which, to guard a railway, but because of the Japanese coming into the war, we were diverted and thrown into the breach at Singapore. I was on a ship called the *Empress of Asia*, where, for the first time in my life, I came across a cockroach. I found it in the middle of a loaf which I was carving, and that day I threw that bread and my sausages through the porthole. It was, in fact, the last of that sort of meal I had for three-and-a-half years. The ship was bombed.

It went on fire. The 'abandon ship' bell went and I went up on deck – frightened, I might say. Then I could see land, right on the horizon, but I thought, 'Never mind, I can swim that far.' I couldn't, of course, but it gave me confidence. I didn't get off the ship in a hurry. After about two hours of explosions up forward, an Australian sloop was taking the wounded off. The skipper took a loud-hailer and said, 'Those who can swim should get off now.' So I slid down a hose-pipe at the back, carefully taking my army boots off and placing my socks neatly in them, slid down this pipe, still wearing my tin hat, realized it was silly to try and swim in a tin hat and took it off and floated off on the tide and struck out. There were several hundred people swimming in various directions. With the current and my swimming, I got to the edge of the rescue ship and they pulled me on board and took me on to Singapore. It was all quite frightening and we were all in a state of shock.

We got into Singapore and we were really uncomfortable. I didn't think I'd see my twenty-first birthday. And, in fact, in one

27

journey through the night in the middle of Singapore, when it seemed there were Japanese firing guns all round me, I quite deliberately went to sleep in the back of the lorry I was in, so that I wouldn't feel the end coming. This had a rather funny sequel. Some months afterwards, I overheard somebody suggest that I was a nancy boy – I suppose that was the word – and a cockney voice said, 'Oh, no he can't be. He was wonderfully brave in action.' Well, my wonderful bravery was me going to sleep [laughs] when I was scared of being killed. Also, you notice, you couldn't be gay and brave.

When Singapore fell to the Japanese, I was captured on the Bukit Timah Road. The Japanese came to take us over at seven o'clock in the morning, at which time the colonel was shaving, so the colonel was called out and he'd got lather on his face [laughing] and this Japanese sergeant delivered his instructions, waving a vast revolver. I had the idea that you should never surrender your weapons, so carefully took the bolt of my rifle and pressed it into the mud out of sight, and handed the rifle in knowing that it was useless like that. If I'd known the way the Japanese treated people found doing things like that, I wouldn't have been so brave. We were then herded in a field and then subsequently marched off to Changi.

When I was captured, I felt very much that this wasn't happening to me. Disbelief. I was very relieved that the war was over for me. I mean, it was very frightening what with the unresolved shock from the sinking of the ship, being thrown into action rather violently and things being very badly organized. The Australian troops had had what they call a 'jack up', which anybody else would call a mutiny. They'd just decided it wasn't worth fighting from Malaya and had just turned tail and gone down-country. It was a shambles, and I was profoundly grateful to be alive and settled myself to the idea of being a prisoner-of-war.

I'd assumed that I would be a prisoner-of-war Geneva Convention-wise. Little did I know what was to come as we went ahead. So off we marched to Changi. We had very little in the way of kit – I'd got some books, happily. I'd also got a miniature bottle of whisky, with which I was going to celebrate my twenty-first birthday, and on my first day of capture I poured it into a mess tin and drank it, saying, 'Happy birthday, Dudley' to myself, to the amusement of some people around me. It was about [laughs] two months later I discovered I had celebrated a day too soon. I had no idea what I did on my twenty-first birthday, no recollection at all, and so I became a prisoner.

We were all marched off to a corner of Singapore Island and we had a sort of phoney captivity of peaceful life and educational studies. Then I was gathered up for a working party up-country. It was supposed to be a convalescent thing, but we didn't really believe that. And so we were all carted off to Singapore station and taken up to Thailand, twenty-four to a freight car. In turns, eight people could look on to the scenery and every half-hour or so the whistle blew and we all changed places. It was very organized and I saw this exciting countryside passing by as we went up-country.

Eventually we got to a place called Bang Pon, which is a junction now, and we were marched up-country to the railway. We marched at night. We had just received Red Cross boots and I take size nine but had size ten, so my feet were dreadfully blistered. We eventually got up to the place where we worked on the railway, about a five-day march; after two or three days' working, my boots fell to pieces and I worked barefoot.

What we had to do was to quarry earth and rubble, then carry it up to make the embankment. Teams of six people. Very laborious work, rather unpleasant from being shouted at by the Japanese. At that time, the great 'hurry up' wasn't on and it wasn't too bad, but you'd work there all day and then go back to the camp. I used to drop into the river – we'd got a spring – and just lie in the water a bit and let the cold water wash the ache out of my bones before I went to have a meal. I'd given up smoking but I decided it was good to have a habit to fall back on, so I would have my supper, two cigarettes and then go to bed.

I then got a very bad case of malaria. I had been diagnosed earlier as having pernicious anaemia by a specialist in Singapore, and when I got malaria – which kills red blood cells – I really was pretty bad. I was put on the evacuation party. The Japanese allowed a few of the really ill men to go back. They rejected me first time. Second time round, the Dutch interpreter – we were a camp of 200 British, 2,000 Dutch – advised me to walk with a stick: it was no good looking so healthy. So I walked with a stick as instructed, waited for hours being examined on this sort of parade ground. We all had diarrhoea and nature called, so I

29

Aged 15, on holiday in Switzerland, 1936

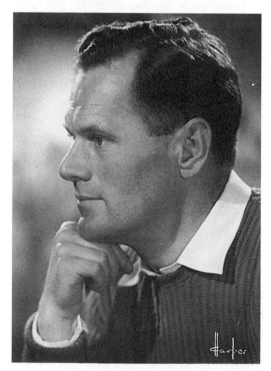

Aged 35

clambered up the small hill where the latrines were, because the place was water-logged. As I stood up afterwards, because we were squatting, of course – what with the sun and being a bit dizzy, I lost my balance and I fell over and I rolled down the hill. Very dramatic stuff, and I think partly that and the Dutch interpreter saying I was bloodless got me on the evacuation party and I went down-country.

I went to a place called Chungkai, which is now a very large cemetery. There was a tree in the middle of the camp where they used to pin the names of the people who had died the previous day and it was usually seven or eight. I know how many people were in the camp and I could divide by seven and I realized that in ten months we'd all be dead, so I thought: 'I've only got ten months to live if I stay here.' You notice I was going to be the last person to die – a usual belief. They subsequently moved me to Kan'buri', which again was fairly foul, where I developed an ulcer in my ankle which was really rather frightening and grew at great speed, but an Australian surgeon cut it out. Eventually, I got back to Singapore.

I should say that I made one fairly close friend, a guy who had his twenty-first birthday in the days of our phoney captivity. It so happened that when I got malaria, I was next to him in the hospital tent. Because we were short of tents, you had either a tent or a fly-sheet but not both, so when it rained – which it did constantly – the water would come through. This guy, called Fred Smith, was pretty bad and I had to channel the water like a boy scout so that it didn't fall on top of him. I also stole onions for him and myself and nursed him, but he got sent further down-country.

When I eventually got to Singapore I met him again in a hospital ward. He was on four eggs a day and suddenly the medical officer said, 'Finish eggs,' and one of the other boys who was on four eggs gave him one of his. The medical officer caught him and said, 'Look, I stopped Smith's eggs because no number of eggs are going to save his life, and we want to keep you alive. So you eat your eggs: don't give them away.' And Fred died.

By this time I'd got myself a job as a nightsoil remover in a dysentery ward, which meant carrying latrine buckets of very fluid excreta. It was quite a nasty job but you got over it quickly. One day, having emptied the bins into the appropriate place, I cut back through and I found Fred Smith's body on an improvised mortuary table, opened up for post-mortem – just skin drawn over fine bones. I suppose that's the one time I really raged about the Japanese, because just the other side of the island there was medicine and medical help which I felt would have saved Fred's life. That's the only time I really felt everything go.

It was mainly a question of day-to-day survival. I'm fairly even-tempered, and I'm fairly philosophical. I'm reasonably sensible. For example, I saw somebody die of beriberi malnutrition after I'd been a prisoner for about three months and I realized that it was worth making an effort to get vitamins, eat rice polishings, and it was very important to do that to keep alive. So I was fairly sensible that way. I stopped smoking and used my cigarettes to buy vitamin pills. I'm not a dramatic sort of person, so I was able to cope. And there is luck, of course.

We were liberated about ten days after Hiroshima. By this time I was back in Singapore in Changi jail, sharing a cell with three other men. One night I was woken up and told that the atom bomb had been dropped on Hiroshima, and I didn't get back to sleep again that night. In the morning our sergeant-major told us that he could neither deny nor confirm the rumour and gave the official instruction, that we were to carry on as normal. In other words, we knew; the Japanese didn't. For about ten days we knew and the Japanese didn't. Eventually, I saw the Japanese being told. I saw a Japanese officer talk with his hands, moving his arms, which is most unusual, and the soldiers' heads literally fell. They were standing at attention and their heads just dropped forward and we realized they knew. It was a very dicey situation, because the Japanese were not likely to take lightly that two of their cities had been razed to the ground.

I was pretty poorly and I was first transferred to Singapore general hospital and then flown home. I was put in a Sunderland flying boat and flown to Madras and, on the good food there, sexual feelings occurred again and I went with a young man who I had groped on the troopship on the way out some three-and-a-half years earlier – which had a nice roundness to it, somehow. And I came home to cold England and away we went.

During my captivity I'd realized I was gay. In our prison camp church, they had a series of lectures on sex. At the end of the six lectures, they arranged for a medical officer to be in the church every evening from six till eight for personal questions. The gay thing had been worrying me and I screwed up the courage and eventually went in and sat on a sort of penitents' bench in the dark, when I realized that the medical officer on duty had given me the anaesthetic when I had my ulcer done. He said, 'Hello, Dudley, what's your trouble then?' And I said, 'I'm homosexual.' He said, 'What?' There was a hush and he said, 'Look, I don't know much about this subject, but we're fortunate to have quite an eminent sexologist in the camp.' Well, I went along and saw this guy. He talked to me and said, 'Yes, you're homosexual, fine.' He lent me Havelock Ellis's *Sexual Inversion in Men*, which made me laugh, but it was an immense revelation to me and he suggested I went to see him when the war was over. I couldn't afford a consultancy, so I thought, 'Well, see if you can get this done under the army.' So I told the colonel at my discharge medical examination that I was homosexual. He again said, 'What?' And I repeated it and a little vein in his neck started throbbing and he went quite purple at the thought of this dreadful thing they'd been nurturing to their bosom all these years. And he said in a slightly choked voice, 'Better see a psychiatrist.'

I eventually saw a psychiatrist at Millbank, who sent me to Sutton EMS hospital [Emergency Medical Services], where I was an in-patient. And I thought, 'No doubt they'll give me hormones and make me better'! What I'd hoped was that somebody could wave a magic wand and transfer that excitement I felt at seeing a good-looking man to a good-looking woman. You know, I thought that was all it was. I was there for the weekend, saw the doctor on the Monday and he said, 'Well, my advice to you is to find somebody of like mind and settle down with him and stop bothering.' When he said this, there was an elation. And I said, 'But I'm going to be a cinema manager and I can't go chasing page boys round the Circle.' I'd got flippant by then, so he said, 'I'm not allowed to chase my female patients round the consulting-room and you're not to chase your staff round the Circle.' He said, 'No, you might as well go home.' There was one other patient there, who said, 'We all come back sooner or later.' I could have wept when he said that. So I came home. The only trouble was the doctor didn't tell me how to find somebody of like mind to settle down with.

Before I went into the army, I had a holiday with a friend of

33

mine, called Ralph, in Wales, where we had slept together. We'd had sex together off and on as kids but this was a little bit more than that. When I first came home on leave, he got leave from the navy to see me and what was rather a pleasant little schoolboy had suddenly become a very beautiful sailor, and I was all sort of excited about him. He was not gay – in fact, he said the only gay experience he'd ever had was with me, and we went on having it right up until the time he married.

When I told him I was going to hospital to try and get this thing changed, he said,'Oh, don't do that.' I said, 'Why not?' He said, 'Well, it would probably change you in other ways too.' He was very keen that I should remain gay, but he wasn't gay. So this was in my mind as well and I was really quite bright and happy about the whole thing.

I also had to go into Roehampton hospital for a Far East prisoner-of-war check-up, and after I'd been there a week the doctor asked me why I had been in Sutton mental hospital. I said I was referred because I was homosexual. He referred me to a psychiatrist, who was quite an eminent doctor, and he said that the only advice he could give me was not to solicit in public!

Well, I'd just entered the gay world and I'd found a gay pub for the first time in my life, the Greyhound in Brighton. I'd picked up somebody in a cottage who had taken me there and I had learnt that what I thought were lavatories were in fact called 'cottages'. So I realized I belonged to this great freemasonry of – I think we were still called 'queers' then.

The point was that by this time I realized that gayness was not changeable and although I wasn't entirely glad to be gay, I wasn't unhappy about it. I think if somebody had come along with a magic wand, I'd have said, 'Well, give me time to think about it.'

I met Bernard in '52. I was in the Fitzroy Tavern, which was rather sleazy – the Coleherne of the day – having a drink and feeling very depressed because my father was dying of cancer. Bernard came over and started talking to me, but I brushed him off because I wanted to be left alone. He persisted and I found that I was pouring out my life story to him, which shows his good counselling qualities. I gave him a lift home and he invited me in – 'But only for a cup of coffee' – and I stayed till three in the morning. The next day I waited for him outside his house and we've been together ever since.

I was a cinema manager by this time. I'd been relieving at another cinema and I went up into the projection room and there was a boy mopping up tea on the floor and the others were taking the mickey out of him pretty badly. Now, that's unusual. Projectionists would do things like that, but when a manager comes in they close ranks. And I was really quite shocked that they were allowing me to see this.

In the evening, as I came out of the cinema, I called: 'If anybody wants a lift down the road, I'm going that way.' And one of the people said, 'Oh, young Monty' – it was the time of the Montagu trials* – and they called him Monty. So I gave him a lift and he brought up the subject again and I said – I'm embarrassed to say – for him not to worry, some of the best people in the world are gay and aren't bothered by it, and gave him a few famous names. That was all right, but he wasn't wildly bright and some weeks later somebody was again taking the piss out of him for being gay and he said, 'Oh, some of the best people in the world are gay, there's Michelangelo and there's Dudley Cave of the Majestic.' [Laughs.]

The manager got to hear of this and an investigation started, which I happily got to hear about through my projectionists, who all stood behind me – I mean, the fact that I'd played with two or three of them at different times, you know. The staff were very much for me. In any case I was suspended and called up to head office, and I admitted the matter – I use the word 'admitted' advisedly. I was sitting outside, thinking that I'd wanted to get out of the business for years, here's a chance. Television was already eating into audiences. In any case, they decided I should go so I went. They gave me three months' pay in lieu of notice and I was out.

Cinema managers were not exactly marketable; it wasn't a talent that people were looking for. They thought managers were the ones who wore evening dress and stood at the front of the cinema, flicking fingers and getting usherettes to do this or that. In fact, I kept a wage sheet for forty people and maintained quite a large stock.

Eventually, I got a job as a clerical officer in the hospital service

---

* In 1954, in what many regarded as a 'show' trial, Michael Pitt-Rivers and Peter Wildeblood together with Lord Montagu were charged with indecency and conspiracy.

and floated slowly upwards. Then when my health packed up I retired on a full pension at the age of fifty-seven.

Q: *Do you think you were sacked because of the climate of the Montagu trials?*

No, if anything the Montagu trials were favourable to us. Generally, it was felt that Peter Wildeblood and Michael Pitt-Rivers were rather harshly treated. No, I think there was no question the Lord Montagu case did make the opening which made the law change. I think the fear was that I might do something that might bring shame on the theatre. They didn't know that I'd had sex with a large number of projectionists around the place – including, on one occasion, in that very cinema, behind the screen!

Q: *So when did you first become involved in the gay movement?*

Well I realized I was a Unitarian as a prisoner-of-war. I came back to this country and the local Unitarian church wasn't very inspiring and I did nothing more about it until '71, when I went back to the local Golders Green Unitarian church. I was very impressed by what I heard on theological grounds; it was a permission to be a humanist. You didn't have to believe in God to belong to the church and the second Sunday that I went along I picked up their national newspaper and there was an item which said, 'Gay/Straight Integration'. The first line was: 'Bottle party opens club for homosexuals – so ran the banner headline of the local newspaper.' And it went on to tell about a group called Integroup, which Tony Cross and Rose Robertson had started in Catford, and the idea was that gays and straights met on the basis of mutual esteem. There was a full-page article and it ended with a delightful glossary: 'Gay – homosexual; straight – heterosexual; affair – long-lasting relationship. Gay ghettos – segregated homosexual group. Drag queen: gay liberation,' and so on. And I thought, 'This church has really got something,' and I became involved.

And then the minister of our church invited Tony Cross and Rose Robertson to come over and talk to our church about it, and I went to the first meeting. I had no desire to come out but my lover, who is not a Unitarian, said, 'Speaking as a practising homosexual . . .' Anyway nobody paid the slightest attention. When the talk was over, the elderly church secretary – an impeccably respectable woman – said, 'Now, Dudley, coming down to more mundane subjects, I think I've found some good chairs for the hall.' That's as much attention she paid. So I was 'out' in church and I became more 'out'. We started our own Integroup and I became secretary and remained secretary for ten years, and we made a very great move forward – basically pushing the local paper to print good, positive stuff about gay things. Instead of it being 'gross indecency', it became 'Rabbi Says Yes, There Are Gay Jews' and that sort of thing.

Around this time, the local paper was running a campaign to close the cottage in Hendon Park, which quite honestly deserved to be closed, but they were writing in rather extreme terms and the minister wrote in on one occasion after a headline which said, 'Children flee from Lavatory' at the sights they'd seen, asking what sights they'd seen that had frightened them so? In any case, GLF mounted, believe it or not, a march on the *Hendon and Finchley Times* and the editor, Denis Signey, just couldn't believe that this number of gay people should come out on the streets and protest at his newspaper. We were pumping good stuff to him about three months later and he published it, and he kept on and he's been extremely good with it.

When I was fully and publicly 'out', I was appointed assistant to the minister and, as such, was authorized to marry people in church. Although I'm not keen on 'gay weddings', I am willing to take services affirming and confirming loving relationships between same-sex couples. If a mixed couple can have a church service, it would be quite wrong not to give a lesbian or gay couple the same treatment.

When *Gay News* started it so happened that their office was near where I worked, so I bought twenty copies and sold them at Integroup and therefore, in a sense, I became involved in the gay community. I was involved in Gay Switchboard from the start. It had been set up by *Gay News*, partly to relieve them of the need to deal with problem calls. The calls were important, but they made producing a newspaper difficult. As a 'contact', I was called in at the first dreary meeting at the Boltons. From that meeting emerged a working party committee. When we started, I did a regular Wednesday evening-shift, firstly as a duty, but I soon learned to enjoy the work. At one time I was their press officer but now I just do a regular Thursday afternoon-shift and look after the Religious File.

The Gay Bereavement Project started in church, when three women were widowed suddenly and a bereavement project was started for them, and it immediately struck me that if three widows who were all well connected with the community needed help, then how much more so do homosexuals who are isolated. The minister agreed to set up a gay bereavement support group and it was jointly sponsored by the Golders Green Unitarians and Integroup. It soon became clear that a telephone counselling and support scheme was needed, not a self-help group, so the present project was set up.

Lesbians and gay men who are bereaved can't grieve publicly: they're likely to be at the back of the crematorium, not in the front row. Sometimes they'll be excluded altogether. Also, a widow or widower can talk about it openly – at the office, for instance. A lesbian or gay man probably can't. The bereaved gays are usually older and the majority of those over sixty are very closeted. I suppose Bernard and I are two of the very few people of that age who are very much 'out'. People say to us, 'We always kept ourselves to ourselves, we didn't like the scene.' They hadn't got any friends, or perhaps they'd got a couple of friends they used to have dinner with.

From the counselling, we discovered that one of the major problems was that people would not write wills, so consequently when one died the other lost a home as well as a lover. They'd make no provisions, like having joint leases or having a car in both names. There's another problem, too, that this house is in my name. If I die before Bernard, he inherits in my will but he'll have to pay inheritance tax on it. If it was my wife, she wouldn't.

For the future there are problems. I'm sixty-seven and have a bad heart. When I die, Bernard will be bereaved and have to pull out of the Gay Bereavement Project, since he and I are the only two people who do the daytime-shift and, by our rules, nobody can be a counsellor who has been bereaved within the previous two years. But, by being aware of this problem, we are on the way to solving it.

I've been back to Thailand. A Japanese soldier has built a

temple on the banks of the River Kwai in memory of all who died building the railway. Sadly, not very many Japanese supported him. They didn't see they'd done anything wrong. They weren't ashamed and it's true likewise with us: most of my prisoner-of-war colleagues are a bit against it. I went along and I took with me a letter from my church, saying we thought it was a good job. I wrote the letter. It's a bit pompous and flowery, but it ended up, 'We believe that the bridge you're building between the previously warring nations will last longer than the iron bridge built during the war.' I feel fairly strongly about this. Next Remembrance Sunday, I plan to get some gold-leaf and not exactly consecrate it, because I don't believe in consecration, but when I go there next February I will apply the gold-leaf to the Buddha image. In Thailand it's appropriate. People show their respect by applying patches of gold-leaf to the images and I would rather like to go along to this image and put a little patch of gold-leaf on it as my sort of token.

POSTSCRIPT BY DUDLEY CAVE, MAY 1988

Our church raised enough money to buy a temple bell for the shrine and I went to the hanging ceremony in February '87. While I was there, I did apply my bit of gold-leaf! As a result of that, I was invited to Japan to speak at a peace movement alternative to the militaristic ceremony at the main Shinto shrine in Osaka and I had a wonderful week.

Incidentally, Philip Bloom, the sexologist I saw in Singapore, became the director of the Kensington Marriage Guidance clinic. About twenty-five years ago, when Bernard's and my togetherness seemed in danger of flying apart, we went to see him and he sorted us out!

1988. Portrait by Sunil Gupta

JOHN ALCOCK

INTERVIEWED IN JULY 1985 BY PAUL MARSHALL

I was born in Ladywood, Birmingham, in 1927 of very ordinary working people. My father was a caster in a brass foundry and made ingots and things like that and my mother was a housewife. Both given to booze. They used to drink quite a lot. I was the eldest of five; one brother and three sisters and they're all still alive. My parents are dead.

Although father was in full-time work there was no money and there were always fights and arguments, usually over domestic things. We lived in a very small house, just three rooms and an outside toilet. My father and mother used to nearly always fight on a Friday night. I hated Friday nights for that reason. It was payday, you see, and they would go out drinking and they would invariably come back drunk. They would start arguing and it would always get violent and they'd throw bottles at one another and things like that. I've always had a tendency to be anxious and I think that's where my anxieties sprang from. It was very, very unpleasant.

I went to the local elementary school when I was five. I didn't like playing games at school – football and cricket. They tried to encourage me, but I just didn't like them. I always made a point of making up to the school bully so that he would always protect me on the side. I remember his name, Jimmy Flood. He was a Black boy. We were great performers together – always playing around. I remember him with great affection. When the war came we were evacuated. I was twelve and I never went back to school, so I lost the most important part of my education. I remember that I used to knit and sew and also do my sister's hair, comb it and curl it with iron curling tongs. My grandmother taught me to

41

knit one, purl one. She was a very dear old lady. She had an oil lamp in the centre of the room and she had the lamp very close to the table and would be attaching buttons to a card. She used to do homework and when you went in she had to lift the lamp up, which was on a weight, so she could see you. Otherwise she was too close to the light. She did this work to make money and, when the war came, she switched over to making wound-clips.

I can't really remember the build-up to war. I know it was an exciting time for us kids but, you see, newspapers were scarce; we couldn't afford them anyway. But I remember my father used to read a newspaper called the *Daily Herald* which was a socialist newspaper. We had no radio – or 'wireless' as we called it – but there were one or two houses that I'd be invited into that had one. I remember the Chinese war from the newsreels at the cinema, but I didn't particularly like the newsreels in those days. I wanted to get on with the business of cops and robbers. I used to go to the pictures as often as I could and I used to bunk in nine times out of ten. We'd get the money together with one of us in and that one would go to the lavatory and push the bar on the door and let the rest of us in. Sometimes I used to collect horse manure and sell it for a penny a bucket and then I got the two pennies which was all it cost to go to the cinema, tuppence.

Q: *Can you remember having any sexual feelings when you were a child?*

Oh, yes, yes. I can remember clearly back to ten years old and I was getting sexual feelings then. I used to deliberately go to places where that kind of thing would be going on – along the canal and places like that. I was coming up to thirteen years old and I met this particular man and he offered me a cigarette. We walked along and we smoked a cigarette. Then he took me on to an incline and we lay in the tall grass and he took my clothes off and he made love to me. I remember it with gratitude. I wanted to tell the world. It was a fantastic experience and, even at this late stage in life, I like to go to Birmingham and I always make a point of going to the canal and reliving those early childhood memories.

I was twelve when war broke out and we were evacuated to Herefordshire. We were looked after by a Mr and Mrs Davis, very practical and down-to-earth country people. I used to spend a lot of time at the local farm and get myself in the hayloft with the farmer's son, which I found very enjoyable. I was there for about eighteen months and then my mother came to get me because I was old enough to go to work. She and my father would be thinking what all working-class people thought at that time – another pair of hands working and bringing in money. So I went to work in a factory, making parts for tanks and things like that. It was all munitions work then.

Birmingham, looking at it from a child's mind, was quite beautiful and exciting then. There was a blackout and, because Birmingham was industrial, it was very foggy. Consequently, in the winter months you could hardly see where you were going. Food was rationed and cigarettes were in short supply and it was difficult for Mother to get enough food. There was a joke at the time that whenever you saw a queue outside a shop, you joined it before asking what it was for! I remember that I used to like to go out and collect shrapnel after the air raids.

I was getting on OK with the people I worked with at the factory. They used to call me cissy and make remarks like that. I seem to remember I just regarded myself as being like that – a cissy or whatever – so it didn't bother me. I got on fairly well with people. I was fortunate enough to have a nice disposition as a kid and I was full of life, too, always singing the latest pop records.

I used to meet a lot of soldiers and American airforce men in the street and I'd stand outside the USO canteen and ask American soldiers for chewing gum. I was a very pretty boy and I was always being taken for cups of tea and things like that. I used to stand outside public toilets, not knowing what I was there for but I knew that there was action of some sort there. And I remember a lovely lady by the name of Nellie, who was a prostitute. She warned me about the police and said that if anyone was to ask for a woman to come and fetch her, and if anyone asked her for a boy then she would fetch me! I can't remember her ever bringing me any customers and I'm sure I didn't take her any either, but I would always get a constant supply of cigarettes from Nellie.

In about '44, I went to work at a camp in Herefordshire for voluntary land-workers. I wasn't old enough to into the Services, so I was in a sort of limbo period. I worked in the kitchens, peeling potatoes and things like that. Then I was sent out to a farm to work alongside Italian prisoners-of-war. They were looked on very differently from German prisoners-of-war. They had a certain amount of freedom. You weren't supposed to fraternize, but I didn't allow that to put me off. I always managed to miss the truck back, so I would be left alone there and I'd go for walks with some of them. They couldn't speak a word of English and I couldn't speak a word of Italian, of course, but we got along very well. I would make it very obvious that I wanted to be made love to and invariably that would happen.

There was a dance hall within the hostel and a Jewish girl called Lisa Levine taught me to dance. She became my partner and we even won a prize. In those days you always had one particular girl that you went dancing with, but I was more interested in the boys than I ever was with the girls. The soldiers fascinated me. I remember that some conscientious objectors used to come to the dances and I used to like to spend my time with them. They were kind, gentle men.

One important point that I remember from that period was when the director of entertainments at the hostel went on a trip to America. He was homosexual and he came back and he told me that the boys in America didn't call each other 'queer', they called one another 'gay'. That was the first time I heard the word 'gay', so it's been around a long time. But we still referred to one another as 'queens' or 'queer'.

I met my first lover at the hostel. He had the unfortunate name of John Thomas and with my name, Alcock, you can imagine: we were like a music-hall act together. But he was a very possessive young man and it made life more of a misery for me than anything else.

It was about this time that I went to London for the first time, for a weekend. I found myself in Leicester Square and it was fascinating for me to see young airforce men in uniform with make-up on! I went back to the hostel and told my boyfriend that I wanted to go to London and he said that he always knew that would happen, that once I saw London I'd never be able to keep away from it. So we packed up and went to London and stayed there until I went into the army.

I didn't particularly want to go into the army, so we kept on moving addresses and eventually the police caught up with me, so

I had to go. I was in the Army Catering Corps, and I remember lying in the dark on the first night, aware that quite a lot of boys around me were crying, but I didn't cry. To me, it was a lovely situation to be in. I was there with all the fellows and I knew that I was going to enjoy it. I wasn't afraid of dying. To me, it was just one big laugh.

I had basic training. I was absolutely useless at that. I couldn't hold a gun: it terrified me. I had to be on the rifle range one day and I had twenty rounds and I shot all twenty and then I had to go to the board and bring back my score and there was one hole on it. I said to the sergeant, 'I must be the best shot in the battalion. I got twenty bullets all through the same hole!' He wasn't amused by that at all.

I met my first gay friend in the army, Ken Starkey, and then it was virtually plain sailing. We'd go to pubs together and we'd camp it up and once, when we were walking along the road, an officer was coming towards us, and he said, 'Come on, girls, straighten up your shoulders and give this officer a salute'! I had a marvellous time with Ken, it was just one big laugh. It wasn't a sexual relationship. It was regarded amongst the queens of that particular period that it was not the done thing to have sex with one of our own kind. We only had sex with what we regarded as the men, not the queer boys. With the men we called it 'trade' – with one another we called it 'tootsie trade' and not the proper thing. I think it probably was the stereotype that had been planted on us. We were queer, so we were much more like women than we were like men and so you had to go with men and not with your own kind. Of course, I realized years later that we were playing it all the wrong way round. We should only have gone for our own kind.

On my first leave I found myself in the West End of London and I met two other queer soldiers in Leicester Square and I remember we walked along arm-in-arm, our berets cocked at a jaunty angle. We were staying at the YMCA in Victoria for the night and were very amused, lying in bed, listening to one or two of the other soldiers mentioning the fact that they saw three queer soldiers walking through the West End of London.

Places to go to in those days were a bit thin on the ground, but the Regent Palace hotel had a men-only bar called the Shake Up Bar so I went there. I was sitting at the bar and I became aware

John Alcock (left) and his lover, Hughie, 1946

John (aged 4) and his sister, Audrey, 1931

John in 1954

47

John (right) and friend, Maida Vale, London, 1956

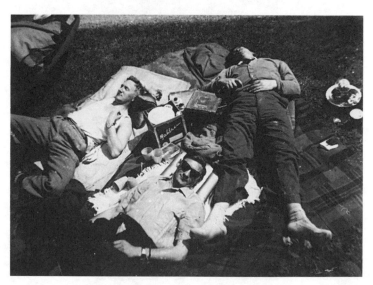

John and friends, Scotland, 1958

of the amount of officers that were standing around, including two from my own battalion in Portsmouth, and that all the officers were homosexual and it gave me a tremendous lift to realize that other ranks were queer the same as I was. On the following Monday when I got back to the battalion, one of these officers was coming towards me and we saluted each other and, as he passed, he said, 'Had a nice weekend, dear? Keep it to yourself.' And that sort of gave me strength.

I didn't do my full two years' service. I'd had enough, so I went to the medical officer and I told him I was homosexual and, of course, if you admitted to being homosexual in those days you were automatically released from the army. We called it 'taking the veil', so I took the veil quite early. The war was over by then. I also had gonorrhoea and the treatment was rather unpleasant. There was no penicillin, so a tube was put down my penis and it was washed out with some kind of solution.

I was discharged from the army directly from the hospital. I was standing at Netley station and there was an airforce officer, a squadron leader, looking at me. He got in the train with me and sat with me and we went to the Imperial hotel in Russell Square and we spent a couple of days there together, which was very nice. We watched the Victory Parade together from the doorway of Wyndham's theatre in Charing Cross Road.

I then went down to Hayling Island and stayed with a friend. One particular night I went over to the Criterion, a gay pub in Portsmouth, and that was where I met my lover Hughie. It was the first time I'd ever fallen in love and it was very much love at first sight. It was very sad because we didn't really know how to handle it. We used to cry a lot because he was still in the Marines. It was very painful if he was away for just a couple of hours and invariably he would have to leave me for at least eight hours, so it was fraught with unhappiness. One day I went to meet him and he wasn't there. He'd left a letter for me saying that he would always love me but he had to go home to see his mother and father. He would think about things while he was away, and he'd come back to me as soon as possible but not to follow him. Of course, being impetuous, I didn't wait at all. So I got on a train and I went up to Scotland and he was waiting for me. We got the next train back and we lived here, in Randolph Avenue, for the next ten years.

I did the shopping, cooking and housework – the domestic side of life. That's the way I wanted it to be. In my ignorance, I wanted to play the female part of everything in our life and he played the male part. He was a very clever engineer. He could take a car to pieces and put it back together again, which always amazed me. I loved him. I realized I depended a great deal on him. I was very stupid in that sense, but I was also very young and very naïve in many respects. But I loved him dearly – passionately. I sometimes look at him now and I'm always pleased that I loved him to the extent that I did, because that love has taught me a great deal about life and about myself. He in no way feels that way about me. I think now that he just looks at it as a friendship. We never talk about our relationship in any deep way. He won't allow it. He doesn't like to examine himself, it frightens him and he doesn't like me at all when I get on to a serious thing. He won't have me talking about politics or anything like that; he just likes me to be very nice and gentle and quiet, which frustrates me terribly. In the end he joined the merchant navy on the *Queen Mary* as an engineer. He met someone else eventually and our relationship came to an end. Unfortunately for me, I carried a torch for him for a long time and I realize now that that was a mistake on my part. But what else could I do? That was how I felt.

Then I met other people. One- or two-night stands. I was very promiscuous and I started drinking heavily, too. I was working as a waiter at Lyons Corner House, but then I got a job on the dining cars of the old Great Western Railway, which operated out of Paddington. I worked with two ex-merchant seamen and, of course, as soon as they spotted me they knew I was a dizzy queen. They told me that I should be working on the boats, because that's where the real queer life was. It was very difficult to get into the merchant navy, but I persevered and finally I sailed away to sea. I ended up on the *Coronia*, which sailed round the world. It was a period of my life which I live on to this very day. It was beautiful, the ten years I spent at sea.

Of course, it was hard work, but there were at least thirty of us on the ship – thirty gay queens – so I managed to have a wonderful time. A world trip took three months and, of course, you had your shore leave. You were sleeping with a Japanese one night, a Chinese the next and a Puerto Rican the next. It was

JOHN ALCOCK

wonderful. I never had sexual relations with anyone on board the
ship; we'd always have our romances on shore. The queer men
would always be together; we had cabins which were designated as
ours. I soon discovered that if ever there was a scandal on board
ship – like somebody touched you up or tried to get in between
the sheets with you – it always involved somebody that no one else
knew about. It was the closet people who did things like that, the
people who did not want to be discovered. Those were the ones
who got themselves into trouble.

Q: *What sort of places did you go to on leave in London in the
fifties?*

The Fitzroy Tavern was still going and there were the clubs. The
Pink Elephant in Soho, the A and B which used to be in Rupert
Street, and there was the Festival club behind the Coliseum. Gay
bars in that particular period were so oppressive. You went in
them and you felt that every pair of eyes was on you all the time:
'Who's this new predator that's arrived?' Every time the door
opened everybody's eyes would go round as if the police were
going to come in at any moment. There was always that uncertainty. It was extremely unpleasant. I had a tendency not to
frequent gay bars because of that. I would go to my own local bars
and I found that I met men just as easily in those bars as I did
anywhere else.

Q: *Can you tell me something about the language you used to use
with other gay men at this time?*

This was known as Parlyaree. I don't know the exact origins of
it. It's a mixture of taking words and spelling them backwards,
but there's a Romany influence there as well as a strong merchant
navy one. We created words for our own use and it came in from
the ships into the dockside pubs and then the gay pubs. This was
the language we spoke. It was great fun, of course, and it also
enabled us to communicate with one another without other people
being able to understand what we were talking about, though I
think some of the words – like 'bona', meaning *good, very nice, it's
great* – was used by all kinds of underground-influenced people.
Another word was 'riha', meaning *hair*. 'Lallies' means *legs*; 'bats'

51

– *feet*; 'Martinis' – *hands*; 'ogles' – *eyes*; 'ogale fakes' – *eye glasses*. *Ears* – 'Aunt Nell', which means *hear* as well. If you say 'Aunt Nell', you're saying to someone that you want them to listen to you. Then of course there's 'drag', which is quite universal. So you have 'valley drags', which are *trousers*. Quite a lot of people use it, particularly in the theatre. 'Camp' and 'butch' are both used by everyone now, of course.

While I was at sea I used to read a magazine called *The Psychiatrist*. The word 'homosexual' caught my eye and I saw that it was an advertisement for the Homosexual Law Reform Society. At about this time I decided to have a rest from the sea and went back to work as a waiter at Lyons Corner House. It was just around the corner from the Law Reform Society at 32 Shaftesbury Avenue. I had imagined that it would be a little office in a dingy block, but when I went there it was five rooms and a hive of activity, with women – I had never imagined women to be there – beavering away. I became instantly interested in it and I devoted all my spare time and spare money to getting the 1967 Act through.

The list of people backing the organization was incredible: the Archbishop of Canterbury, Brigid Brophy, Leo Abse and other Members of Parliament. J. B. Priestley was the president of the Homosexual Law Reform Society and the vice-president was the Chief Commissioner of the London Police, C.H. Rolfe. That gave me a kick. I think that he knew that it was time the law was changed because there was an awful lot of sadness. Men were committing suicide and people were being blackmailed and robbed, being beaten up – all kinds of things like that were happening.

I personally became very frightened during the time of the Peter Wildeblood trials in the fifties. I thought that every policeman coming up to me in the street was going to arrest me. I always looked over my shoulder when I was bringing a gentleman home to entertain, usually a labourer – I always had a tendency towards men who worked on the road. The temperature of the time was quite unpleasant. We thought we were all going to be arrested and there was going to be a big swoop. The newspapers were full of it. I got so frightened that I burnt all my love letters from Hughie. Fortunately, things became a little more relaxed in the early sixties. Films like *Victim* with Dirk Bogarde – we were able to identify a little with that.

But the law was definitely a blackmailer's charter. It was a piece of legislation that we had to rid ourselves of and yet – I can say this with all sincerity – at the time our worst enemies were our own kind. I think it was because they had been conditioned to think that a change in the law would somehow expose them, or if the law was changed it wouldn't be so good as it was then.

When the Bill was actually passed, it was two in the morning, and I came out of the House of Commons with Antony Grey and all the crowd and we all said goodnight to one another. I walked down to the Embankment and I stood and lit a cigarette and was looking down into the water and I was very aware that I'd been part of making history. Part of something that people will be very glad about. I feel quite sure, for instance, that young people will look back and not understand how we could persecute men in such a barbaric way. [The Sexual Offences Act 1967 decriminalized male homosexual activities in private for consenting adults over the age of twenty-one.]

Q: *Can you tell me what your politics were at this time?*

I voted Conservative until '66. It's very easy for me to pinpoint the date because that was when I first became involved with the Homosexual Law Reform Society. Until then I didn't even know what left and right meant! I had never been interested. It just seemed the natural thing to me to vote Conservative. I realize now that that came about because I was a waiter and I depended on the money that I picked up off the table. The more wealthy people were, the more service that I gave, the more money I made. I now realize how dreadfully wrong I was. During the Law Reform days I did a television interview. I spoke to Antony Grey about it. I wanted to arm myself with answers to any political questions the interviewer might ask me. Antony Grey pointed out, at the time, that the Labour Party would be more in favour of a change in the law than the Conservatives. Also, through spending a lot of time at the House of Commons, I was exposed to politics and how they worked.

Now I would say that I am very much over to the left. Although I do not embrace communism in all its aspects, I am moving towards it. I look at politics as a very wide spectrum, which involves conservation. Greed ruins the atmosphere and the earth

53

and, of course, capitalism represents greed. My vote would be wasted if I voted Communist, so I always vote Labour, although sometimes the Labour Party has annoyed me intensely.

Part of my move towards the left is because I am an 'out' gay and I mix with a lot of gay people, particularly on Hampstead Heath, on the gay lawn where we all congregate. There is one group of communist boys who go up there and they always appear to me to be so lovely and gentle. There's no aggression amongst them whatsoever and I instinctively like them. The heath is a very important place for me now. One of the sad things is that I didn't discover it until I was gone forty years old. It was on Hampstead Heath that I saw a boy reading *Gay News* and I didn't know there was such a newspaper. I started to read it and I saw an advert for a Campaign for Homosexual Equality fair, and I went along to it and then I got hooked and I became very interested in CHE from that time.

In the late sixties I was going through a period of heavy drinking. I had always drunk a lot from the time that I went into the army and it sort of escalated from brown ale to the heavier stuff in the merchant navy. I had a tendency to be overweight and the doctor suggested I only drink Scotch and water and nothing else. Unfortunately, you become addicted to alcohol and I became heavier as the years went by. Of course it was very tied up with sex as well, because when I'd had enough to drink it was very easy for me then to go out and chat up gentlemen in order to have sex with them. Of course it was a terrible waste of time, because invariably I was quite incapable of performing. I suppose it was like what a lot of men go through, both homosexuals and heterosexuals: a period of uncertainty, dissatisfaction with life. I made a great many friends during that period and I still have some of them, but some have fallen by the wayside because friendships that are made in pubs are not very permanent – they're like clouds, they come and go. I'm glad to say that I don't drink at all now. I don't moralize about it at all; I understand people getting drunk. They're very unhappy people; they just want to get away from themselves.

Q: *How do you feel about getting older?*

I'm aware of it from the point of view of physical things but, if anything, I'm now in a period of my life which is definitely better – happier, more solid. I'm more aware than I've ever been in my life. I think I look better now than I've ever looked before, and I also feel more confident.

From the point of view of money, what I have now is just sufficient to cover basic necessities. I have a Social Security disability pension. It's not really sufficient to live on. My colour television has to be paid for and my telephone: two things that I will not give up – I would rather cut back on food. But my benefit could and should be three times more. I think that the average pensioner in this country, who has worked for forty years, deserves at least £100 a week. I should be able to go to the theatre and cinema at least once a week and buy birthday presents for people and entertain a great deal more than I do. All that is part of enjoying life and you shouldn't be denied it. The government – any govern ment – should get around to thinking that way, because, after all, what is given to us in the pension is spent, so it's merely another way of putting money back into the system.

I have a very close, wide circle of friends: actors, writers, dancers, a betting-shop manager – oh, you name it! Most of them are young – around thirty years old. I enjoy living on my own and having the freedom to do what I want, when I want. I wouldn't be without my cats, mind you. I talk to them. They're a very important part of me; they're very important for my health.

One of the side-effects of the medication that I'm taking for my high blood pressure is the lack of an erection. This doesn't cause me any particular problem because I'm passive by nature anyway. On the occasions when I do have sex, I manage OK. You don't necessarily have to show by an erection that you're enjoying yourself and partners understand that and sail along with me.

Q: *Do you have an image of yourself – see yourself in a certain sort of way?*

Yes. I have an image of myself as a kind of camp, slightly corpulent, mincing queen, in love with life, full of chat and trying to be as understanding as I possibly can. That's the image I see of myself, but definitely camp. I adore people breaking into a smile when they see me. That's great. Very, very rewarding.

1988. Portrait by Sunil Gupta

BERNARD DOBSON

INTERVIEWED IN SEPTEMBER 1985 BY PAUL MARSHALL

My parents were both very young when they married. I was on the way, so that's why they married and I was born in Shipley in Yorkshire in March 1927. My mother was the daughter of a miner. I remember in my early childhood living in a one-up, one-down terraced house just outside Bradford and my father being out of work. This must have been '31.

When I was four, my parents both developed consumption. I remember being taken to a children's home with my sister and waiting in a room with wooden benches and my parents going away. I was frightened and bewildered. My parents died shortly afterwards. It was in the days when people died of TB.

Eventually, we were moved from what they called the Central Home and put into a smaller home, with eight other children and a foster mother. I disliked her very much. She used to give us a whack across the head at least once a day. I don't think she loved children very much, or, if she did, she'd lost that love over the years. I wasn't happy there.

I was twelve or thirteen when I was taken out of the home by an uncle and aunt. Another uncle and aunt took my sister. I was with them for about a year until I proved to be a delinquent lad, stealing and playing truant. I was too difficult to cope with, so the uncle and aunt who had taken my sister took me as well, and I called them Mum and Dad.

I left school when I was fourteen and went to work in my dad's health food shop. He was a herbalist, a member of the National Institute of Medical Herbalists. People used to consult him and he would prescribe them herbal medicines. Working there, I wasn't in a situation where I met other lads, so I was very lonely.

57

It was at that stage that I began to have rather romantic sexual feelings. It was during the war and there were soldiers in town, and I used to dream of encountering some marvellous soldier or sailor. I didn't know what we'd do together, I just thought it would be marvellous to meet one, to have a great friend – maybe somebody about twenty, a grown man – and it would be wonderful. Looking back on it, I realize that I was living in a period of patriotism. All the ideals of manhood were embodied in soldiers and sailors and airforce men. These were the heroes in films and in the comics that I read. Perhaps I identified – this was the ideal male, this was the sort of man I wanted to be.

One day, my dad decided that I'd reached the age when he should give me a talk about the facts of life. He said that sometimes I might find I'd got an erection when I woke up in the morning. But an erection to me was a building! So I said, 'What do you mean by an erection?' He said, 'Well, your penis may go hard.' And I thought, 'Oh, that's an erection!' He told me that this was perfectly natural, that boys quite often played with themselves and when they did they produced this sticky fluid. It was a nice feeling, so maybe they did it again and again. All boys did it and I wouldn't come to any harm.

The funny thing was that I'd never done it before, so, the very next day when I was alone in the house, I lay on the bed and masturbated. I thought, 'This is fun.' So I promptly started and went at it like mad for the next two or three years. Needless to say, I never told my dad that he started me doing this!

At weekends the family used to go walking over the Yorkshire Dales, which I loved. I was also encouraged to read a lot. My dad was a member of a book club called Readers' Union. So I discovered H.E. Bates and read all his novels and short stories, and then went on to other books in the house: John Buchan, Stefan Zweig, J.B. Priestley and Ethel Mannin. I read poetry as well.

I first became interested in politics then. My dad was a member of the old Independent Labour Party. Fenner Brockway was one of the members then and James Maxton. I first started reading political things through the *Daily Herald* and the weekly *Socialist Leader*. So my politics were shaped by my dad.

He used to get a magazine called *The Countryman*, which I used to read. It all sounded marvellous – a romantic life in the country with the birds singing and the apple trees blooming. I decided I wanted to do that sort of work. My dad arranged a job for me, on an estate in Hampshire, near Borden, which was a huge army camp. And that's where I had my first sexual experience.

There was bombing going on in London, this would have been 1943-4, so a lot of West End theatres were closed and they used to bring the shows down to the garrison theatre, in the army camp at Borden. I was crazy about the theatre and cinema and film stars like Don Ameche and Tyrone Power. I lived in this world of fantasy, to escape from what I thought of as my dreary world. So I used to stand around outside the theatre and get these soldiers to take me in. One night, there was this army sergeant sitting in the row in front of me. During the interval he turned round and started talking to me. The theatre was half-empty so he came round and sat next to me for the second half. And during the second half, there was this knee jammed up against mine and this hand wandering, and I thought, 'This is terribly exciting, this soldier doing this to me!'

When the show was over, he asked me where I lived and I told him – it was about a mile-and-a-half walk away. So we walked out of the camp. It was a long road and there were pine woods at the side, and he said, 'Let's walk through the woods.' It was a light summer night – May or June. We sat down and I knew something was going to happen. He put his arms round me and started kissing me. And I thought, 'Oh, this is marvellous! This is what I've dreamed about!' And he made love to me and I thought, 'This is wonderful that this soldier wants to do this to me.' He found out that I'd never done this with anybody before. He didn't fuck me or anything like that. He was a very tactful fellow. His name was Alex and he was in the Royal Army Medical Corps, part of the Red Berets, an airborne unit who were dropped by parachute. I started seeing him quite a lot. When I used to meet him, I would be standing near him and I would tremble. And if he just touched me I'd immediately get sexually excited. If he just touched me!

After I'd been seeing him for two or three weeks, he told me he was married, and I thought this was extraordinary. I couldn't understand that he could be married, because I knew that married men were interested in women. They wouldn't be interested in boys. I thought that some awful thing had happened in his life – that he'd met me and that was the end of his marriage. So I said to him, 'Now that you've met me you're going to get divorced, aren't you?' He didn't say anything for quite a long time and then he said, 'Well, it's wartime; you mustn't talk about things like that.'

I must have known I was homosexual by then. Along with loads of other books about politics and sexual politics, my dad had books by Havelock Ellis, and also *Towards Democracy* and *The Intermediate Sex* by Edward Carpenter, who was a socialist as well. I read *The Intermediate Sex* and thought that it must be about me. But at the same time I hadn't met anybody like that. I imagined I was the only one in Keighley, except for Stanley who was friendly with the people next door. My mother and father used to talk about him: 'He's a pansy boy,' and, 'Here's Stanley; he's effeminate.' And I used to think, 'Well, I'm not like him. But he must be one of those people as well.' And even when I went away to the farm and met Alex, the soldier, I didn't think of him as being homosexual, because he was married. So I don't really know what I thought.

It was '44, the start of the invasion of France, and Alex's unit was transferred. Meanwhile, I'd got fed up with life on the farm so I went home. Then Alex came home on leave from France and came to see me at the shop. He was a Mormon and he'd come to Bradford for a Mormon do, which was near where I lived. My mum and dad, who were both at the shop that day, thought it was very strange, this man of thirty coming to see me. So I took him home and as soon as we got in the house we got on the sofa and started carrying on like mad. My parents asked him to stay the night and discussed where he should sleep. I was thinking, 'Oh, I want to sleep with him but I can't let them see it.' Eventually, it was arranged that we should sleep together and of course I didn't get any sleep all night! I didn't see him again. He kept up a correspondence but gradually it died away.

I was called up in April '45. I didn't believe in wars. I thought they were bad. But this was supposed to be a war for democracy. I kept thinking, 'I hope to God it stops before I've been in very long, because I don't want to go to the Far East.' The war in Europe was coming to an end, but the war against Japan was still going on. So I was filled with trepidation but excitement as well, because I was going to escape from the oppression of living at home and meet a lot of fellows of my own age, which I did.

I was posted to the HQ of the Durham Light Infantry for basic training. It was supposed to toughen you up – make a man of you. I thought it was horrible. I didn't like all this stuff; having to charge with a fixed bayonet at straw men. I thought it was awful having to scream and shout. But mixed in with it was a feeling of comradeship with all the other young fellows. I just liked being with a lot of lads.

Eventually, I was sent to Epping in Essex to the Royal Army Service Corps. They did clerical work and driving. There were a lot of older men there. Some of them had come back from abroad and were waiting to be discharged. They used to fuss around the younger ones a lot. There was a distinct sexual element there. There used to be a lot of jokes made about who were the prettiest lads and they used to make cracks like, 'I fancy that one'.

I would quite often go up to London on my own, for a weekend, and stay at the Red Shield, a hostel for servicemen, or at the YMCA. I used to go into pubs, such as Ward's Irish Bar in Piccadilly. Invariably, someone would come up and talk to me and make sexual overtures. I met one or two people like that. I also met an actor in St Martin's Lane one day. He lived above the Duke of York's theatre and invited me up for a drink. I thought this was a very strange thing to do, have a drink in the middle of the afternoon! I wasn't what you would call streetwise. Even after having had several sexual experiences, I was still very naïve. I thought he was a bit hoity-toity – he spoke posh – but I went up to his flat. I saw him several times. I was still very passive. I just let him do things to me – kiss me and suck me off, and so on. I wasn't emotionally involved with him at all, but I think at that age you respond to anybody.

I had several sexual encounters during those visits to London. One was with a Canadian soldier I met at the hostel. We went out drinking together and he suggested we find some cheap hotel so that we could spend the night together and have sex. But he wanted to fuck me and I wasn't into this at all, even though he was a nice handsome chap. We ended up having sex, but it wasn't as satisfactory as he would have wanted. But I didn't want to be fucked.

When I went home on leave, I went home as a soldier. I was somebody who was grown up and glamorous – in a uniform. I was a new person. I enjoyed that. I had now become one of the men that I'd wanted to be, or idolized. Not a hero exactly, but part of the army.

61

Reading 'Evil Men', an article about homosexuals, in the *Sunday Pictorial*, Hampstead, London, 1952

In the army, 1945

Bernard and his sister, Betty, Christmas 1945

Before I left home, I'd had great difficulty getting on with my adopted mum and dad, particularly my mum. Looking back on this I realize it was because of what happened to me as a child. Having left my real parents at a very early age, there was a succession of women I had to call Mother, one of whom I disliked intensely. My aunt was my fourth 'mother', and I couldn't get used to calling her that. My father told me that she was very hurt by this. I was also jealous of her. I thought my adoptive father was marvellous and I actually had fantasies of my mum going away, so that there'd just be me, my dad and my sister. I had sexual feelings about him as well. I thought it would be marvellous to sleep with him in his bed. I used to upset my mum a lot. She was a good, kind woman, but I used to think that if she wasn't there, I wouldn't upset her! That terrible antagonistic way in which teenagers sometimes think. It was her fault for being there! Crazy adolescent 'logic'.

It got better after I left home and it wasn't until then that I started giving my mum a kiss on the cheek when we met. There hadn't been many displays of physical affection and, never having been cuddled as a child, I was very wary of physical contact of a non-sexual nature. It's sad looking back on it, because I think it's very important. I wish it had been different.

From Epping I was transferred to Hessle, near Hull. There was mud everywhere and it was very old. But there was this close feeling there, that you get with a lot of men together, a lot of horseplay that had sexual undertones – lots of groping and grabbing and playing around.

There were two particular fellows there who were physical training instructors. They were great chums. Both of them had good physiques and I was really attracted to them – one of them in particular, Ben. I used to cause quarrels between them, because Ben would want to bring me along if they were going out somewhere and his mate would object. They were both married. I had to go into hospital for a while when I caught impetigo – a skin disease – and while I was there I used to write to Ben nearly every day. I told him that I was feeling miserable because I thought about him all the time and that I loved him. He came to see me but he never mentioned what I had written. But when I left hospital it seemed we were even closer and he seemed to drop his mate.

63

He became my special chum and he moved his bed so that he slept on the bunk under me. I remember going out for a walk with him one spring day, across the golf course. We sat down and we started messing around. He was tickling me and acting the fool, and then he'd got his arm around me and we were wrestling. Eventually, we were in a position where he was on top of me and I put my arms right round him and pulled him close and he kissed me before he knew what he was doing. I thought this was marvellous. He pulled himself away and said, 'Oh, I shouldn't have done that. That's wrong, fellas shouldn't do this to each other.' I told him that I was glad he did it, that it was lovely. And he did it some more and then he was just making love to me! Of course, we were much closer after this and we often used to find places where we could carry on.

Then he told me that his wife was coming up for a holiday and staying in lodgings nearby, and so we stopped the sexual carryings-on. He used to slip out at night and see his wife. I felt rejected. I didn't talk about it, I was just very, very cold about it. But after she left we started up again!

Ben was demobbed eventually and I was very upset. I went out for a walk with him and I was crying. Afterwards, I kept in touch by letter for quite a long time. He went home and resumed his marriage, but it was me who finally didn't reply to one of his letters. I just dropped it. But I remembered him for a very long time. I still remember him with affection.

After an unhappy time at another posting, where I fell for a boy who couldn't return my feelings, I asked to be sent abroad. I wasn't; instead, I ended up at a camp near Leeds for German prisoners-of-war who were awaiting repatriation. Our contact with the Germans was strictly limited but nobody felt any hostility towards them.

Soon after arriving there I was made a sergeant in the Education Corps. I ran the camp newspaper. I was interested in current affairs and I used to pinch news from other papers and type it up myself – discussions about life after the war, politics and all sorts of things. I used to get the *Daily Worker* in those days. I wouldn't have said I was a communist, but I was left wing. I was pleased that Labour had come to power in '45, but my politics were rather vague. I didn't have any long-term political views. My politics were basically emotional.

I made friends with another sergeant at the camp. He was quite a tough fellow – a Welshman. I was mad about him. One night, he was in the next bed to me and he said he wanted to get into my bed. We were the only ones in the hut that weekend, and I wanted him to, but I felt rather shy about it. But eventually he did get into my bed and we made love. After that we did it at every opportunity. We used to go swimming in an old, abandoned quarry in the woods and we'd make love. It was a very intense relationship and he had very strong feelings for me, even though he had a girlfriend back home. He used to say he loved me. And I loved him.

Everyone in the camp seemed to know we were crazy about each other. It became accepted that we were special friends and that there was a sexual relationship going on. I had told various people that I didn't like girls, and one day I said, 'You've heard about queers? Well, I'm a queer. I'm homosexual.' They didn't take it seriously; they thought it was a romantic pose. But they eventually accepted it. I felt much easier after that – I felt released, somehow. The year I spent in that camp was a very happy time.

I was demobbed in March '48 and I felt absolutely desolate. I didn't want to go. I liked it there. I'd got loads of friends; discipline was non-existent; I didn't have to think about looking after myself, and I was earning 49s. a week, which, in those days, was a lot of spending money.

On the day I left the army, as I was going around saying good-bye, my stomach was turning over. Some strange, unknown thing was going to happen to me. I was given civilian clothes and a sum of money and I went home. Eventually, I had to get a job, so I moved to Leeds, found a room and a job as an invoice typist. It was very boring. I tried to get a grant to go to drama school at the Bradford Civic Playhouse. I'd been going to weekly classes there whilst I was in the army. I auditioned, was accepted, but was refused a grant. But I'd made contact with a chap in this gay pub in Leeds, called the Mitre. He knew people at Scarborough Rep Company and I managed to get a job there as an assistant stage manager and walk-on actor. I wasn't very good and they got pissed off with me, so I left. I then spent the summer of '49 as a deck-chair attendant on Scarborough beach. I'd been in touch, by letter, with the writer Ethel Mannin, who wrote to me saying,

'Why don't you come to London? All young men come to London eventually.' So I did.

I went to stay at Ethel Mannin's house in Wimbledon for a few weeks, to look for a job and find somewhere to live. Her husband, a writer called Reginald Reynolds, who was a pacifist and a Quaker, was going to India for several months. He had a room in Chelsea where he used to write, so I lived there while he was away. I went to work in Bush House as a messenger. It was awful, so I left and got a job as an invoice typist at Robert Hale, the publishers, in Bedford Square. This was in late '49/'50.

I was quite bewildered by London but I thought it fascinating. Chelsea was quite a different place in those days. The King's Road was really interesting. It was still regarded as a sort of artists' quarter. But I was desperately lonely. I didn't know anyone in London. My room was so small that I couldn't stay there in the evenings, so I used to go out every night into the West End and buy myself a half-pint of beer in some pub. I would go to the Standard, which used to be in Piccadilly, next to the Criterion theatre. That was a gay pub. There was also the Fitzroy, off Tottenham Court Road, which was quite a famous pub especially during the war, and one or two others in Soho which are still there.

I invariably used to meet somebody interesting and I went through a succession of one-night stands for months on end. But I was still very naïve because whenever I met someone with whom I had good sex, I'd think this was the one, and I'd insist on meeting them again but of course they never showed up. This went on for ages.

However, one night in the Fitzroy I did meet somebody, a chap called Jackie, and took him back with me. I thought he was marvellous and he moved in with me, in that little room, although later we had to move out and I found another room in what was then a very slummy part of Chelsea, called World's End. Then I found out that Jackie was a compulsive liar and that he'd been in prison. At about this time I'd broken my arm and so I was off work. Both Jackie and I decided we hated London, so we went up to Scarborough. I still couldn't work, but Jackie got a job in a shop, but he stole and so he had to go to prison. I was left there on my own. Eventually, through a friend, I got a job in Jersey and I lived there for eight or nine months. Then I went back to London.

I got a job in a bookshop, at Kegan Paul's, opposite the British Museum in Great Russell Street. At the end of the street was the old YMCA. In those days it was for men only and it was full of young fellows and I thought this was great. You weren't allowed to wear swimming trunks in the pool – it was considered unhygienic – so, as you can imagine, a lot of people who were gay were members of the YMCA. It was easy to pick people up. There weren't any people snooping around to see what was going on. Later on, there was a bit of scandal when it was brought to the notice of the authorities that there was quite a lot of sexual goings-on taking place. Then you had to wear your swimming trunks and there would be an attendant at the baths, whereas before there wasn't one. But in those days, the early fifties, it all seemed fairly easy, although it wasn't talked about – it was ignored – pushed under the carpet.

Q: *How did you feel about your sexuality?*

Although I was having quite a lot of sex, I think I was analysing it in a very adolescent way. I was thinking that I was homosexual because this or that happened in my childhood, and that it was not the 'natural' thing and it was no good pretending it was. The norm was heterosexuality and although I couldn't do anything about it, it wasn't normal. So although I didn't feel guilty, I had a feeling it was somehow wrong. This went on until I was about twenty-four, then it became irrelevant whether it was right or wrong: this was what I was. I didn't proclaim what I was. In those days you didn't come out at work. It just wasn't talked about very much, except among those of us who were gay, and that's *all* we talked about [laughs].

Although I'd had a lot of sexual encounters, I hadn't made many friends or had any long-term relationships, but in the late summer of '51 I was introduced to Jimmy. Jimmy was a working-class London fellow. He had a very good physique, was sweet and nice and gentle, and yet manly. I was very smitten by him. He'd had a very unhappy childhood; been drafted into coalmines as a 'Bevin boy' and then joined the RAF. When the room under mine, in Hornsey, became vacant he moved in and we became lovers. We then got a flat together and were lovers for the next three or four years. In the meantime, we were both picking up people on the side and not telling each other! Eventually, we did tell each other, but we didn't part and went on living together.

In '55 we gave up our flat and went on a cycling trip around France for five months. France was beautiful and when we got to Provence it was just like riding through a Van Gogh painting, the cypresses shimmering in the heat and the olive groves and the rocks . . . It was a marvellous experience. We went all the way down to the South and stayed at a nudist colony on the Isle de Levant. This had a very liberating effect on me. I felt really like a 'child of nature' with the sunshine and the sea and cooking in the open air. I also met a French boy there, and had an affair with him.

When we came back from France we moved to Hampstead, where we've been ever since. By this time, Jimmy and I rarely had any sexual thing between us – our sexual relationship dwindled away. It was mutual. We were both interested in other people. He had a very intense affair with a chap younger than himself and I had an affair, too, but we didn't split up.

The Peter Wildeblood trials were going on when I was working in a bookshop in the City in the early fifties. John Gielgud was arrested: he was caught importuning in a public lavatory. There was a great scandal about it and of course we talked about it a great deal.

There seemed to be a sort of witch hunt of gays in that particular period that went on for two or three years. It didn't worry me because by that time I had got over all that 'although you're gay you should really be normal' stuff. I'd got past that. I must have felt defiant about it because the *Sunday Pictorial* ran an article that was headlined 'These Evil Men', about homosexuals. Jimmy got a camera and took a photo of me out on the lawn reading this article and holding it up to the camera. It meant that I was saying, 'Up yours!'

It must have been in the early sixties that I read in the *New Statesman* about a meeting to reform the law on homosexuality. I went with a friend of mine to Central Hall, Westminster – it was the first such meeting that had taken place – and we went early, feeling very self-conscious. It was packed out. By going to a place like that, you were proclaiming in a blaze of lights that you were one of these hundreds of homosexual men – they were mostly men – meeting, not in the usual situation, cruising the place, but going there to talk about law reform. On the platform there were people like J.B. Priestley, Kingsley Martin, who was editor of the *New Statesman*, and one or two MPs. There had been quite a spate of articles in the liberal newspapers and left-wing weeklies after the Wildeblood–Montagu trials, about reform. On the platform was a man called Antony Grey who was instrumental in founding the Homosexual Law Reform Society, which went on to become the Albany Trust. I was very excited by the meeting, so I went up to him and told him that he had given a marvellous speech and that I was very interested. He gave me his address and I joined the society.

We used to meet in each other's rooms and talk about how we should spread the word and influence people. I became part of it for quite a long time. I think it was more a social thing for me than it was for Antony Grey and some of his friends. They used to lobby MPs and write articles trying to involve prominent people.

When the law was reformed we were very pleased – we thought it was a marvellous thing to happen, that you weren't considered to be a criminal anymore in the eyes of the law. Although before, the law didn't worry me in the least. I didn't think about risk in those days. There was a time, from '60 to '70, when the sex drive in me was really strong. I'd go down to the West End at least once a week. I'd invariably pick up someone and bring them back for sex and then off they'd go, into the night.

I used to cruise Primrose Hill quite a lot. It wasn't crowded like Hampstead Heath. I only went to the heath a couple of times and it was so dark that I kept falling over tree roots and into puddles. It was really a farce. Like something out of Joe Orton! But Primrose Hill was different because it had lights on the paths.

One night, I got this uncontrollable urge to go out and meet somebody and have some sort of sex. That particular night there was nobody about. Then I saw somebody enter the park. He was walking about fifty yards behind me. So I stood under a tree and this man stood under another tree about twenty yards away. I moved and so did he. I saw another man further down and I thought, 'There's two people around now.' Then the first man moved again. This all took about five or six minutes. Eventually, he moved towards me and I moved towards him and I started rubbing myself. He came a step closer to me. I reached out to him and was just going to touch him when he said, 'Righto, you're under arrest'! I thought he was joking. The other man came up, and he said, 'And my colleague has witnessed what you were doing.' He also claimed that I'd touched him. I could tell he'd been drinking. I could smell whisky on his breath. He was very unpleasant.

They drove me to the police station and charged me, searched me, and took my fingerprints. One of them took me back home. When we got back, we sat in the car and he started talking to me. He said that I wasn't a bad-looking fellow and I didn't have to go up Primrose Hill looking for chaps because there was a pub for homosexuals up the hill, the William IV. Everyone went there. He said that they knew all about what they did up on Hampstead Heath but that the police didn't go up there. Then he asked me why I went up on Primrose Hill, didn't I get any sexual satisfaction? I said that I sometimes felt like going up there to meet people. This conversation went on for about a quarter of an hour. It was very strange.

The next morning, at the court, the police advised me to plead guilty, otherwise I might have to go to another court. If I pleaded guilty, it would be just a small fine. I noticed a journalist sitting there and I was worried that my case might appear in the local newspaper, although the *Hampstead and Highgate Express* had recently written an editorial stating that they weren't going to report on those sorts of cases because of the misery that was caused. Anyway, I went in and the police gave their evidence. They said that I had been observed up there for half an hour, which was untrue, and that I'd been seen to approach various men and touch them and, eventually, I'd approached one of them and importuned him. I listened to this in astonishment and I thought, 'You bastards!'

I was asked if I pleaded guilty. I said that, yes, I was up there looking for somebody, but it's quite untrue what they said because there was nobody up there except those two men. There were three magistrates, and the middle one said, 'Are you telling us the police are not telling the truth?' I said, 'That's right.' They then had a little confab and asked if I'd been drinking, which would be 'mitigating circumstances', of course. I said that, no, I was quite sober. They said that I would be fined £20. Nothing was in any of the papers, so that was that. That was my experience of being

70

arrested. Of course I was up there importuning, but they still lied. It didn't happen the way they said it happened.

Q: *Were you involved in the Gay Liberation Movement?*

Yes, that was the beginning of the seventies and I went to a meeting of the GLF which was held in a large room at the London School of Economics. It was full of men, considerably younger than me – I was about forty then – and I was fascinated to see all these handsome-looking lads around me who were all gay. They were not the sort of gays that I had often mixed with in bars and seedy clubs in Soho and had met in cottages. They were very militant and quite open in their attitude about being gay – not at all worried about anybody in the outside world knowing they were gay. They were very defiant.

The meetings were very 'free' and they didn't like to have any committees, so anybody could speak. The people on the platform were not supposed to be any more privileged than the audience. You could tell them to shut up. I thought this was really anarchic.

The press had begun to take notice, so things were appearing in *The Times* and the *Guardian* and in some of the popular papers. There were rather scandalized reports about it and I remember, at the second or third meeting, there was a great to-do made because they wanted to know who was there from the press. Somebody was there from the *Daily Express*. There was uproar because this paper had been unsympathetic in their reporting. The reporter was immediately asked to leave. I was one of the very 'liberal' types, thinking, 'The freedom of the press – they should be allowed.' I thought it was democratic to let them be there, but I would wholeheartedly agree with banning them now, whether it's undemocratic or not.

It was all quite revolutionary, full of this fire and enthusiasm and this defiance. We could buy badges which had 'GLF' on them. I remember a friend and I used to walk around wearing these and we thought everyone was staring at us. We were quite self-conscious about it; we were proclaiming for the first time to the world that we were gay. It was a very strange time, very exciting. I thought that everybody was going to change; everything was going to get better; everybody was liberated, and all these young people were growing up and they were going to lead quite

71

different lives – they were going to conquer everything. Everybody was going to be accepted and there wasn't going to be a stigma about being gay.

That was when the word 'gay' started to be used. I don't remember encountering it before. I'd stopped using the word 'queer' – it was a nasty word, meaning something odd, ill or sick – so I'd started using the word 'homo'. That sounds awful as well. But when the word 'gay' came along it took me a long time to use it. It took a long time for the press to use it as well, and they then remarked on the fact that this word had been misappropriated. Now everybody knows what it means.

I went to the first big GLF dance at Kensington Town Hall. It was like a first night, what with the police outside and flash bulbs popping and fights going on with the press. Inside, there was this great hall and there were all these men dancing with each other like at an ordinary dance. I was a bit self-conscious about it, but I noticed that so many of the men younger than me weren't. They didn't care – bugger anybody who didn't like them. It really went to my head. It was like drinking champagne!

I went to a demonstration on Highbury Fields one night. A young man had been arrested and fined for soliciting there. His name was Louis Eakes and he had his name in the press because he was leader of the Young Liberals, and so he had been disgraced and all that sort of thing. We all took a candle with us and had a candlelight procession through the gardens. Everyone was staring at us and the police were walking with us. We stopped at one point and we all had to kiss each other and hold hands. I found it a very moving experience.

It was a really exciting period and I think it did liberate me. It did all sorts of things to me which are very difficult to explain. I think it was being able to be open, and also the support – not just from one or two people, but from lots of people. I felt a kind of strength that I'd never experienced before. Using the word 'gay' was symbolic – I was casting off the word 'homo' and using a word which was a good word. It was lighthearted, positive, something you didn't have to be heavy about. I challenged people who used 'homo' or 'queer' after that. I was casting off a tag that society had put on me. It was some sort of liberation of the spirit and the mind. I thought we'd never go back to the old days.

Q: *What about what's happening now, with Section 28?*

This fills me with dismay and rage, because we see every day in the newspapers horrible things about gays. The tabloid press use the word 'poof' now. That's crept back into fashion. I feel really depressed about that – not that I mean I've sunk into a clinical depression! But I feel this impotent rage about what's happening, because I see that it's a return to those old days, thirty years ago, when the *Sunday Pictorial* ran the piece on 'These Evil Men'. It seems as if that sort of mentality is coming back in a much more powerful, virulent form than before. I feel I've reached my age – I'm sixty – and I think, 'God! I've seen something that I thought was a revolution and been involved with it and now we're going back to the bad old days. People are being stirred up to hate people who are gay. We're being made scapegoats again!'

After the trip to France with Jimmy, I worked with him as a gardener for many years, then we worked as tree-pruners on Hampstead Heath. I really enjoyed the outdoor life, but when I was forty I was offered a good job in an antiquarian bookshop. After some hesitation, I took it and worked there for seven years, but eventually I left, thinking that I could work on my own, selling books. I knew a great deal about antiquarian books. I couldn't afford to rent a shop. I bought lots of books and sold them by post and catalogue. The first year I did very well but, by the third year, it became very difficult. One of the reasons was that I didn't like working on my own. So I stopped and took a year off. Then I decided to do something completely different and I got a job with Camden Social Services as a care assistant at a day centre. I was promoted and got a job at another day centre, as a deputy, where I am today.

What I seem to have done in my later life is what many gay people do and, I suspect, what some heterosexuals do too– that is, separate my sexual life from my love/friendship life. The few very close friends that I've got are friends with whom I can be very honest about everything, especially sex. We can tell each other about our romances and our adventures, if we pick people up, and all the things we may have done with other people, all the details – the humiliations, the funny parts and the times when we've done something foolish. These good friends understand these things, so we can be quite open about them. And then, on the other side, is my sex life, when I've picked people up or had a mad, romantic, passionate interlude. My life is divided into these compartments. On one side, close friendship where you can reveal yourself, warts and all. Your friends can see you naked, literally and metaphorically, and accept you. Then there's the sexual side, where what you reveal to your sexual partner is your sexual desires. You present yourself in a certain way – often it's as you think your sexual partner wants to see you, and quite often that's not the real you. Or is it?

Over the years, Jimmy and I have got on better and better. It's a sort of marriage, putting it in those terms, without any sex in it. We often kiss and cuddle each other, though, so there is a sexual element there. I like the feel of him and presumably he likes the feel of me. He's a combination of friend and brother – he's a lover without the sexual side. It's a very, very close relationship in which we see each other at our worst and at our best and still accept each other. We accept each other's sexual carryings-on and don't feel jealous, so I feel that nothing now can break the relationship. After all, we've been living together since '51, which is a long time. He's my best friend and always will be.

TODD BUTLER

INTERVIEWED IN MAY 1988 BY GLEN EVANS

My parents were seniors in high school when they married, but it wasn't a question of 'Whoops! She's pregnant, let's get married.' My mother was the town beauty and my father was also a catch, in that he came from *the* family in Phoebus, a dinky little coastal town in Virginia. My grandfather was at one point the fire chief there and my father ended up being the fire chief, years later. I was born about eleven months later, in 1936.

My mother and father divorced when I was two-and-a-half and my brother was six months. Very unusually for that period, besides actual divorce, was that they agreed that my mother would take me and my father would take my brother, who was given to my grandmother as a 'birthday present' as they shared the same birth date. My mother and I went to Baltimore.

The neighbourhood we lived in was pleasant. Baltimore is famous for its terraced houses and the white marble steps in the front, called 'stoops', which on hot summer nights people used to sit out on. We lived with an elderly French couple who let out rooms. Mr Lebrun was a masseur and his table was at the front. If you came in off the street, it was the first room, with a massage table and the ointments and everything. I used to love the smell of it. Mr Lebrun used to smoke in bed and periodically he would fall asleep, of course, and there was this comedy of every six months or so the mattress flying out the window and the Fire Department showing up. Oh, dear!

My mother was working as a waitress, and when I was around six she remarried. I don't remember disliking my stepfather initially, but I certainly got to the point where I did dislike him and I was very frightened of him. I mean, if he'd looked at me

75

1988. Portrait by Sunil Gupta

the wrong way I'd burst into tears, not that I can think of anything that he actually ever did to me. There was trouble between him and my mother. Later on I discovered one problem was sexual, in that he was one of these guys that had an orgasm, rolled over, and went to sleep. That was it. The idea of the woman having an orgasm – he couldn't care less.

My childhood was spent with my mother and stepfather living together for a while and then separating, then living together for a while and then separating. One night I distinctly remember. I was getting into my pyjamas and my mother came in and said, 'Get dressed. We're leaving.' So I got dressed and she whisked me off again to one of her girlfriends. She would leave my stepfather and it was a question of 'What am I going to do for money?' So then she would go back to work as a waitress until they got back together again. There were moments when there were just beans on the table. I never went hungry, by any means. But we'd go back and forth from pretty close to the poverty line to a certain middle-class affluence.

I must have been an incredibly cissy little boy. Well, not so little – I was always tall for my age – but I was very cissy. I identified so much with my mother. To give you an example: one of my mother's girlfriends was getting married and, after the wedding, I was sitting out in a car crying and someone came over to ask 'Why are you crying?' 'Because my mother's crying.' I figured if she's crying, I should be crying too. I identified with her exclusively – totally rejecting my stepfather and all of his values – and I think my mannerisms aped my mother. She is a very feminine woman.

I went to a Catholic parochial school with strict separation of boys and girls, so it was only boys all the way through the first eight grades. By that time I had converted and then I went to a Catholic high school. The hell I went through in school! I was called 'queer' and 'cissy' and life was not pleasant. One nun discovered, by showing an interest in me, that I was very smart and then you had the combination of being the smartest kid in the school and the cissiest. It was not nice. I can remember a graduation ceremony from the eighth grade – the cap and gown and all. My nearest rival as far as brains was concerned was the big, butch football player, so we were in competition in that sense, and after this ceremony we were walking down the aisle and out of the church and he goes, 'Queer!' This just reduced me. I was just wrecked by that. Obviously it was painful, but for some reason I was also shocked that he said it in church.

I was thirteen then, and by that time I was diddling with several boys. I thought of myself as a good Catholic because I dilly-dallied with the idea of becoming a priest. And even after I came out, a couple of years later, I still considered myself a good Catholic. I just decided that being gay was all right, that God made me the way I am, so therefore it must be all right. I remember having a conversation with myself at fourteen. I'd been coming to downtown Baltimore looking for sex and having sex regularly with men and I really liked it. So I was reviewing this in my mind and thought, 'Sweetheart, I think you're queer and you may as well live with it as best you can.' That was pretty much it.

I remember something that presaged what my sexuality was going to be like. It was in the middle of the war and my mother and I were on a train. It was an overnight ride and it was very cold and the trains were packed with people standing in the aisles. Two marines were standing next to our seats and my mother said, 'Why don't you let one of them sit down and you sit on his lap.' I was maybe eight or nine. So I'm sharing this Marine's lap and am consciously wriggling around and, of course, he got an erection. He had his arms around my waist and at one point he had his hand on my cock. I remember a look passing between him and his buddy, because his buddy must have realized something was going on, and he moved his hand away from me and I took it and put it back on. It's an incident I will never forget because it was terribly erotic for me.

There was also something erotic about VJ Day [the end of the war between the United States and Japan]. My mother, her girlfriend, my aunt and I were in downtown Baltimore. The crowd was packed with all the sailors and everybody kissing everybody else. And I remember during the war, in periods when my mother was separated from my stepfather, that inevitably a boyfriend appeared. It wasn't a constant stream. My mother is a one-man woman, but just one man at a time. I'd wake up in the morning and find some sailor sleeping on the living-room sofa, which had a certain erotic quality to it. Throughout this time there was certainly an erotic tension in the air.

At thirteen I was told the facts of life by my mother and

stepfather, which was an interesting experience. My stepfather gave me good practical advice – you know, if you go out with a whore make sure you wear a rubber. It was a very male-chauvinist viewpoint and I guess he must have told my mother that he had told me the facts of life, because the next night she decided to sit down and tell me her version of it. The two had nothing to do with each other. Hers was around satisfying of the woman, making love and being affectionate and tender. My stepfather hadn't told me any of this.

I had an extraordinary amount of independence at a very early age and, at fourteen, I had already started to arrange my life to the way I wanted. I ran away from home and hitch-hiked to California. One reason was that I had actually failed a subject in school, which to me was appalling. I had suffered a tremendous shock to my ego. It was mid-term break and I was going to a private tutor. One day I just decided to play hookey, to go downtown to the movies. One movie was about New York and I decided I was going there, so I just blithely got a bus ticket and went. There I was with $10 in New York and my school books under my arm, not knowing what the hell I was going to do. So I walked, for ever, and ended up in Jersey and decided, 'I've got this far, I may as well continue this trip and hitch-hike to California to see my favourite aunt.'

Hitch-hiking to California was certainly an education. I had a sob-story for whoever picked me up. If I hit a town, I would go into a hotel or a restaurant and say I'd need some money or food or a place to sleep and that I'd do some work. I remember mopping down a hotel lobby floor. The trip took two weeks and I finally appeared on my aunt's doorstep. She had been notified that I was missing. There were police bulletins out for me and stuff in the paper – the whole thing. There were phone calls to my mother and stepfather, and my stepfather actually cried. I had used him as a convenient excuse for running away, but he never really mistreated me. Why I ran away, I don't know. Probably the sexuality thing, though I'm not aware of any great angst about it. More than anything, it was the blow to my ego about school.

I was shipped back to Baltimore and by this time the school year was blown out of the window. So I had an enormous amount of free time, and my mother's attitude was that if he can hitch-hike to California unscarred, he can pretty much deal with things on his own. Since I wasn't going to school, I was sleeping late and then started going downtown to the cruising park where all the young queens (as we referred to each other) met. There was a little restaurant in this park, and we'd sit there and dish and camp, to use the terms of the day. If you're 'dishing' somebody, you're talking about them in a malicious way: 'camping' meant being outrageous in an effeminate way – doing silly things out loud on the street where people could see you.

The cruising was mostly in cars. You stood on the corner and cars would circle around you. They'd drive by and slow down and that was it. You got in the car and went off and parked somewhere. The guys in the cars were quite often very closety types and probably chicken-hawks – men who like young kids – and then there were the types who liked young queens, the queenier the better. I was a very pretty kid, so I made out very well and was very popular.

Queens never went with other queens. I mean, we were sisters and you did not go to bed with your sister, except in very rare circumstances. And I wasn't interested in effeminate people; a queen to me was not a turn-on at all. I have perhaps some problems around that, but certainly the more masculine a man was, the more interested I was. I met the first love of my life during this period. I was back in school but still cruising downtown. He was eighteen and I was fourteen and I seduced him. I developed an enormous crush, but he was having a lot of trouble about whether he was gay or not, and one night he stood me up on a date. So for no real reason – I mean, I'd been stood up – I packed a bag and headed for California again.

This time I was 'out', so it was always in the back of my mind that there would be the possibility of having some sort of sex with just about every lift. Indeed, something I won't forget is one officer and gentleman of the US army making it with me and then telling me, 'Now get out of the car, faggot.' I was very angry about being abandoned in the middle of nowhere, and I felt bad that I was a queer and the one at fault. I was only fourteen and my consciousness hadn't been raised!

This time my aunt was not terribly surprised to see me. She made some arrangement with a local parish priest to get me into a preparatory school north of Los Angeles, run by the Dominicans. They managed to get me a scholarship, as it was very expensive. It was supported by Irene Dunne and Loretta Young and most of the boys were children of divorced parents or very rich parents who did not want their kids around. Some of the kids were millionaires in their own right, and they were all certainly outside of my economic class. But I don't remember being uncomfortable there. The thing is – no rhyme or reason for it – I ran away again.

I managed to get a job as a bus-boy at San Francisco State College, lying about my age of course. And I even managed to get a place of my own, after living at the YMCA for some period. I thought, 'I've got a job and a place to live. I am proving that I can take care of myself.' So I let my aunt know where I was via a postcard, and two days later the police arrived at the door and I was sent off to my father in Virginia. I was only fifteen.

Being sent to live with my father, for the first time since I was two-and-a-half, was a hoot. I mean, they were getting desperate. My father had remarried not too long before I appeared. My father had not really made any attempt to get to know me and here I was – living with two people, neither of whom I knew, and my brother who was living in the same town with my grandmother who he called Mom. It was a peculiar situation, very bizarre. My stepmother was a perfectly nice woman, but totally unprepared for having a fairly recalcitrant teenage boy dumped on her doorstep. This was a difficult situation for her, because at this point I was very wild. I was used to doing anything I wanted to do. It turned out that a first cousin, who was nineteen, was gay and let me know where the cruising spots were in Norfolk, the naval base nearby. So I was having a very good time. I woke up one night and heard my stepmother and father having an argument about me, and I thought, 'Right. I'm off.' It was the summer – I had finished ninth grade – and I left the next day for New York, got disillusioned with it, and headed for California again.

In Tennessee an eighteen-year-old kid gave me a lift. He was working for the summer on road surveying. We were chatting and I was comparing myself to him and thought, 'I'm nowhere near this. It's time to go home.' I sent my mother a telegram asking for money to get home, and she sent me one saying, 'Get home the same way you got there' – which was fair enough. Looking back on it, I'm sure they were going through emotional wringers every time I disappeared.

This is when I came out to my mother. I went back to Baltimore and started the tenth grade, and was back downtown with the young queen crowd where I met this guy Burt. My mother was separated, renting a room in a house full of strippers, and working at night as a waitress. One night Burt and I were in bed when all of a sudden there's a knocking on the door. It's my mother and it's like, 'What do I do? Help!' Then there's Burt grabbing his clothes and climbing out of the window and me stalling my mother. She's shouting, 'What's going on? Why aren't you letting me in?' I got my pyjamas on and Burt got out of the window and I let my mother in. She's immediately looking under the bed and in the cupboard. She knew somebody was there. There's a bow tie that Burt's forgotten and my mother knows I don't wear a bow tie, so I've snatched it and was hiding it behind my back. She's looking out of the window and sees white shoes. This is back in the white buck days – you know, Pat Boone and white saddle Oxfords. Oh, dear God! Burt of course was wearing these goddam white shoes, pressed up against the wall. She goes, 'Whoever you are, you may as well come in.' Poor Burt comes in, looking like this is it, he's had it – my mother's going to call the police. He's looking very dejected and finally she says, 'Well, get out. Just get out of here.' He flees as fast as he can and as he goes out the door I hand him the bow tie. I came up with some convoluted, ridiculous story which I can't imagine she believed, and shortly after I do just tell her that I'm gay.

It didn't enter my thoughts at all that homosexuality was illegal. Being a minor, I was aware that if I was caught by the police it would be hell for the other person, even though I could be as willing as I was. I always thought it was ridiculous. I certainly was quite capable of seducing people, and did. I have no memory whatsoever of being hassled by the police. Once I was making it with someone in a dark alleyway and a cop caught us. I came up with some silly-ass excuse, trying to get my voice down as far as it could go, and the cop just let us go. The cop obviously knew what was going on but he couldn't be bothered.

My mother finally decided to divorce my stepfather. So while this was going on it was decided that it would be better if I was sent down to Virginia, to be near my father. I was sixteen and it was legal to leave school, so I got a job in an offset-printing place and my own room in Norfolk and proceeded to go out to the gay bars every night and have every sailor within reach. This was during the Korean war and there was a certain atmosphere – you know, 'Let's do it tonight because we don't know what the fuck's going to happen tomorrow.' That whole area was one gigantic navy base.

One afternoon I was with a friend on the beach, fooling around, and these two sailors up on the boardwalk made some smart comment. Before I knew it, all four of us were down in the dunes in their car, guzzling a gallon of sloe gin fizz. Anyway, it was all finished and over with and they said, 'We'll take you back to the barracks.' I had enough sense to say, 'Now, wait a minute, that's a little dangerous.' They said, 'Oh, it's all right. We're the shore patrol.' So off we go and indeed their buddy is on the gate, so no hassle. There were twenty-five guys on the lower floor of the barracks, and the shore patrol went around and woke everybody up. They pushed two bunks into a corner and then somebody else appeared. It was, like: next, lay down, take the towel off, do it, next, out, next – an assembly line. My jaws were very tired.

Everybody was having a good time. There was one guy my friend had, but he was very cute and I decided he was not getting away from me, so I said, 'You! Come here. Get!' He thought we were wonderful, so he was running around to all his buddies, nudging them on to us. There were people who didn't want to know about it, but there were no hassles. I've always been amazed that, in that large group of men, there was not one hint of aggravation. It was just, like, 'Isn't this fun?'

On my seventeenth birthday I joined the airforce. My mother was now living with my present stepfather and there was a proper household going and a place for me to live. I tried going back to school but I was used to leading my own life and it just did not work. Other sixteen-year-olds seemed like such kids to me that I was unhappy and wanted to quit school. The only way my mother would agree was if I went into the Services, which is pretty much what I had in mind. I had realized that there was more to life than being an outrageous, screaming queen and that I was going to have to butch my act up or my life was going to be absolute misery. So part of joining the airforce was to put myself in a situation where I had to do it. And it worked fairly well.

One of the nicest compliments that anyone ever paid me was in a bar in Paris, where I was on leave. There were two young

American lesbians and we were chatting and I mentioned something about having been such a queen and they said, 'Oh, my
God! We thought you were straight.' I was practically in ecstasy
because I had always thought it was written all over my face. It
may have been gay self-oppression, but I do not find effeminate
people sexually attractive and so I didn't want to be what I didn't
like.

We all go through periods in our lives when you can't do
anything wrong, when everything gels. It was like that in Paris.
I was taken to a gay bar where people were actually fighting to
get to me. I was the star and loved every minute of it. There I
was with my crewcut, very obviously a GI and not making any
bones about it. I was a young, fresh, well-built, good-looking
American GI who was available for just about anybody. It was a
moment in my life when it all came together.

I was stationed at a little tiny radar site on the edge of the
Sahara Desert for one year and I think the airforce thought I liked
deserts because they next shipped me to the Mohave Desert in
California, where I had essentially a nine-to-five office job.

Since I was fourteen I had always thought I wanted to be a
dancer, but my mother was not interested. Now was more or less
the first opportunity I had on my own to do it, so I began to take
classes on weekends with one of America's leading ballerinas. The
people on the base knew I danced because, believe it or not, I
entertained at one of the officers' dances. I must have been awful
because I had had no real training. It came time, going on three
years in the airforce, when I had to make some decisions about re-
enlisting – I was officer material in the force's eyes – or seriously
trying to become a ballet dancer. Though I started late, the
woman I was studying with said I happened to have the correct
muscle structure to be a dancer.

It was being diagnosed as having syphilis that decided me. I
could very easily have said it was some whore I picked up in LA,
but I decided to tell them it was with a guy and that I was gay.
At first there was some reluctance on the airforce's part to accept
this, saying it was an isolated incident and it doesn't matter. But
I said it wasn't an isolated incident, that I'd been doing it every
weekend. They thought it was a con to get out and they didn't
want to discharge me. I had just been named 'Airman of the
Month' on the base. I was sent to see a psychologist, and

interrogated for incriminating evidence, which was very stressful, and given a dishonourable discharge. They just washed their hands of me. The thing is, I found out later that it had been a misdiagnosis. I didn't have syphilis and if I hadn't been told that I had, I would never have thought to tell them I'm gay or leave the airforce. Being told that I had syphilis was very shocking.

There was never enough money, so as a dance student in New York I was always hungry. I took classes at the Ballet Theatre School, known later as American Ballet Theatre, and lived for a while in the House of Flowers, a building full of bed-sits managed by a woman who looked like death warmed over. She was cadaverous, with pure white hair and skin, and cheeks that couldn't get any more sunken in. She loved theatre folk, and everybody who got into the house was given the name of an actor of the opposite sex. I was 'Adele Jergens', a grade-B blonde movie star.

Everybody was starving, and poor Steve – the woman who ran the House of Flowers was called 'Steve McNally' – had to put up with people always being behind in the rent. A group of us got together and would eat lunch in my room, because it was cheaper and I had a hotplate. It was illegal to have hotplates and every now and then there'd be a fire inspection. We'd get word of the inspection and you'd get all the queens dashing to hide their hotplates. Looking back on it, it's more amusing than while I was experiencing it.

I was working in a Greenwich Village bar called Lenny's Hideaway, probably the most famous gay bar in Manhattan at that time. Lenny was a front. I mean, the Mafia used to come around to make their pick-ups, and the police came in to get their pay-off too. You couldn't see in unless it was summer and the door was open. Gay bars at that time always had blacked-out windows. You had to look in and they were always gloomy. You could barely see to the other end of the bar, it was so dark.

The bars in New York are open until four o'clock in the morning, so I could be working until that time. And then there were the parties. It could be a party every night – marvellous. In '56 me and Freddie, another dancer, moved into the Village, sharing an apartment. I was one of the few dancers that actually had my own apartment, so there would be dancers' parties. Needless to say, my dancing was going right down the drain.

It was during the period when Freddie lived there that we met

Ginsberg and Kerouac. Freddie had gone to school with Diane Di Prima, who was a struggling young poetess very much into the beat generation. For some reason, she was staying with us. Ginsberg and Kerouac were in town and she got a hold of them and brought them right into our apartment. There was a lot of chatting and bullshitting. Diane was really hot to talk to them, and Freddie much more. I was the outsider in this, though I was impressed that they were there – particularly Kerouac, because he was very sexy. We ended up all of us in bed in the front room. I sort of worked my way down the line. I mean, I made love to Freddie, just kissing, then I fucked Ginsberg and played with Diane, and I blew Kerouac. It was funny, because the whole point of this for me was to get to Kerouac. I knew he was straight and if he was going to turn me down I was going to upbraid him about how he was a phoney with his whole liberal philosophy. But he didn't turn me down at all. Then they disappeared out of our lives.

I was a starving ballet dancer and definitely did not consider myself a beatnik. At some point I had a reaction to all this, and tried to put a stop to all these weird people marching through the apartment. There would be bodies sleeping everywhere, and it seemed things were sort of disintegrating. I remember screaming and jumping up and down at Freddie about this. Freddie moved out and I believe went on to fame and glory as the person who sleeps all the way through Andy Warhol's *Sleep*. He became very involved with that crowd and eventually committed suicide when he was on acid and decided he could fly and went off the roof.

I managed to struggle to class during all of this, and then the landlady finally threw me out because I had no money to pay the rent. That was probably the nadir of my life in New York. I had no place to live or to sleep. I decided that if all those creepy kinds on 42nd Street can hustle, I can hustle. Lo and behold, I went to 42nd Street but ended up on the benches of Central Park. Some rather nice man came along and God was with me because I was hauled off to an unbelievable apartment on Park Avenue. He very kindly ensconced me in the YMCA, paid for a month's room, gave me money and generally said, 'Pull yourself together. All is not lost.' I began auditioning for shows and ended up in *Gentlemen Prefer Blondes*.

I was starting to be a good enough dancer to get a series of jobs, going on the road on national tours, in musicals. The life was as a gypsy, going to auditions in New York, maybe doing summer stock, going on the road for nine months. You took whatever job came along, as soon as somebody said they would hire you. I did not go about my career in the right way at all. What I really should have done was concentrated on the ballet and get into a company instead of disappearing every six months, taking the first job that came along. I knew that I was company material and I was definitely scheduled to go into the Joffrey Ballet. Later, I worked as Robert Joffrey's administrative assistant, and he told me that this disappearing was the reason why I didn't get offered a place.

One day in '60 I met this guy at the Village Art Show. He was in the process of moving, and I'll never forget sitting in this pitch-black, real New York old cold-water flat with the tub in the kitchen. We both enjoyed ourselves and made a date for the next weekend, after which I went off to summer stock. I had had to give up my apartment while I was away, and I had no place to live. I wrote to him saying I needed a place to stay for a couple of days, 'May I stay with you?' I mean, I absolutely was setting out to trap him. This was *the* man. I had no intentions of moving out, none.

Norman was the sexiest thing I had ever met. Just looking at him, he struck all the chords. The poor man didn't have any hair then, either. He was only twenty-seven, but looked thirty-five. He did not look or act gay, which was important for me. It was unusual for somebody to be fully 'out' and leading a gay lifestyle to be that butch. Usually, if you met somebody who was gay and butch, they were very uptight, closety types and very, very neurotic. Norman was fully 'out' and totally masculine and he was interested in art, music, dance.

He agreed I could stay for a couple of days and I've been here ever since. The relationship was idyllic for the first year, but after I got over the infatuation there was a period when it was very rocky. Norman wanted me to be faithful and I would not be faithful, so we were having lots of arguments. I was not about to be anybody's little wife and did not want this kind of attitude and straight standards imposed on me or the relationship. By the third year I realized the whole question of fidelity was never going to be resolved until Norman felt all right about himself having a trick outside the relationship – which did happen when we were on a business trip and met some guy who was obviously cruising both of us. I said to Norman, 'It's entirely up to you.' He finally decided 'yes', and we had a threesome. That started it and eventually he realized that my having sex with somebody was not the same as going off into the sunset. It was also in the third year that I decided that I really did love this man, that this was a lifetime thing.

In '63 Norman went into business for himself, as an art dealer, and after wandering around Europe a few months getting together some stock, he came back and was doing very well. As most of his time had been spent in London, we decided to move to London. I didn't know what I was going to do, but I didn't care. A week before sailing date, Norman met a collector of old-master drawings who was interested not only in buying for his private collection, but in starting a business together. Before I knew it, it's thirties Hollywood movie time. I'm sailing off by myself, with handkerchiefs waving from the dock, streamers, the band and the whole thing; and Norman's still hanging around New York, making plans to open a brand new old masters' gallery with him as director.

I ended up in a bed-sit in Baker Street for a year. This was the swinging sixties and the curious thing is, I look back on the period and think I had a good time, but there weren't many gay places to go. There was something like a milk bar down on the King's Road, called the Gigolo, where they only served coffee or Coke, certainly no liquor. There was a vague little dance-floor, and at the back was one section that was very dark and very crowded and nothing really went on. You showed up at eleven o'clock or twelve at night, because it's just not done to get there at ten. This was when all public transportation stopped at midnight, so I'd walk from Chelsea to Baker Street.

There was another club further down the King's Road where, because of the sixties feel of experimentation, you'd get the odd 'straight' guy wanting to find out what it was all about. I certainly met a lot of people there who would deny being gay, saying they'd stumbled in by accident – but off you'd drag them, home and into bed. They included cops. For some reason, I must have met six bobbies during that year in London.

I was just waiting for Norman to come over and leading a life of leisure, in that I didn't have any work to do. I got vaguely involved in teaching dance, and I was taking ballet class. I couldn't get a job as a dancer here, though, because of the work permit: they didn't really need American dancers coming in. The gallery in New York took off. After a year I went back and into being a gypsy, doing the shows again.

Q: *Could you talk about the gay scene in New York in the sixties?*

In the early and mid-sixties New York went through a period when they were closing every bar in sight, so that at one point I think there was only one gay bar left open. That could have been '65. Norman and I worked and were not bar people particularly. Many of our friends lived in the East Village, and were smoking dope and taking acid, and it was like an extension of the beat generation, getting into the hippie period. This was my experience of the build-up to Stonewall. It was just a question of everyone feeling tired of being hassled – really tired of it.

Actually, I never went to the Stonewall as it was not the kind of bar I particularly liked. It was grotty and you got grotty Village types in it. I was getting too old for that at that point. It was raided by the police and there is an apocryphal story about a Black drag queen starting the whole thing by taking off her heels and beating a cop over the head with them. I was down in the Village visiting friends, and word got out that the police were around and that barricades had been thrown up. It electrified the gay population and I remember my reaction was 'Right on. I'm glad someone's finally done it.' By the second night there was a riot going on and I decided to join in.

This had a liberating quality for, I think, all gays in New York. Just after Stonewall was one of the few times that Norman and I ever went on a march. It was a march and demonstration outside the house of a city councillor who was holding up the passing of a gay anti-discrimination Bill by the city, and it was organized by the newly formed Gay Activists' Alliance. And we were founding members of the Eastside Gay Organization, a consciousness-raising group concerned with developing a positive gay image, and some political things like getting a Bill passed by the council prohibiting discrimination against gays in housing.

The Gay Activists' Alliance bought an old fire house from the city and turned it into a meeting-place with a disco and bar, and rooms to have meetings and some offices. It had an atmosphere that was wonderful, particularly for those of us who had gone through the fifties and early sixties. It was enormous. On weekend nights there must have been a thousand gay men there and there was no tension, no looking over your shoulder.

One wonderful night in the summer, when it's so hot and humid, we came down to dance at the disco and there was a queue literally a block long to get in. Evidently, there was a bomb scare because all of a sudden the big doors open like the fire engines were going to come out. Everybody poured out of the building and it turned into an instant block party, with everybody dancing on the streets, having a wonderful time. Then the Fire Department showed up and the fire engine makes its way, very slowly, through a thousand guys and pulls up in front of the building and stops – the firemen wouldn't get off. They were terrified, absolutely petrified. They thought they were going to get raped. And one marvellous little queen up on the third floor who did not vacate the building leans out and looks down on this fire engine with these firemen clinging to it for dear life. I mean, they were absolutely wrapped around the stanchions – they were not about to get off the engine – and the queen shouts, 'You don't live here anymore!' And the entire block of people just went up in flames. It was just great.

The cops finally showed up and, of course, they were much cooler. There was one cop who was very young and good-looking and he was being sent up as he made his way through this mob into the building. I'm sure he must have been groped on the way, but he was very cool and he kept a smile on his face, loving every minute of it. Once the firemen saw that the police got through it was all right for them to get off their fire engine and go in.

The movement against the war in Vietnam did not affect our lives, but I remember the whole Tricky Dicky period of Nixon and the atmosphere of America becoming a conservative country with the rise of a fascistic Right. The Fundamentalist preachers and the Moral Majority started having a good deal of power around the early seventies, and then there was the repression of the students and the race riots happening. It is one of the reasons why we moved to England in '74.

I gave up dance in '70. Part of it was disillusionment with the theatre, and I just wasn't hungry anymore – I just didn't have the drive. And the body was giving out, saying, 'You've done enough. You should slow down.' I had a job as vice-president of a furniture-importing company, but I wasn't committed to it. Norman came home one day and asked if I'd like to move to London. And that is pretty much how I became an art dealer, because I had to do something to make money in England. With Norman around, I could pick his brains, but it was very much my own business and I've kept it very separate from his. It's an agreement between us that he does not interfere, or he gets his fingers smacked.

London is about ten years behind New York in that it's slower and much less hassle, which is why we like living here. New York is fast and zippy and full of energy and has some wonderful things going for it, but it is not an elegant city and it doesn't have a 'grand manner' style of life, if you want to call it that. Norman and I have withdrawn from the gay scene. We have a gay social life, but when I think of socializing now it's having people for dinner or going to their place, or going out to a restaurant. It never occurs to me to go to a pub.

I'm certainly not politically active at all. Both of us feel that we have had a good life and that we would like to give something back, particularly to the gay world. And so my 'activism' is doing volunteer work as a counsellor and as a buddy for the Terrence Higgins Trust, that sort of thing.

I remember being aware when I first moved to London that some sort of gay activism was sorely and desperately needed. I will never forget watching the police raid Holland Walk in Kensington, which used to be a cruisy place at night. I was there and I suspected there were some plainclothes men around and I warned a couple of people. I watched these men arrest about twenty guys who very meekly marched off to the police station. Now, the cops here don't have guns and there were only four of them and there were twenty gay guys. Why in the hell didn't they run? But, no, they very calmly, very meekly, all with their heads bowed down and their shoulders bent over, very calmly marched off to the station. There's no reason to put up with that. And there's no reason to put up with what still goes on outside the Coleherne on a Saturday night after the pub closes. Kick the fucking cops in the nuts and then they'll stop breaking balls, you know. Once I was cruising and I was in the light and everybody else was in the dark being very furtive behind bushes. It was not a question of this being a perfectly natural, normal thing to be doing – to want to find somebody to go home and to go to bed with. Victoria still reigns in this country in certain aspects.

Within our circle, only one close friend has died of AIDS and he's primarily the reason why I decided to do something about working in that field. I was visiting him in hospital and there was another guy on the floor who had no visitors. I had been thrown out of my friend's room while they were doing some tests, and I asked the nurse if the other guy would like some company. It may have been his choice, but he had never had a visitor and I was very upset at that. I was also very upset at my own behaviour with my friend. The first time I walked into his room I kissed him on the forehead very consciously. Then, through to the next day, I kept thinking, 'How could I do something like that?' This was one of my dearest friends and I was appalled at my behaviour. So in the afternoon when I went it, I kissed him on the mouth and decided that I had to do something for people.

I haven't really changed careers but I realized that if I wanted to work with people with AIDS, I wanted some skills behind me – rather than just waltzing in like Pollyanna saying, 'Here I am. I'm here to make you feel better.' So I'm now in my second year of a training course in counselling and doing volunteer counselling with the Project for Advice Counselling and Education, working with gay men and women. Slowly but surely, my career as an art dealer is getting eroded and I have visions of in a couple of years listing myself as a counsellor-cum-psychotherapist with a speciality in AIDS counselling.

My career as an art dealer was exhausting: buying in Europe and getting on the road with heavy portfolios, going from museum to museum, a few hundred miles a day, for six weeks at a time. In '86 at the end of a business trip, I had a heart attack out on the street near my home. I was going into shock but I managed to get home and call the doctor, went into cardiac arrest and woke up in the coronary care unit with lots of IVs in me and this damn monitor with the squiggly lines going, and they put this self-inflating blood-pressure sleeve on that inflates every hour, on the hour. Every time it inflated it would wake me up and I would see poor Norman in the corner, trying to look cheerful – as cheerful as he could in that situation – but thinking, 'Twenty-seven years of togetherness is going out of the window.'

By the way, there was not a hint of homophobia at the hospital. The only time they tried to get rid of Norman was when I was in cardiac arrest and he kept standing in the doorway of the emergency room. They kept showing him out – mainly, I think, to make it easier for him – but he kept sneaking back in. When I was in the intensive care room, he said he wanted to stay and the nurse said, 'Fine, I'll get you a couple of chairs and some blankets and a pillow.' He stayed all night with me, which was wonderful. I'd wake up and there he would be, dozing, and it just made me feel better. They were very aware of the relationship and they couldn't have cared less. At one point, a nurse asked how long we had been together. When I said twenty-seven years, she said, 'My God! that's longer than I've been born.' That was lovely.

1988. Portrait by Sunil Gupta

DAVID RUFFELL

INTERVIEWED IN AUGUST 1986 BY WILL TODD

I was born in Shepherd's Bush in 1940. It was the start of the war and I was pushed off to an aunt in Sevenoaks in Kent until I was about six. Being evacuated was about the happiest time of my childhood. It's the earliest memory I can conjure up. My family used to come down about once a month and then my mother moved down with us, so it was quite a nice time.

I know absolutely nothing about my father. He was stationed during the war in Kenya. The story I've been told is that he was demobbed over there, decided to stay, sent for my mother and my brother and myself, and she wouldn't go. But I think the true story was that that 'father' isn't my father. I've got another father to my brother and I think that caused the divorce. Before the war my mother must have met somebody.

I have a brother who's two years older and completely opposite. I mean, he's into sport and he's a sports teacher now. When I was a kid I wanted to be a monk; he wanted to be a footballer. We shared a bedroom, so we didn't get on at all. I always used to get beaten up by my brother because he was older and obviously more 'masculine'. That's what it was, really, because my grandfather and uncle (who lived with us) always used to support him and they were very masculine. They didn't understand me at all.

When I had the choice, I used to go for quite outrageous clothes, whereas my brother was always very sober. My interests were reading the Bible and collecting crucifixes. I think I was just always fascinated by religion. I used to go to Methodist Sunday School quite voluntarily, and to the evening service as well. In a simple way you were being told the stories from the Bible and, at the end of it, you got given a stamp with the text that you'd been discussing that day.

95

I do remember as a child dreading the thought of Christmas coming. Both my uncle and my grandfather knew I was petrified of Father Christmas. There was a particularly ugly one in Hammersmith who would come up to me when I used to be dragged out shopping, and I used to scream. My uncle and grandfather used to go outside at Christmas and knock on the window with their fist and say, 'That must be Father Christmas' – just to watch me get all agitated and start running to my mother. I remember asking for a pram for Christmas when I was very young, and my family were horrified. I remember everybody saying, 'You can't possibly give it to him.' My mother was saying, 'Yes, if he wants it he'll have it.' And, sure enough, I had this pram on Christmas morning. I was very close to my mother. She was my only friend. There wasn't anybody that I would share anything with, discuss things with, except my mother. When you went out with the kids it was to do something specific – like go scrumping or play football. I mean, you never sat and talked.

But there used to be a boy and I was aware that he was totally different. I was fascinated by him. I must have been about nine and he was a year older. He was extremely feminine. He used to get people together to do plays and everybody would dress up and I used to love that. It was a way of expressing myself I quite enjoyed. The plays were fantasies. There was always a wicked witch in them. I never played a star part. It used to piss me off, but I was always one of the chorus or the background or the gang.

I loved going to school. By that time I was gay. I'm talking now about when I was eleven and had passed the 11-Plus. I can remember my first sexual experience quite clearly. When I was eleven I went to Wembley Stadium for a speedway match. I was very conscious in the interval of this man standing just behind me. I knew what he wanted and I actually went back into the toilet and he followed me. We didn't speak at all and I was really quite excited. He said to me, 'Shall we go into there?' and pointed to the lock-up. I said, 'Yes.' So we went in there and he sucked me and I came and I couldn't believe it; it was fantastic.

My school was co-educational anyway, so it wasn't too bad; there were always girls to be friends with, so it wasn't difficult. It wasn't difficult because I led a double life quite easily. I had to lead a double life. I was very aware that I could end up in prison, that's what I used to think. I had a best friend who was a girl.

We were interested in the same things – music and records and we enjoyed each other's company. It was a great thing to have a record-player and you actually saved for weeks for a 78 because you did a paper round and you got paid something like five bob. It was modern jazz, Gerry Mulligan and Chet Baker and then, of course, rock 'n' roll came along and Elvis Presley and that was something totally different. We both flung ourselves headlong into rock 'n' roll, going to all the strange places that people went to in those days – the Two IIs coffee bar in particular, in Old Compton Street in Soho, the coffee bar that Tommy Steele was discovered in and all those people that were famous in the fifties, Cliff Richard, the Drifters. I went there every Friday and Saturday. Hundreds and hundreds packed into the place and there was never enough bar staff to serve everybody.

Q: *Did you have any sex education in school?*

The only sex education I had was about worms and that's very confusing because they can be both male and female, whatever they choose. I remember a boy that I really fancied in my last year. I remember hearing him making an arrangement with a girl that they would go on Barnes Common one night and he would fuck her. I mean, I used to stand there and listen to them – it was amazing. That was sex education. But it was very exciting to learn that way.

By this time I'd met a boy called Gerry who was obviously the same as I was. I knew and he knew and we sought each other out. We used to talk to each other and then one day we had sex together. Through the conversation it transpired that we were both doing exactly the same thing after school: going home, doing homework and then going out, going from one public toilet to another, which you could do in those days, and spend a whole evening doing that. We felt we belonged to some secret club.

There was always a threat from the police but it was very, very unusual. I mean, it was against the law and you could have been blackmailed or imprisoned but it didn't stop that sort of thing.

It was around the time of Lord Montagu's famous trial and that affected everybody that was gay. If you were very feminine, you suffered. I used to get up in the morning and read the newspapers, mainly because I was fascinated that there were other people around doing the same as I was doing. It was just a bit more serious because they'd been caught. All this news was coming out in open court and the newspapers were really making a heyday of it. I just resolved to be inconspicuous and that would be one of the reasons why I even went with women. It was very important. Nobody ever laughed at me or took the piss out of me like they did with people who were fairly obvious, and of course they got teased so much that I would avoid them like the plague. I probably took part in it, I've got to confess, because it would help to throw suspicion away from me. If I laughed at a queer, I could hardly be one: that's what I thought.

I left school when I was fifteen, in '55, to become an apprentice printer in a firm in Notting Hill Gate, which was a very gay area. I used to spend my lunchtimes at the local toilet in Notting Hill Gate station having a marvellous time. I was an apprentice for about two years and then I met a guy who took me off to Spain for two months. NATSOPA, the printers' union, frowned upon it and dismissed me. I had a nice holiday in Spain, though. The relationship lasted two years. I introduced him to my mother and he was obviously gay. It didn't worry me. Although I never came out verbally, I was always 'out' at home. I lived at home and he used to come and see me every evening. We used to either sit in my room and play records or go out to the theatre or to the cinema or he would drive to Richmond. He was very kind. A lot older than me. I still had contact with Gerry, my oldest friend, because of the bond that was there when we both thought we were utterly different.

After Spain I came back to London and beatniks were just starting to become fashionable. It would be '57/'58 and it was a whole new different life for gay people in London. I became part of it. The craze started in Venice West in California. Allen Ginsberg and Gregory Corso and Jack Kerouac and all those writers, bumming around, and certainly taking dope. It's the first time I became aware of drugs, and I got into that sort of scene that was around London at the time. I had a girlfriend and we used to go to all the jazz clubs in Soho. We went to Cy Laurie's in Great Windmill Street, and it was like wearing a uniform. We would all be in black. She would have long black hair and black stockings; I'd have a large black turtle-neck jumper and jeans. I then discovered my first gay bar in the West End, the A and B, which was in a little alley-way off Wardour Street. Probably someone I'd met in the cottage told me about it. Once I'd discovered where it was I used to wait downstairs. When somebody came along that looked like they were going in, I would say to them, 'Are you a member of this club? Could you sign me in?' Nine times out of ten they would. They were all private clubs then. And of course, being that age, you could never afford the membership fee. I'm talking now between sixteen and seventeen. I lived a very complicated life, because I was still having a relationship with the guy I went to Spain with as well as my girlfriend. They both thought that I was being monogamous.

I also remember seeing James Dean in *East of Eden* in about '55 and being absolutely devastated. His portrayal as one of the brothers was the best piece of acting I'd ever experienced and he was the first man in the cinema that I fell in love with. I used to pin pictures on the walls and have a shrine to him with candles. My mother used to pick up these candles and these framed photos and dust around them and put them back – as though it was the most normal thing in the world. I used to go to the American import shops, Cecil Gee's in Shaftesbury Avenue, and buy stuff there and return to Hammersmith and be quite a freak. I mean, I'd search London for a pair of pale-blue jeans because I'd seen James Dean wearing them.

I was twenty-one when I got married. That would be '61. If you weren't married you were obviously queer, people would say that. Out of sheer desperation I was working in a supermarket delicatessen and there was a girl there who was quite fantastic. We were like brother and sister. I was always honest with her; she knew I was gay. I liked her a hell of a lot; we always had something to talk about. I decided that I would like to go and live in Cornwall and I was looking for work. We talked one night about how we would miss each other. And for some strange reason, I said, 'Well, we don't have to. You can come with me.' She thought it was a fantastic idea. I really did think that marriage was the way of cementing the relationship. I would imagine she accepted me being gay because she loved me and thought if she didn't, I might not stay with her. So I think she accepted it with a silent protest which became a very loud protest after we were married.

I realized what a dreadful mistake it was, very early. There was a life ahead of me which I might not be able to cope with eventually. Or there was a nice quick easy way out and that would be to split up before anything drastic happened – and by 'drastic', I mean if a family were to start. Of course, that's exactly what happened. I guess it must have been three months into the marriage when I realized that things were going wrong, and then of course she told me she was pregnant, which put a completely different light on it. She really wanted the baby.

After the birth, I tried to suppress the gay part of me. I was quite together enough to know that I couldn't suppress it completely; I just thought I'd calm down. After my son was born, things changed dramatically. I still had little assignations but they were always probably in toilets in the lunch-break and after work.

Eighteen months later, my first daughter was born. By that time we were living with my brother and his wife. It was a terrible time. We lived with them for about a year and then we managed to get a council house in South London, where my wife comes from. The twins were born exactly a year after my other daughter. The marriage really deteriorated when I got a job in the music business. I ended up as promotion manager for the Who, Jimi Hendrix, T. Rex, the Crazy World of Arthur Brown. They were huge groups and I worked for their record company called Track Records. Everybody was taking Mandrax; it was the age of Flower Power by then and I think with the drugs I became totally irresponsible, totally selfish. The job didn't help; it took me away from home a hell of a lot. There were four children, all very young, at home with my wife. It just got a bit too much for her and she started having an affair with my brother, which was the thing that finally made me leave home.

My son was terribly affected and I had to go and see the headmaster who openly said it was because I'd left home. He wasn't coping with the situation too well. I had to tell him that I was leaving him. And he couldn't accept it at all. He started to cry and was stamping his foot on the floor and saying, 'That means that I don't have a daddy anymore.' It was really affecting me.

The day I actually left, it was the worst thing that I'd ever done – to walk away and shut the door and know my four kids were tucked up in bed. That really did me in. But it had to be done, it was necessary. I couldn't stay there any longer and I don't think my wife could have coped with it either.

It actually made me closer to my brother because I wasn't

reacting like the rest of the family were. Oh, they were going hysterical – and, of course, because I wasn't playing the injured party there must have been something wrong with me. Eventually, my brother and my wife split up. I had left the marriage anyway .by then. So she was alone with four children. I used to have the children every other weekend. They used to come and stay with me and my lover in Hammersmith and the kids grew up with it. My lover helped bring them up; he was friendly with my wife and with me. Whilst I was living with him, if he had a day off in the week, he would go over to my wife and the kids. To my kids, it wasn't strange that I slept in my lover's bed and if they were up early in the morning, they used to come in and wake me. Something that they'd got used to.

As I've said, the guy I was living with was extremely friendly with my wife; they got on tremendously well and the kids absolutely loved him. And I went out and met somebody else and fell in love with him. I was with my lover seven years and hadn't even gone with anybody, never even wanted to. I don't know, I just went out one night and was particularly miserable and went into a cottage and met a guy. It was just rather strange – we hit it off straightaway. I went home that night and remember laying next to my lover and not being able to sleep. This guy I'd met that night was in my mind the whole of the time and that was very unusual for me – I wasn't prone to fall in love at the drop of a hat. I ended up leaving my lover and living with this guy within six weeks. My wife resented it. She thought I was really disloyal to the guy I'd left who she was very good friends with. So I got letters from her solicitor saying that she was going to contest the joint-custody of the children and she was going to stop access to them.

I went into court and as soon as the judge started to talk I knew there was no hope, so when we broke I said to the barrister, 'I'm not going to contest the custody of the children. I don't stand a hope in hell's chance with this man. He's really anti-gay. He's giving me a rough time. I know my wife; she can have custody of them; she'll look after them. It's the access that I'm concerned about.' So voluntary custody was written on the legal documents and the judge looked at me more sympathetically. He referred the case to the probation department, who interviewed all my children and then made an assessment afterwards that to stop them seeing me would cause more harm than good. So I had access every other weekend – providing my lover wasn't around. He had to go home to his parents every other weekend while my kids came over, and that eventually affected our relationship.

I didn't want it to happen but my children did come first, I must admit. They were important. I don't think he could accept that. But, once again, we lasted seven years and all four of us now – my first lover and my second lover and my wife and myself – are all friendly.

Q: *Talking about your social life, are you involved in the commercial gay scene at all?*

When I said years ago I used to go to the bars, it was always on a Saturday and it was something special to do. It was rather glamorous because it was not only underground, but there was the excitement of being taken home that night and ending up in somebody's bed. That was the only place where you could meet people who were gay. Now, my two exes and my old friend Gerry are my closest friends. Those three people really know me; there's never any pretence. We discuss everything.

Q: *When did you find out that you had AIDS?*

I was in a relationship which lasted ten months. In that tenth month I began to feel very peculiar. It's something I can't explain, but other people with AIDS recognize it. It's a feeling where you give up without being physically ill; it's a mental thing. I didn't relate it to any disease or illness, I just thought maybe I was having too many late nights. I said to my friend one night, 'Look, I don't particularly want sex.' He said, 'I think our friendship really doesn't need sex anymore.'

That was in October of '84 and I began to feel a lot worse. I thought, 'Well, maybe I've got VD.' So I went to the clinic at Hammersmith and I saw a doctor and she took all these blood tests and urine samples. After I'd got the blood result for syphilis, she said, 'You're perfectly healthy.' That week my twin daughters said, 'Look, if we're going to have Christmas here we'd better start thinking about getting all the shopping.' Walking round the local Asda I felt so ill I thought I was dying, and it all seemed to come on that evening.

102

DAVID RUFFELL

Aged 10, Lena Gardens Primary School

Innsbruck, Austria, 1956

So I went back to the clinic the next day and I remember the doctor saying to me, 'My God, you've deteriorated in the past week. You look absolutely awful.' I was X-rayed very quickly. When she brought the X-rays back she said, 'I'm going to let the senior registrar talk to you.' He introduced himself and then he held my hand and he said, 'You're quite seriously ill. I'll be perfectly blunt: your X-rays are telling us that you've probably got a rare type of pneumonia called pneumocystis, which is connected with the AIDS problem. Until we can do a biopsy on your lung, we're going to admit you into Charing Cross Hospital immediately and treat you for that pneumonia.' I said, 'I've got to go home and make arrangements for my animals.' And I don't even remember coming home here, to be honest; I must have been in a state of shock. I'd called the twins from the hospital, so they were at home. I sat them down and I said, 'It's only guesswork, but the doctors think I've got AIDS.' They'd known I was gay and we'd often talked about AIDS. And one of them started to cry but quickly pulled herself together. When I left, both cried.

At the hospital I was kept waiting behind curtains in the casualty department. No one would come near me. I had to shout for a nurse and when I said, 'Could I have a glass of water?' she said, 'I'll have to check with your doctor.' She eventually came back into the curtain with a mask on and rubber gloves. The doctor sat and explained everything in detail. He was incredibly good, and they took me up to a side ward with big signs on the door saying 'Important: Barrier Nursing'. There were all these slogans that said 'Bio Hazard'. I went into this little room and I stayed there for about two weeks and never saw anybody unless they had a mask and a gown and rubber gloves on. They were concerned that the pneumonia was really building up very quickly, stopping oxygen getting through the lungs and into the blood, and I was deteriorating quite quickly. They used to come and check me every half an hour and I knew I was very ill. I didn't eat for a week. My children used to come every day. The few people at work and my friends who I'd decided to tell that it was AIDS, came to see me frequently.

As you can imagine, lying in that room in the clinic and being told I had AIDS, I thought, 'Well, I suppose in a week I shall be dead.' I just thought I was on the way out and it was a hell of a shock, but I certainly didn't panic. Everybody kept telling me how brave I was, but I wasn't brave at all; I was really going quite mad inside. I was dealing with it very silently. I thought, 'I've got to quickly make plans.' So I said to the doctor, 'I desperately want to speak to someone from the Terrence Higgins Trust.'

At about six o'clock the next evening, the door opened and in walked the guy from the Terrence Higgins Trust in his mask and his gloves and his gown, and introduced himself. And he said, 'Are there any questions you want to ask me?' And I said, 'Well, there's hundreds of questions. When were you diagnosed?' And he said, 'Oh, I don't have AIDS.' That really disappointed me. He answered a few of my questions, but I still wanted to speak to someone with AIDS. He did say that he could introduce me to the support group at St Mary's hospital. I was well enough to go home after the two weeks. I was on very heavy doses of antibiotics whilst I was at home and I wasn't allowed to go back to work. My employers knew I was in hospital but they were told I had pneumonia.

On 2 January I went to the support group and I was quite frightened. There were about seven people there, five with AIDS, and I kept wanting to stare at them. All I'd seen were scary pictures of people on the TV and in newspapers. These people just looked ordinary. One looked ill, but everybody else looked very healthy, and that impressed me. I expected people, not quite to be covered in sores or scabs, but certainly to look terribly gaunt and ill. I sat and listened the first night and learnt enough to want to go back. Two things I remember from that first night. One is what type of sex one of them was having with his lover who he lived with. The other thing was one of them was having problems finding a dentist that would treat him. That was something I hadn't thought of. With a person with AIDS they have to take stringent precautions, and sometimes it's too much trouble for dentists. More often than not, they will refuse you.

Something that struck me when I went there was that they were all planning for the future. They certainly were concerned about having their teeth fixed, and that struck me as being slightly odd. I thought, 'Well, is it worth it?' I've since learnt that it's acceptable on the first occasion to think that, but it's certainly not acceptable after a while – unless you're just morbid.

The group has been a tremendous help. I wouldn't hesitate to

105

recommend it. I often go and talk to people who are recently diagnosed, like I wanted to speak to someone.

You learn quickly to do whatever your body tells you to do. I actually ask people to leave if I'm feeling tired and I do explain that I've got to get to bed. I'm also very aware of exercise and I try to walk everywhere. I'm very conscious that I've got to eat, not necessarily the right things, but the things that make me happy. If I come home on the bus thinking, 'I'm looking forward to sausage and mash,' then I shall eat sausage and mash. I couldn't possibly come home and have a vegetarian diet or a macrobiotic diet. I think mentally that would be doing me more harm than good – a bit like taking a spoonful of horrible medicine. The trust are trying to educate doctors, once the diagnosis has been made, to then follow through with help. You can't just say to somebody, 'You've got AIDS, you're going to die.' What you can say is, 'You've got AIDS. It's inevitable at the moment that it will result in death. In the meantime, you can do this and prolong your life.' But they don't do that. Medically, of course, there is hope and the longer you keep yourself alive the better chance of getting a cure. But you think, 'Well, can I hang on in there for five years? Yeah, I think I can.' It's a life full of quality then. I mean, once we'd been diagnosed, the majority of people led lives we wished we'd led years ago.

When I went back to work I had wanted most people to think it was just pneumonia and nothing else. I thought the quicker I got back, the better. In February I knew that the symptoms were coming back. I let it go on for a week to see whether it would disappear, and then I went back to the hospital. My doctor gave me a thorough examination and he said, 'I want you to go home, keep a temperature chart, do what you have been told to do, take these tablets and wait.' It started to snow heavily and became bitterly cold. And I really couldn't cope. It used to take me about three-quarters of an hour to dress to walk the dog at ten o'clock at night. I had this raging fever and I was going out in the freezing cold. So I phoned my daughters again and said, 'Would you mind moving in with me for a couple of weeks and see what happens?' The doctor phoned me the following morning. I read my temperatures out to him and explained that I couldn't walk, all my joints had gone stiff, and my mouth was full of thrush. So he said, 'OK, you'd better come in.' I went in that afternoon.

This time it took twice as long and a bit more to sort of clear up. And I've been warned that each time the symptoms come back, so it'll take that little extra bit longer.

Q: *And it was during this second time that you were in hospital that there was a lot of negative media coverage of AIDS?*

Yeah. In between me coming out of hospital the first time and being admitted the second time, the prison chaplain who used to be at Wormwood Scrubs had died with pneumonia. This is the prison where I work. The newspapers printed all of his symptoms which, unfortunately, were all of mine the first time. There was an awful lot of publicity on the TV about him. And when a prisoner at the Scrubs was suspected of having AIDS, the media were filming at the Scrubs that Saturday, talking to the Prison Officers' Association and the regional director who'd come to talk about stopping movements in Wormwood Scrubs. They then talked to a prison officer who said, 'Things are so bad in that prison that even a member of the admin block is in hospital with suspected AIDS.' ITN followed it through with the hospital, who then confirmed it, and an ITN camera crew then spent the evening outside the hospital.

The hospital certainly didn't tell me until it was too late, which pissed me off more than anything. The administrator made the statement and it was pointless to retract it. It was all over the newspapers the next day and all on the news and the TV that evening. It's the first time I ever cried with the illness. It's the first time I ever felt sorry for myself.

Eventually, after I'd calmed down and my anger wasn't quite so strong, I was able to sit and think about it and I realized it was the best thing that could have happened. All over that weekend, my main concern was that people at work would all react like I've read everybody else reacts. They would refuse to work with me; I would lose my job; I would then have financial problems; everything would collapse. But it didn't turn out like that at all. The first thing on the Monday morning, the sister came in and told me that the person outside waiting to see me was the administrator of Wormwood Scrubs and asked did I want to see him? And I thought, 'Oh, God! This is it.' They let him in and he looked kind of sad, standing there in his gown and his gloves and his mask. I mean, he's usually in a very smart suit behind an enormous desk. And he said to me, 'Oh, David, what on earth are we both going to do now?' He said he was going back to the prison to discuss my situation and be back to me. The next day he came back and said, 'I'm absolutely staggered. All the staff are 100 per cent behind you and you're going to have no problems.'

They immediately had a collection for me and that evening I had the most incredible book on James Dean. And the next day a huge bouquet of flowers, and then an enormous basket of fruit. And all these cards and letters started to come and I was very conscious that their response partly changed the direction in which I was going at that time. I realized exactly what a fortunate situation I was in.

I think I realized in the beginning that honesty would give a lot of people around me the strength that they might require. My daughters, in particular. The friends I've got now have been with me most of my life and I really know that, if the time comes when I die, those people are going to be absolutely devastated. So about two weeks ago I sat down and made my will. Accepting the fact that I'm going to die, I thought I should now really take control of that, so I wrote to all my close friends little letters and I did find that extremely distressing. It was a bit like writing a suicide note. But it was important to me that it be done. And I phoned everybody up and we laughed about it and I said, 'Look, I'm not going to be morbid but if you don't tell me what you would like, I'm going to leave you something really horrible and you're going to really hate me for it.' It was distressing but necessary.

I really want to read unbiased interviews with people with AIDS; that's what I wanted to read originally and this is what prompted me to contact the [Hall Carpenter] Archives. I think the experiences of people with AIDS should be documented now. The guy I admired most of all in my group died a month ago and, apart from what I can remember, all his problems, his struggles, his fears have all been buried with him. He was like a pioneer; everything that he went through was all trial and error and it's just sad that it's all been wasted.

The doctors used to come and see me and talk in such strange language. I used to cling on to certain words if they were repeated often enough, and I would remember them phonetically and then look them up. The doctors went into this medical spiel and I was lost – therefore I was ignorant about something I was suffering from that might kill me.

I recently read about a guy who has planned his funeral, even down to the flowers. The flowers are a very American thing, but it made me think, 'Well, look, you're not being morbid. You're just taking control. You've controlled everything else you've done, so what the hell.'

POSTSCRIPT BY DAVID RUFFELL, CHRISTMAS 1987

Such a lot has happened since this interview took place. Firstly, three years after diagnosis, I am very much alive, which I had not expected. Nor did my doctors and, instead of encouraging me and trying to discover why that should be, they look at me, obviously quite baffled, and declare, 'It looks like we could have made a mistake.' Just like that, without a thought to the added confusion, misery and, at times, fear and damage to my mind. I prefer to think that the original diagnosis was correct. That way, the longer I remain healthy the more of a bonus it is.

Since diagnosis, my life has changed a great deal. It has become much more valuable and I try not to fritter it away quite like I used to. I have started painting and am currently working on a series of pictures which I have collectively entitled *Diagnosed AIDS* and which shows the despair and confusion that surrounded me in those early days. I also have a video camera and am in the process of making a video of the paintings with a suitably atmospheric soundtrack which I am composing with the help of a synthesizer.

I have given up smoking, become a vegetarian and, at the time of writing this, have been celibate for just over a year. I am investigating the Buddhist philosophy and at present my life is full and worth while. Death from AIDS is a million miles away. I don't think I have the time to die. Besides, I want to learn how to play the steel drums next.

This interview was edited by Margot Farnham.

David Ruffell died on 5 July 1989.

1988. Portrait by Sunil Gupta

PHILIP BAKER

INTERVIEWED IN JULY 1988 BY PAUL MARSHALL

It was wartime and my father, who was in the US airforce, was playing the saxophone in a jazz quartet at a night-club called the Café de Paris. My mother went there for a night out with friends and met my father. They had an affair, and I was born on 25 May 1942 in Croydon. My mother was white and my father Black and my mother, partly through family pressure, decided not to marry him. She saw him a few times after I was born and they kept in touch after he'd gone back to the States, but gradually they lost contact.

My mother's parents owned a boarding house in Chichester, Sussex. My mother helped run the place because my grandfather died shortly after I was born, apparently from the shock of seeing that I was coloured. My mother had quite a hard time over that and also from other relations, so she had me looked after by two ladies in Kent. I was quite happy there, but they didn't keep children after the age of four, so I was adopted by some distant relatives of my mother's. They told her that she could still have access to me but, shortly after the adoption, access was stopped. I don't think they approved of what she had done – having an affair with my father – so I think that was their way of punishing her.

Even though I was adopted, I thought of my adoptive parents as step-parents. My stepfather managed a bicycle shop and we lived above it. The first night at my new home they dumped me in a tin bath and took a scrubbing brush to me because they thought my skin was dirty and not actually coloured. My step-mother used to beat me. I can't remember when this started – perhaps it was because I used to wet the bed. They used to take

111

me down to the basement, which had a stone floor, tie my hands and legs and put me in a makeshift bed – two chairs joined together – and leave me there until about six o'clock in the morning. Then they would bring me back upstairs and make me stand outside their bedroom door until they got up and had breakfast.

It was mostly my stepmother who ill-treated me, but my step-father would join in. He was the one who tied my arms and legs and once – I don't know how he got away with this – he chased me all the way home from school for about a mile, hitting me with a leather belt.

They were religious – Methodists – and pillars of the community. They had a son who was older than me. I found out later that my stepmother had beaten him when he was a baby out of sheer temper because he wouldn't eat. I ran away a couple of times and played truant. When the police brought me back, it was all smiles; but as soon as the door was closed, they would beat me all the way up the stairs. I don't think anybody else in the community was aware of what was going on – they just thought I was ungrateful.

I could just remember the early part of my childhood, which I enjoyed, so I suppose I had some sort of yardstick to judge that I was being badly treated. If I misbehaved I used to get the whole saga, 'Well, your mother didn't want you. Nobody else wanted you, so that's why we adopted you.' I don't know what went on in my stepmother's head. When I was older we talked about some of the things she did and she denied a lot of it, but I've still got the scars. I also found out that my mother had been paying them £2 a week for my keep.

I went to the local schools. I can't remember much racism at the time; that came later. I was aware that I was different, but I wasn't sure how different. If there had been other Black children around I would have been more aware of it. Colour is a strange thing. My step-parents used to make remarks about it because, according to my mother, my father was very black. I suppose, in a sense, I went into my own world because I can't remember having any friends. After school I had to go straight home. In a sense, I climbed into my head. Sometimes I would spend my time watching my stepfather in his workshop, and sometimes I spent it in the house – but it depended on what sort of mood my step-mother was in. I was put outside in all weathers. I remember to this day finding corners and sitting hunched and rocking myself – that was a way of keeping warm. I remember talking to myself or to an imaginary person because I didn't have any friends.

I used to go to Saturday morning pictures. I can't remember much about that time in terms of the toys I had, or whether I listened to the radio or not, and I suppose it's because I blocked that time out of my mind. That whole area was very painful and, until I was well into my teens, I used to say that my parents were dead and I didn't start talking about it until I'd made some friends that I could trust.

When I was ten years old I got up one morning, was told to put my suit on, had breakfast and the next thing I remember, I was standing in a juvenile court. My stepmother told the court that I was a difficult child and she'd even taken me to see a psychiatrist. I think she was trying to find an excuse to get rid of me. The next thing I knew, I was being driven down to a children's home in Sussex. I enjoyed it there. It was a very open atmosphere. There were ten or twelve of us and we were allowed a lot of independence and there were large grounds to play in. I liked the school I went to, although I was very bad at lessons because I was dyslexic and it wasn't recognized at that time. My teacher tried to help me. I wasn't aware of how good she was until later. I liked geography because there was something going on that wasn't communicated through just writing and reading – there were maps. I enjoyed art but at that time it wasn't a big subject.

I made friends with both sexes at the home, and at school, for the first time in my life. There was a wide range of ages amongst the kids at the home, from eight to eighteen. I opened up and became more curious about what was going on around me. There was a girl there – she must have been eighteen – who opened my eyes to sex.

I woke up on my twelfth birthday to be told I was leaving, and I was sent to Dr Barnardo's in Ifield. It was such a shock to the system that I ran away on three consecutive days and went back to the children's home. I was brought back each time. There were about forty kids – half from the South of England and half from South Shields in the North, from a home that had been closed down. It was everybody for themselves. There were eight or ten in a dormitory, and that's when I encountered prejudice.

113

Some were better at it than others and some did it all the time. There was one guy called Dennis who was very clever. He was the same colouring as I was, but he had straight hair. He managed to get the others in the dormitory, who were all white, to pick on me. This went on for quite a while and I used to lose my temper quite frequently. One day I'd had enough. I remember throwing a snooker ball at somebody because he called me a 'nigger' and throwing a jack-knife at somebody else for the same reason. It was bad and the superintendent and the matron didn't stop it. The matron decided I was good at sport because I was quite tall, but I wasn't. I was only good if I didn't have to do it, if I *wanted* to be good at it. It was very competitive with races against other children's homes and they stuck me in the hurdles. There were comments like, 'You ran like a girl.' I remember the matron saying that. When I went to school there was racial prejudice and there was also a lot of prejudice against the Barnardo boys, so when I was at school we all used to club together.

Then the home slowly changed. The superintendent and his wife, the matron, were asked to leave. It was nothing to come down in the morning to her study and find her pie-eyed with a half-empty gin bottle beside her. She used to swear a lot and she was prejudiced. There was another boy who was the same colour as I was, called Tuppence. He was about eight. The rule was, if you didn't eat what was put down in front of you, you had it served up to you again later. This went on for ages with him because he refused to eat, and he was found curled up in a field one day and rushed to hospital. They never found out what was wrong, but they operated and he died soon afterwards. If he had been white, he wouldn't have died. When I went to Dr Barnardo's it was all boys. There were a couple of boys there who were – I don't think 'gay' is the right word – but who did do things. Also, one of the housemasters used to toss some of us off and vice versa. One of the boys split on him, there was an investigation and the police came round and he was arrested. They twigged who was involved. We were witnesses and had to go to court. He got two years. Looking back, I think half of us encouraged him initially – he didn't do much. It wasn't heavy sex. I didn't think there was anything wrong with it – it was just something some of us used to do.

I was sent out to work when I was fifteen and went to a plastics factory on the Crawley industrial estate. I was a storekeeper. It was quite a happy place to work at and I stayed for five years. The manager was into theatre, music and literature, so it was like a second schooling for me. He was also gay. Everyone knew this but no one took much notice – this was in '57. He used to go up to London to the theatre and he used to recommend plays to me, so through him I became aware of that world.

I was fostered until I was eighteen and I was sent to a lot of families and some of them were horrible. I began to have a social life when I started at the factory because it had a social club, and around that time I remember buying my first record – Fats Waller's 'Red Sails in the Sunset'. I don't know whether it was the way it was sung or what, but there was something about the record which did something to me. The same thing happened when I heard Edith Piaf and Judy Garland. There was something about them which hit the emotions and I responded to that. Perhaps it's got something to do with being gay. I went to London with a coach party to see the stage show of *West Side Story*, and it was incredible – the dancing and the singing, everything looked so real. I felt as if I was right in the middle of it. I'd never seen anything like it and it altered my whole outlook. When I got back home I felt as though I was on another planet, but I couldn't really talk about it to anyone. The couple who were looking after me were old fashioned and straight-laced and didn't approve of that sort of thing, although, strangely enough, they used to read the *News of the World*. They were caring in their own way, though, and I think they were trying to protect me. I remember them saying to me once, 'Remember where you come from – your background – you were born into it and you can't escape it.'

There was another musical which had quite an effect on me and that was the film *Carmen Jones*. I saw it when I was feeling very down, but I remember thinking that Pearl Bailey and the other Black singers and dancers were wonderful. But, again I felt I couldn't go home and talk about the film. I don't know how I felt about *Carmen Jones* in terms of a Black identity. In Crawley at that time there weren't that many Black people. People were rather curious about my background, but I used to cut off rather than talk about it, because it was too painful. I've been accused at times of not being that Black. Because I was brought up with whites I didn't really know what Blacks were going through but, at the same time, I was aware of prejudice – there was no way I could go round making out I was white. Perhaps I was slightly cushioned by where I worked and the friends I had. It was later on when I came to London that I was more aware of it.

I knew that I was attracted to men more than women at this stage – perhaps it had begun at Dr Barnardo's – but I had nobody to talk to about it. I had girlfriends until I was eighteen or nineteen, but it seemed that every time sex reared its head the girls would cut off – you'd kiss, but they would draw the line at heavy petting. There were four other gay men at the factory where I worked and I had a sort of fling with one of them and we'd do it when we could, in lunch breaks or we'd stay behind late or go into the grounds. But in Crawley there was nowhere to go. I even shared a flat with someone who I thought was gay and it turns out that he was, because years later we bumped into each other in the Salisbury. There was a boy at Barnardo's who later got married and had children and we had a thing going on for a while, but whenever he was short of money he used to show up on my doorstep and ask for a couple of quid or he said he would tell people. But he basically came round for sex. It was very strange because part of me got off on him and part of me was petrified someone would find out.

Once, I was in Brighton for the evening with some friends and I met someone I used to work with at the factory. He asked me to go for a drink with him and my friends said, 'Go on, you haven't seen him for ages.' So I did and he asked me to go home with him and I stayed the night. But I don't know whether my friends twigged that I was gay or not. Perhaps they were more innocent in those days – they were from the Baptist youth club which I belonged to – they were aware of gays but nothing was said. Perhaps people were nicer in those days.

In Crawley in the sixties I was a mod. There were a lot of mods in Crawley. It was a new town that had been built up slowly in the fifties, and a lot of people moved out from London. Also, Croydon and Brighton were nearby and people like Georgie Fame, the Moody Blues and Spencer Davis used to play at the local college. I remember seeing Stevie Winwood playing when he was fifteen and thinking, 'God, he's a genius.' I used to wear Italian suits with cloth buttons and a 'bum freezer' jacket. It was a smart outfit but I had to hide them from the couple I was fostered with, so I used to leave the house in one lot of clothes and go to a friend's to change. I also got my first pair of winkle-pickers – a bit late, but I got them.

I went down to Devon and Cornwall with a friend on a scooter. There were lots of other mods and that's when you used to get the rockers as well, so we used to go around with the other mods for safety. I don't think I was tough – I think my experiences as a child made me a bit of a coward. I was quite arrogant – I had a big mouth. It made me stand up for myself and I remember in my first job people saying to me, 'You can't say that, you'll get your head knocked off.' But I tend to say things when I go for a job and it's obvious that I don't get the job because I'm coloured. I don't let them get away with it. Going back to the mod thing, I never had that much trouble. It depended on what scooters you had. I had a Lambretta and it didn't have all the gear on it and when we went down to Brighton other mods used to pass us on the much better Vespas and jeer at us. We used to enjoy ourselves, so we used to avoid the trouble. We were mods because we liked the music. We used to travel a lot to hear bands play – blue beat, jazz, Manfred Mann, Ginger Baker and people. It was a cross between drinking and music. Then when the Beatles hit the music scene it all seemed to change.

Seeing *West Side Story* and *Carmen Jones* made me start going to dance class. I had a very good teacher and studied for about five years. I was good at dancing. For the first year I did classical ballet and then jazz ballet–contemporary dance. They were private lessons – I always did things on my own. It wasn't until I came to London that I did classes with other people.

I used to go up to London for auditions for the good shows like *Sweet Charity* and *Golden Boy*. There were only about ten coloured dancers in London – five women and five men at that time, the mid- to late sixties. You weren't aware of prejudice straightaway, but you realized that you would be called to auditions and then you weren't recalled. *Golden Boy* had Sammy Davis Jnr in it and he was so appalled that he actually brought his own dancers over from the States. Once I cancelled a holiday to audition for a show that actually called for coloured dancers and none of us were chosen! I auditioned for *Irma La Douce* but the director said, 'We can't use him because he's out of context with the show.' The same thing happened when I tried fashion modelling: it wasn't

Aged 2, Kent, 1944

Aged 5

Aged 9, with Ivan, Horsham, Sussex, 1951

Philip and Gennaro, Stockwell, London, summer 1988

that open – you thought it was, but it wasn't. I felt both bitter and resigned. It was like banging your head against a brick wall. If you complained, you got labelled 'stroppy'. That barrier seems to have been broken now but, then, it was hopeless.

I shared a room in Bayswater with David, a friend from Crawley, and it was through him that I got into the gay scene. Although he was straight, he had a lot of gay friends and one night they took me to my first gay club, Studs, in Poland Street. When I was living in Crawley I used to think that I was one of the few homosexuals on the planet, but in London I realized I wasn't, because I met people that I could relate to and I realized there were more and more of them. So I came to terms with being gay. It was a gradual process, but coming to London crystallized it and made me make that decision to be gay – to go forward rather than backwards.

I was working at a late-night coffee bar called As you Like It in Monmouth Street while I was doing auditions, and about this time I met Michael at Studs. He was the first person I fell in love with and I think I was attracted to him because I thought he was sophisticated. One night I took him home to Bayswater and, for some reason, David was very upset when he woke up and found me in bed with someone. My relationship with Michael only lasted about a month. I went to a club one night and he was with someone else and, of course, I was very upset. I went round to his place to find out why it had ended but he didn't want to know.

I used to go to a few of the early GLF meetings in King Street in Covent Garden in the early seventies, but I'm not very good when it comes to groups. I was working in a men's clothes shop in the King's Road when the King's Road was still very fashionable. But although it opened new areas for me, I didn't like it – it was pretentious and I like people for what they are, not who they are. That was also when I became aware of Black gays in London. Black gay men would be invited to dinner parties because it became fashionable to invite us. You were patronized. It was quite vicious. It was all right if you sat there and said nothing, but not if you opened your mouth and had opinions and ideas of your own. You were invited because you were Black and good-looking and some Black guys seemed quite happy to accept that. That was the scene. There would be party after party, but that wasn't where I was coming from.

In my experience, on the gay scene there are divisions between the Blacks and the whites. Then there's the whites who will only go with Blacks and the Blacks who will only go with whites. I remember going with one white guy who didn't think I was Black enough, so I said, 'OK. I'll swing from the lamp with a bunch of bananas, if that's what you want.' [Laughs.] All his lovers were Black, but he had a fantasy of what a Black man should be.

Q: *What about politics?*

I've voted for the Conservatives, Labour and Liberal in my life but now I tend to vote SDP because I think that the Labour Party is doing what the Conservative Party is doing – looking after its own thing. The Black movements in the Labour Party are treated appallingly and it seems that, in any party politics these days, in order to get on you have to sell your principles down the river. I don't like labels – I wouldn't join a Black political movement because I don't think that's the way forward. I don't know what the answer is – but I don't know how long the political parties are going to sit there and ignore us, who are a large part of the population. Perhaps we need a Jesse Jackson. The strange thing is that I don't have a lot of Black friends who I talk politics with. The way I've grown up, I'm not sure whether I would be accepted in the Black camp – but at the end of the day, I identify as being Black. I am Black.

I lived with Alan, who was a teacher, for a time but he seemed to want me to be more intellectual than I was. Then I lived with Dennis, who was a dancer, for about eighteen months. Dennis taught me quite a lot in terms of how to see things. I used to worry about what people thought of me, but Dennis was very loving and caring and gave me the confidence to be myself – to be natural.

I was sacked from the job in the King's Road and got a job at the Savoy hotel doing costing. Then I had to get out of London because I was trying to get over a relationship which I'd been hurt by, so I went to Amsterdam for a while and then to Nottingham. I came back to London and eventually moved here, to Stockwell, where I live now. I worked in restaurants and clothes shops and then started working for myself as a fashion agent, and also working with someone who did knitwear. I did this for a couple of years, but I ended up nearly bankrupt.

In '76, when I was thirty-four, I decided that I wanted to see my mother again and, through some relations, I got her address and wrote to her. We met and it was a bit strained on the first meeting. She was pleased to see me but was curious as to why I wanted to see her – whether it was to rake up old things. When I said it wasn't she was pleased. She had remarried and had two children, Ruth and Steven, and her husband had died quite a few years ago.

It was as though some part of me had found another part of myself. I also met another family, because my half-sister was married and had two children. My mother had never told her other children about me – she had explained me away as being a friend of my grandmother's – but when I met her again she asked for a photograph of me. As soon as Ruth saw it and then saw me, she twigged who I was. I don't know what my half-brother's attitude to me is – he wasn't too pleased when he found out – but Ruth and her husband were entirely different about it. They thought that my mother should have told them. Apparently, my mother had always sent me Christmas presents when I was at Dr Barnardo's but I never received them.

My mother died of cancer soon after I met her again. It was a shock but I was glad I had found her again: I think it would have been a bigger shock if I hadn't met her. At least I knew who she was and found out more aspects about myself. She talked about my father and said that she would have married him, but she suspected that he had other children by other women. Maybe I would like to meet him – to find the missing part of the jigsaw – but I don't know where he is.

Because I had met my mother again I was quite happy, but the business thing was getting me down. One night I took an over-dose. I don't really know why I did it because, the night it happened, I partly felt OK. I suddenly grabbed a bottle of sleeping tablets and washed them down with a couple of glasses of Martini. I hadn't planned it at all. I think that's what happens: you suddenly do it. I mean, I wasn't sitting there planning on suicide. I suppose I did it because I had too much going on. This happened at about two in the morning. I came round a couple of hours later and phoned a friend and told her what I'd done. She said she'd phone an ambulance, and I don't remember anything after that until I came round in hospital. Apparently, I was screaming at the doctors and telling them to keep away. There was another strange thing. When I got back from hospital a friend rang me and said, 'What's this strange message you left on your answering machine?' I'd put a message on there saying, 'I'm awfully sorry, I may be away for a few days and I'm sorry for any inconvenience I may be causing.' It was as if another part of me had taken over. I left the hospital on the condition that I see a psychiatrist, but I didn't. It took me about nine months to get over it. I'm not sure how you get over that sort of thing – there's nothing to measure it by, it's a strange area. It's difficult to talk about trying to take your own life. I remember reading James Baldwin – *Go Tell It on the Mountain*, *Giovanni's Room* and, in particular, *Another Country* – and the part where Rufus jumps off the bridge and kills himself. That really did something to me and I thought, 'My God, his insight into people is amazing because he's really experienced it!'

Q: *What was your response to AIDS?*

Perhaps I started looking at myself in a different light. Part of you says, 'Oh, God! There's this virus and I might have had it for years and not known I've got it.' And a lot of the media attitude was a bit like shutting the stable door after the horse had bolted. I got slight paranoia about it and then, slowly, one person you know dies from it and then it's another. Before, people you knew didn't die – they might be hit by a car – but suddenly there's this virus which can take you at any point. I suppose part of my life did alter. When I went out on to the scene I looked at things like one-nighters in a different light, but my sexual habits changed in any case, because I grew to dislike the scene when the clone period started in the late seventies. But all the things you used to do in a relationship were suddenly wrong. We've all gone through that phase – sex, poppers and backrooms – but suddenly, if you're going to do those things then you're going to catch AIDS. Part of me has always been rebellious and I'm not sure whether I did the things you were supposed to do. I carried on and took the precautions I thought were necessary. I suppose it made me look at homosexuality or any sort of sexuality in a different light.

In mid-'85 it was diagnosed that I had a tumour on the right kidney. So at that point my life really did change. You tend to think that if you're going to get something like that, it's going to be in old age. I used to think, 'God, I hope I don't get cancer.' It was the last thing I expected. I put the symptoms down to the fact that I wasn't eating the right food and that I'd put myself into a sort of self-destruct mechanism. I was smoking a lot of cigarettes and dope as well, and I was getting into foul tempers. I don't really know why. There is a part of me that self-destructs every so often. I tend to do it in relationships – push people as far as I can and see just what the limit is. I think it's something that comes from my childhood. Again, I'm not very good at shouting for help. I had just finished a relationship with someone who went to live in America and I was using that time to try and find out who I was. I was very difficult and refused to see my friends. I've got some very good, close friends, both men and women, and I upset them – shouted and swore at them – but eventually we made it up.

I refused to be operated on and sought alternative treatment – diet, looking after myself and homeopathic medicine – and I've recovered. It's strange: the medical profession says that with cancer the tumours subside and reappear again, so they think that I'm just in one of the stages where it's subsided. But I feel well, and everybody that sees me thinks I look well. But in a couple of weeks I'm having a scan and then I'll find out.

One Christmas I was given a set of Tarot cards, but I didn't touch them until about a year later. It opened up other areas because, in a sense, it broke down my dyslexia, since I had to start reading about the Tarot. Because of my pride I hadn't sought help for the dyslexia, so I don't do things like letter-writing – which is a shame, because I like receiving letters. It's made me feel very inadequate throughout my life – there are certain things I would have done if I'd learnt to read and write. To cover up my dyslexia, I'd just tell people that my spelling was atrocious.

It was the part of me which is curious which made me interested in the Tarot. I liked the idea of something where there's two schools of thought – you can explain it, and you can't explain it. I think it's something that works, whether it's Tarot, astrology or the *I Ching*, which has been part of Eastern culture for thousands and thousands of years. I used to believe in God, but I think that's a bit like believing in Santa Claus. I believe in something larger – a form or being – I don't know what you'd call it. Sometimes I fight that side of me. I've never been religious, so perhaps I use things like the *I Ching* instead.

I used to make a living out of Tarot and it opened up other areas for me. I did Tarot readings at the Edinburgh Festival a few years ago. I don't do it so much now – having the cancer took what little money I had and I didn't have a phone for eighteen months, so I lost a lot of the clientele. Now I don't know whether I want to do it again. I want to use that part of me – but whether it's in Tarot, I don't know. Over the past year the creative side of me seems to have gone out of the window.

Since the cancer, over the last three years, I thought that I'd come to terms with myself and my emotions, but it's not actually true – I was too busy fighting the cancer and it was a way of not looking at my emotions. In fact, it's said that the kidneys represent emotions, so it's interesting that it went to the kidneys.

I live with someone now, Gennaro. I met him one day when I was going out to look for a job and, instead of a job, I ended up with a relationship! I'm not good emotionally in one-to-one relationships, although there's one part of me which has opened up quite a lot. Part of me is very wary, so perhaps it's to do with trust. We find there are areas that we're not talking about. He's twenty-three, so there's an age-gap. Those are the areas I'm having trouble with, and so I spend the whole day thinking about them. But it's difficult having a relationship with someone when you're unemployed and they're working – but Gennaro says he likes to know I'm here at home, although that makes me feel like a housewife! A few months ago I got so frustrated about something that should have been quite simple, that I took a knife and cut my hand. As I was doing it I thought, 'What the hell is all this about?' And it's about communication. It's to do with emotions. He had a childhood with a large, extended, supportive family, so he's caring and supportive. But it's that side of me which I block off. In the past, when people have been caring to me I've given them a hard time. It's not meant that way. It's as though I set up things so that people keep their distance. He says to me, 'Why don't you say something? You seem to talk to friends, but not to me.' I'm seeing a psychiatrist and I've opened up a hell of a lot compared to what I was six months ago; but from Gennaro's point of view, I probably haven't.

As far as getting older is concerned there's nothing you can do about age – it's one of those processes. I've always said that it didn't worry me in terms of what I'd done or hadn't done with my life – age is a state of mind. I don't know how long I've got. Thinking about what I'll be doing when I'm sixty-odd doesn't really come into it anymore. When you've got something that people say you can die from, you take each day as it comes; but if you start doing that, you stop planning any further – so it's catch 22. I don't know how to answer questions about age. I don't know how you're supposed to feel at forty-six [laughs]. There are things in my life that I wouldn't have done, but these things happen. Some people seem to have all the answers, but at this point I don't know a damn thing. I feel that I'm relearning all over again.

JOHN FRASER

INTERVIEWED IN MAY 1987 BY WILLIAM PIERCE

I was born in Liverpool in 1947, in a slum area of the docklands that no longer exists. There are even worse slums there now but they're modern slums; then, there were rows and rows of terraced streets. We lived in number 14 and my grandmother lived in number 6, in the same street, with still unmarried sons. My mother's sister lived two streets away and the relatives of my grandmother lived two streets further on, so it was a very, very tight community. I was born a twin, which is quite interesting, in the coldest winter of the history of the world – 1947, in February. I have a sister who is about three years older than me and another sister who's seven years younger and a brother who is almost fifteen years younger. So I'm one of five children.

We all lived in a two-up, two-down terraced house. And when I say to people I can remember going to buy gas mantles as a child they think it's prehistoric, but in fact some of those houses were not yet converted to electricity and nobody had inside water. I didn't live in a house with inside water or even hot water or a bath until I was thirteen, which now seems incredible.

I remember sitting looking at my twin brother, because we had one of those real old-fashioned buggy prams with hoods and we were placed opposite each other, and the very first memory I have is of sitting gawping at this other face sitting gawping back at me.

We've grown up to look very much like brothers but we're not identical twins. My brother is stockier. We are more or less the same height and, in a funny way, as we get older we look a lot more like twins than we did in adolescence or childhood.

I want to say that we had this mystical thing where, if he was ill, I would get ill. To a certain extent that did happen because

127

1988. Portrait by Sunil Gupta

you know if one of you has mumps, the other one's going to get mumps too – but there wasn't any mystical feeling between us. There was, though, a very, very strong bond which we both fought against in childhood and adolescence but which we've now both come to recognize as being quite important to us. It was a fight at the time, because it was two people fighting for their individuality and he is very positive and individual in his way. I am, also, except at the time I was individual in a society that wasn't going to allow my individuality to be witnessed.

I wanted to sit inside and draw and paint and read – things which were totally alien in a working-class society – and my brother was always in the street playing football. So we had antipathy towards each other and friction quite a lot of our lives. I was bright and artistic and sensitive and my brother was those things, too, but he was also very outgoing and sporty and competitive in a way which I wasn't. At school it was more personal and hurtful because he was very academically bright, but I was very creatively bright. But again, those things didn't apply in those days; you had to be able to do your sums and recite your tables, which I was never terribly good at. I wanted to paint a picture.

The big trauma happened at eleven. He passed the 11-Plus and went to grammar school and I didn't pass and went to secondary modern and was told by parents and teachers and friends that from that point on he was the brainy one and was always going to make it. I was going to end up in a factory, on the docks; no future was considered for me in the same way it was for him, and that obviously caused a deal of friction between us, because I always thought that he was getting the advantages that were being denied me. But funnily enough, although these people said these things to me, I never believed them. My attitude was, 'That's what you think; stand back and watch.' So maybe we both had the ambition to get out – it's just that he did it in a different way from me.

I suppose I was a cissy in my parents' eyes. They wanted me to be a tough kid – big in the street and fighting – and they realized what they'd got was a very sensitive child. But instead of encouraging that, they saw it as a terrible weakness and an awful indictment on them.

My father at that point felt it more strongly than my mother, though Dad has completely changed over the years. Now I'm incredibly close to my father because he has allowed himself to become more sensitive as he gets older. He was a sensitive man, you see, and because he was very bright, we were the only kids in my street that had bookshelves. We might have had a cold tap in the backyard, but we had bookshelves and on birthdays and Christmases we'd be given books. Now it was a very important part of my life that those books were there and that I had access to them.

My father worked in a factory, but he was a production manager. He made ice cream – something I don't eat much anymore; as a child it was supposed to be a terrible luxury. To any man in that circumstance, to have a cissy child was a big problem because it reflected back on him. And being a sensitive man, he was doubly freaked out about it, because he was trying to play the grown-up male game, and he probably wasn't doing it successfully himself. Then to have me puncture it all the time must have been tough for him. I've talked about it with him since and he's agreed that it was true. So my twin brother was what is called 'a real boy', playing in the school football team, being team captain and head boy.

Q: *When did you start to draw?*

I cannot remember not having pencils and paper. I can't remember a time when I didn't draw, and I did draw more than write. We didn't do art in secondary school. Boys do woodwork – come on, you don't do art in a crappy secondary modern school in a slum area of Liverpool! But that didn't stop me. I continued to draw and paint and at home I did it all the time too. I'd always known it was going to be a career – although I was in this crappy school being told that my future was zilch.

I used to go to the theatre a lot without people knowing that I went. I was fourteen, fifteen. I would find out that D'Oyly Carte was coming to the local theatre and I'd save up and book tickets. I went to the Royal Ballet when I was about fifteen and saw *The Sleeping Beauty*, with a very famous Oliver Messel design. So, I always knew I was gonna work in the theatre because that's what I wanted and I was always interested in theatre design and that's what I saw. But again, going to the theatre wasn't part of a working-class life. Oh, yeah, panto at Christmas. We'd all be taken off to see Ken Dodd in *Aladdin*, but theatre as a way of life wasn't part of my childhood. Books were, because of my father; literature was – but not the visual arts, not theatre and not music. Not classical music. The radio would be on but it would be *Workers' Playtime* or *Housewives' Choice*.

Q: *What about sexuality? When were you first aware of being attracted to other boys?*

I only have one gay friend who thinks that he became gay out of a conscious decision to be gay, as almost a protest. Every other gay friend I have knew that they were gay long before the word 'homosexual' had any meaning in their lives and I am somebody like that. I was never aware of my difference until I was twelve, thirteen – when you suddenly realize that boys in the playground are looking at the equivalent of page three and I thought, 'I prefer the person looking rather than what he's looking at.' But by that point I was used to feeling different and, like most outsiders, I was class clown, because I was witty and I was bright and I could take the piss out of people without getting a fist in my face. I could make them seem silly by the laughter that I generated from other people, so I took the sting out of any kind of aggression that way. There was one boy in my class I can remember who probably was gay but who couldn't deal with it and had no other way of combating the heavy kind of male adolescent aggression, and I think he probably didn't come out of it very well. But I had a way of batting it away.

But I was very hung up about sexuality because I did still feel myself to be a working-class, masculine man. I couldn't define it in any way, but all the role models so far in my life had been that, and later on, not being a man became more important to me than it was as an adolescent. That took an awful long time to get over.

Q: *How did you decide to go about working in the theatre? Did you get any help from school?*

I got help from an English teacher who will always remain a saint, an idol, to me. I left school at fifteen and I went to work in a department store. And then I joined an amateur dramatic society

– Liverpool Youth Theatre – and that was great because then I was suddenly with a whole pile of kids who felt very similar to me. I'd been isolated in my interest up until that point.

I applied for the course at Bristol but because I'd left school at fifteen with no qualifications, the chances of getting a grant were practically nil, because they ain't gonna give a grant to a secondary modern kid who's got no qualifications to go off and do something; the English teacher supported me and wrote letters to the Education Department and it was really through her that I got the grant and, if I hadn't have got the grant, then I wouldn't be sitting here today talking to you.

When I was fourteen [laughs], this careers officer came around to see everybody and I went in and he said, 'Your teacher's told me you're terribly good at art.' I said, 'Yeah, I think so.' 'Well, what do you want to do?' And I said, 'I'm going to be a theatre designer.' And he looked at me as if I was completely mad and said, 'That's aiming a bit high. There's a vacancy for a sign-writer'! As I was good at art, would I like to do that? [Laughs.] But I didn't take it. I went to Bristol instead.

Bristol was a huge revelation to me, because we were all there with a common ambition, but there was a huge class diversity. Until I went to Bristol I'd never met middle-class or rich people. Now there were some rich people at Bristol who used to take my breath away because I'd never come across anybody so wealthy before or so assured – the kind of security that comes from money. But because I was a bit pushy, I loved it; it was hugely different for me. We also have to remember that I had a very strong Liverpool accent, and this was '64 when the Beatles were really making it, so I had a bit of cachet for having a Liverpool accent [laughs]. But I lost it because I decided nobody could take me seriously while I had this incredibly trendy and fashionable accent. I was also seventeen and being reborn and unaware of any other problems apart from my ambitions, so I sailed away on that a lot.

That really was the first time sexuality raised its head. I realized I was attracted to men but I still thought it was only a short-term problem that I would get over. And there were some very beautiful, very attractive people there then. When I look back, I could kick myself because I realized that I could have done something about it much earlier, but I was still intimidated. I still couldn't come to terms with it. You see, I still equated homosexuality with weakness.

132

There was one particular guy who was the very first extremely effeminate gay I'd ever met – and he was my worst fear. I kept thinking, 'I think I know I'm homosexual, but that's what homosexuals are – and I am not like that.'

I was having great male friendships at the time with other students who would laugh at this person and I would think, 'Well, you know, these people won't be my friends if I am like that, therefore I must avoid being like that.' I couldn't see myself as homosexuals were supposed to be – and, indeed, are still thought to be now – and if I wasn't like that, then I couldn't be gay.

I was incredibly naïve for eighteen. I think everybody was. People didn't talk about sexuality; they weren't as aware of the world as they are now.

But I did fall in love with somebody, a straight person, and I remember one night in my bed-sitter him coming round and talking and me just bursting into tears and actually stating what I felt. He was incredibly understanding and sympathetic. He was as confused as I was, but at least he didn't go, 'Get off, you pervert,' or 'I hate you.' But I realized there was no going back on it, having blurted it out. I had to just get on with it.

It still took time for me to come to terms with the actual physicality of it, rather than the idea of it. When I left the theatre school, I went to the Theatre Royal in Bristol to be a prop-maker and a scene-painter, and again had fun. I had a lot of very straight male friends who again considered me fairly joky and witty, which meant that I could get on with them, without having to let them get too close.

I suppose I thought that if I had a relationship with somebody I would jeopardize friendships, that people would dump me. Keeping strong friendships was more important than a physical relationship. Of course, I found out later that this wasn't the case. What happened when I came out was people said, 'Oh, we've known that for years. Why haven't you been getting on with it?'

After Liverpool, Bristol was beautiful, with lovely architecture and the downs and Clifton and the bridge. Coming to London was another gob-smacker because it was just huge and I really couldn't cope with it. I came to London in '67 – hippies, growing my hair long and wearing beads. That was great. Now that was a liberation, you know, to have hair down to your shoulders and wear bright clothes and tight loons and flowered shirts. That was great fun. A lot about that era is now knocked as the 'permissive society', but it wasn't; it was very open but it was very political, I remember. It wasn't just screwing around. There were big anti-war demonstrations, there were a lot of left attitudes in the air. I was at the big anti-Vietnam demonstration outside the American Embassy in Grosvenor Square, which still chills me when I see it popping up in documentary programmes because it was horrific. People had turned up to be peaceful, and yet there were horses charging and then violence broke out and people were ripping up railings and I just felt general dismay – that something that had started off to be a protest against violence became, in itself, very violent and therefore defeated itself for me.

My sexual life wasn't really taking shape. I did have a relationship with somebody which was bumbling and difficult and painful because he was going through exactly the same things as me. The very first big love of my life didn't come until I was twenty-one. That was the very first proper, real, physical, fulfilling relationship in my life, with somebody who is still a friend. But that didn't last very long. I was twenty-one before I'd done it properly and grown up, whatever it is to lose your virginity. It seemed pointless then to worry about what people might think, but it took that long, and it took the freedoms of the late sixties to do it for me.

I was working on operas, making props, and not earning very much money, but then, when you're that age, you survive. I don't think that I missed out on very much.

Then GLF came along. I think somebody came up to me one day, giggling, with that clenched-fist badge and he said, 'Can you imagine, my dear, a whole army of us.' But he was uncommitted to it. Then I think there was an article on Stonewall in *International Times* and I was much stronger by now and, I suppose, reacted angrily to what I'd been missing. So I went along to the London School of Economics off Kingsway in London and was very nervous. I didn't know quite what to expect or who I'd find there. The meeting was held in the lecture hall, which had an amphitheatre of wooden seats around a dais; on the dais was a table and around that sat what was then called a steering committee. Oh, we didn't have them for very long. I mean, we had to be a democratic organization, didn't want to have people sitting there telling us what to think.

Up until then I'd only met theatre gays, but then I was meeting

architects and students and there was an accountant I remember
very well. It makes it sound very middle class, doesn't it? But
there seemed to be a great cross-section of people. There were
some Americans there who'd been through it a bit earlier in
America and therefore were much more verbal in discussion.

Also there was quite a lot of police activity at that time; people
were still being busted and a great deal of outrage was coming
from us about it, but there was a desire to be constructive about
the anger and to give ourselves a higher profile. I suppose we all
felt like I felt – that I'd been hiding for too long and suddenly
there was a move towards coming out. Out of the closet. And I
really wanted to do it, because I'd had it. I'd been locked up
about it and suddenly there was this whole pile of people saying,
'Let's get out on the streets and do something about it and say,
"Excuse me, you don't say that about me anymore, I'm not
prepared to sit in a group of people and listen to anti-gay jokes
and laugh and pretend that I'm not gay."' There was an opportunity to be angry about all these things that had been a huge part
of my existence just in order to survive. And I reacted very
strongly. Not violently; I'm not violent. I thought, 'Why should
another kid go through what I went through when I could be out
on the streets saying to kids, "You know, if you're gay it's all
right, don't worry about it; you don't have to go through that
anymore."' Which is why I always thought that Gay Pride
marches were hugely important.

Q: *What were early GLF meetings like?*

Chaotic. There were screaming queens who had one particular
idea of what being gay was about. There was another group of
much straighter people who thought it was about something else,
and a middle group who identified with both. I suppose I was in
the middle group. I didn't see anything wrong with looking
straight and being gay, any more than I thought there was
anything wrong with looking faggoty and being a faggot. I mean,
it seemed to me to be perfectly, well, 'human' to be one, either
or neither. But there seemed to be a lot of acrimony between the
groups. And don't forget the GLF movement was only part of a
series of movements like the Women's Liberation Movement and
it was revolution. People really did think that they could change

John and his twin brother, Liverpool

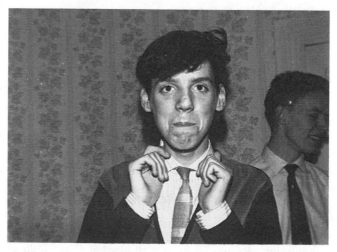

Aged 15, at a party, 1962

John, 1971

society. That was the general feeling in the air at the time and there were the riots in Paris – a universal movement of kids. American kids as well. In those few years, youth culture and youth politics shook the world. Unfortunately, it didn't last. It was very verbal and very exciting because lots of ideas were being thrown around. In GLF we'd long since got over having a committee who held the chair to make sense of it. People stood up and had their say and had arguments across the room or whatever. So it was a great mish-mash and, at that point, there was a common bond – the important thing was being out of the closet. The important thing was being political. The important thing was no longer hiding. The important thing was to be honest and to say that you were gay.

I remember there was a poster at the time and it was very clever because it said 'yes' to everything we had always been denied. It said something like, 'Gays are cock suckers, yes,' 'Gays fuck other men, yes.' And for years and years and years everybody said, 'Well, actually, I don't fuck.' So this poster suddenly galvanized everybody. It meant that we could actually begin to say, 'Yes, and if you don't like it, tough fuck.' From that came a great deal of strength which was very good for me. I remember having arguments with gay friends who were not in GLF and who felt extremely threatened by this boat rocking, because it was getting a lot of publicity. Fleet Street were down there like packs of hounds, of course they were.

I went on the very early marches and, actually, they were quite small. Again I thought it was very important – gaining publicity. I remember the Festival of Light zap in Central Hall, West-minster. It was all part of Operation Rupert and it was a concerted effort from all the freaks [laughs], *Oz* magazine and Gay Liberation and the Women's Movement and God knows who. We all turned up on the Embankment underneath the statue of Boadicea and it was all terribly carefully planned. Normally, everybody schlepped around in flowered shirts, beads and long hair, but all the men showed up in borrowed suits and ties and the women were wearing dresses and high-heeled shoes and there were a couple of terrible queens dressed up as nuns. All in order to get in.

It was very well orchestrated. The Festival of Light at that time was far more powerful, more vociferous than it is now. I think it's still dangerous but it's much more insidious now. Then, it was straight up and down – they were Christians; they were pure; they were right and society was decadent; it was promiscuous; it was permissive and it had to be stamped on and they were out in their multitudes. So we all showed up at Central Hall and we were all allotted spaces to try and get to, so the 'nuns' got into the gallery, other people got into the back of the hall and others into the front. I was sitting with – I think there were about four of us, eight rows back from the podium – and there they were! There was Whitehouse and Muggeridge and Cliff Richard and various other people. The meeting began with hymns and all of that; we all stood up and then talks began and the sedition started subtly, with people throwing stink bombs. It all sounds very silly now. And then the two drag nuns ripped open their habits and showered the people below with pornographic pictures, which caused absolute uproar. And then came my turn for being kicked out. The big discussion was about obscenity: pornography and television, films and literature, and I and the group I was with stood and – I still think, quite rightly – said, 'Real obscenity in the world is starvation in India or Bangladesh – or now Ethiopia – why don't you direct your energies to that instead of trying to curb people's freedoms?' etc. We were seized by great burly Christians who herded us down the stairs and threw us into the street.

So it seemed to have worked, whatever we were doing, because certainly it unnerved people. But the thing that sticks with me was that I was standing in the street after the meeting, giving out leaflets and attempting to say, 'I'm homosexual; I think what you're doing is wrong; I think you need to think about what you're doing to people like me.' While I was handing out leaflets, I was being spat at and I remember saying, 'Oh, great. That's terrific from a Christian. That's Christianity, is it, spitting at people?' Or being told I was the devil's spawn; generally, people were either incredibly hostile or patronizing.

When we moved from the LSE to a basement in King Street in Covent Garden it was the summer, and everybody seemed to be more interested in joining GLF at that point, because it had become much more open – a fashion parade, rather than anything to do with politics or revolution or change. Then it moved to a church hall in Powis Square, Notting Hill Gate. After the meetings, people trickled off to different pubs. One evening a pile of us wearing GLF badges were refused service, so we sat on the floor, saying, 'OK, if you don't serve us, you'll have to have us removed,' and thinking that this was going to upset the rest of the pub and being very nervous about it. The extraordinary thing was that the pub joined in! There were a group of rugby lads in a corner and they were getting pissed off because they weren't being served because we brought everything to a standstill. We sat and talked to them and explained to them why this was happening, and instead of getting abuse from them, they sat on the floor too and were prepared to be carried out by the police as well. And that's when I realized that gay liberation was making some kind of foray into popular consciousness.

Q: *Did you go to a consciousness raising group?*

Yes I did, every Friday for months and months. It was very good. What it did was to bring together a very diverse group of people, about a dozen of us, and we were very disciplined about showing up every week and we did talk a lot, like we're talking today, about our childhood experiences, our brothers and sisters, how we felt at school, what it was like coming out, how we faced up to our sexuality. And the group got very, very close. The sad thing is, of course, I don't see anybody from that group now. But that's not to say that at the time it wasn't a very good thing for all of us. Some more than others because in a group of people you're going to find people who are more articulate and more forceful and open to exposing their lives and their emotions. At this point I'd really changed – like a somersault. I'd gone from being nervous and shy and diffident and worried about my sexuality to embracing it totally, so I really was one of the people who was most verbal, which probably wasn't very good.

The groups were unstructured – not like group therapy where somebody sits and referees or tries to give a form to what is being said – here somebody would begin and people would add to it and then an argument would happen and it was completely unstructured.

I don't understand what happened when GLF broke up. It became very factionalized and there was a lot of in-group fighting. The radical feminists became more and more determined that any sexual revolution had nothing to do with men, even gay men, and therefore they split totally, and then the different attitudes to being male and gay became very, very pointed. The most vociferous group were the ones that grew their hair long and painted their fingernails and wore make-up and lived in communes and generally thought that unless you were totally into your female side, then you were in no way revolutionary. And if you wore jeans and sweatshirts as opposed to tulle and sequins, then you were not radical and therefore they didn't need you. That group went off and formed communes in Notting Hill.

Ordinary gay people who just came along for a meeting, wanting to be involved in something they thought might be important to their lives, were completely alienated by this in-fighting. People like me stuck with it a long time because I had sympathies for both sides. I mean, I didn't want to have a moustache, wear plaid shirts and boots, nor did I particularly want to wear feather boas. But I could understand both. I can't understand why they couldn't get on together. Each group thought that they were correct and that their particular kind of political philosophy and attitude to life was the only one that was going to lead to true liberation. And in the end, of course, it just broke up everything because nobody could agree. Very sad. Very sad.

Then *Gay News* was published and I remember an incident where somebody snatched *Gay News* out of someone's hands – I think it was at a Kensington Hall dance – and ripped it up, saying that they were making money out of being gay. It was all becoming capitalistic.

Q: *How did GLF change you?*

It gave me a lot more confidence and it gave me a lot of attitudes I still hold today, because I don't want to let go of those good things that happened and the good ideas that came from it. I'm depressed that GLF wasn't a vanguard both sexually and politically. I think it ought to have changed perceptions more than it did.

I didn't lie anymore about who I was, and I wasn't about to let anybody get away with anything anymore. Indeed, I remember once even having a line changed in a play because it was very anti-gay. It was a political play about the Heath government and I was having an affair with the actor who had to say the line. I said, 'You've got to look at what you're doing. This is a deeply sexist, anti-gay line and it's got to go.'

After that I went to Australia. I went out to live with somebody who, through meeting me in London, had come out as gay and then returned to Australia with his glad tidings [laughs], which was not considered terrific by family and friends. So at the point I went out to join him, I met with very little except hostility. This was Melbourne, which was still very surface macho. It was like an English provincial town with the worst kind of middle-class attitudes – and it's rich, of course. I was living with an enclave of people of my age, who all had boats or houses in the country and, as a socialist, I suppose that pissed me off rather a lot. That kind of lifestyle for little or no effort, to me, is real decadence. I stayed for six months.

When my relationship with the Australian failed, I came back to England broke. I'd also been out of the country working somewhere else for a year before that and, by the time I got back, I'd been away nearly two years. So it was good to be back but it was '80 and the sixties and the seventies were over, really over!

There was no longer any popular movement. I still listen to the Beatles and think, 'All you need is love' – and then you see the kids looking violent. They say it's only a fashion, but they look aggressive: they look mean; they look hateful; they look lost. I'm so glad I was young then, because there were just more options. The atmosphere was filled with possibilities. Kids are terribly put down now.

In Australia I'd taken a terrible bashing. I was never that promiscuous. I tend to have relationships rather than one-night stands. I've always found somebody, then lived with them for six months or a year and when that finished, I would start with somebody else. But at that point I couldn't pick myself up and dust myself down; it took a long time. Then I met a Latin American architectural student and that was probably the greatest relationship of my life, because everything worked on every level. We didn't stop talking and we enjoyed the same things. We enjoyed the same music. We have a very similar sense of humour which, when you think that I was born in Liverpool and he was born in Mexico City, is really unlikely. But we laughed and we enjoyed each other. And I suppose that was the first time I had somebody who was a real friend and a lover, where everything that's important for a relationship came together. But, unfortunately geography intervened and I cannot work in Mexico and he cannot work in Britain.

This was three or four years ago; he was in his mid-thirties; he was Catholic. He couldn't tell anybody at home, couldn't. He knew when he went back he would have to play the game, get married to a good Catholic girl and have sons. As far as I know, he is doing all this because we've now lost contact. It saddens me because it seems to encapsulate a terrible gay problem – that is, he could have been back in Mexico and six months later walked under a bus and the last person in the world to be told would be me. Because he couldn't tell his parents about me, he couldn't tell his friends, he couldn't tell anybody. All he had was a memory of me.

It seems odd now, though, that I should ever have felt strange about being gay because it's such an assimilated part of my life, and there is nobody who doesn't know I'm gay. My twin brother was quite shocked by it, because he thought, being twins, if I was, then he would have to be. But he's since married and is very happy – as, indeed, my other brothers and sisters are; they're really quite proud of me.

My mother hated it. I mean, she looked like Miss Haversham for about a month after I told her. Didn't wear her teeth for three days. Surprisingly, my father doesn't mind at all and when I go home he never makes any problem of it. My mother still sniffs occasionally. My friends all know about it and I still make new friends.

But I think it is harder as you get older. Not that I'm particularly ageist, but I'm not as likely to put myself in the position of being loved as I would have been a decade ago. So I do feel I'm probably likely to spend long amounts of time being on my own, because I'm not as ready to make myself vulnerable. I'm not pessimistic about it; I think that there is somebody, somewhere, that I will meet and grin at and understand immediately. It's just that I know it will be harder to come by because the people I'm likely to have relationships with are probably going to be as guarded as me. But I am optimistic.

1988. Portrait by Sunil Gupta

KURSAD KAHRAMANOGLU

INTERVIEWED IN MAY 1988 BY PAUL MARSHALL

I was born in August 1951 in a town called Samsun on the Black Sea coast of Turkey, facing the Crimea. I come from a reasonably well-off family and I have one sister and one adopted sister. It's a small immediate family but with lots of uncles, aunts and cousins.

I was born as a Muslim and my parents are still practising Muslims, but were fairly liberal. My sisters and I were never forced to have a strong religious education, and when I was fourteen or fifteen I discovered existentialism and things like that and it was very fashionable to deny God, so I have hardly any religious background at all. On paper, I'm a Muslim and I come from a very Islamic background.

I went to a primary school like other kids but then I went to a boarding school for seven years. You had to take an entrance exam to get there, but it was also a privileged school because your family had to pay quite a lot for you to study there. The medium of teaching for many subjects was English. There are many schools like that in Turkey, most of them in English but there are ones with French and German. Historically, one of the reasons is that they were set up for minorities in Turkey, so that they could send their children there. Over the years this changed. If you are going to pursue an academic career it is really necessary to speak one of the Western languages. You have a better chance of getting a good job, so language-learning is a very important part of teaching in Turkey. Unfortunately, it's not very widespread: it's only reserved for the privileged few.

I was at boarding school between the ages of eleven and eighteen. To start with, it was obviously a bit heartbreaking to be

145

away from home but then towards the end of my studies I really enjoyed it. I think it's a very good place for a gay person to be. I remember quite clearly there were twenty-four kids in my class and, with the exception of three, the rest were having some sort of sexual experience with each other or as a group. The opportunities were always there. I can't believe for the life of me that the people who were running the school weren't aware of it, but it was neither condoned nor condemned. I think if it had come to light, it would have been condemned and people would have been punished, but obviously it was done in secret, so it was there.

I think public schools have quite a lot in common wherever you go. Because everybody was at it, I didn't feel different from the other boys. I didn't have this feeling of isolation which seems to be a major problem for gay men, like, 'Oh, my God, I am the only person in the world who feels like this.' I probably felt that I took it a little more seriously than them. I don't know; it's very difficult to say now. Therefore I didn't have much joy in coming out. One of the nicest things about it is realizing you're one of the millions, but that isolated feeling was never there in the first place for me. I'm sorry if this upsets some of the theories about being homosexual [laughs], but in fact I had a very stable home – loving parents, terribly supportive. It was quite a happy childhood and I enjoyed my teens. The opportunities were there and I had a very good education. I wasn't aware at the time, of course. I was complaining all the time – 'This is too restrictive and I'm locked into this school' – but in hindsight, I was happy.

When I left school I studied engineering. That was actually shaped for me because of the kind of society that I lived in. In Turkey there is a very clear hierarchy of professions which are socially and financially more satisfactory than others, and top of the list are medicine and engineering. I was interested more in things like art and philosophy but I was continuously discouraged to have those interests. I was more or less pushed into becoming an engineer because, once you graduate from high school it is very competitive to get a place in Turkish universities. It is almost impossible to argue against your family and adults around you that you don't want to do that. I resented for a very long time the fact that I had to do engineering.

I went to university in Ankara from '69 to '76. It was politically the most radical university in the country. Student movements are more serious political forces in Turkey than in this country. I was gradually introduced to socialism and there were many students around me who were in active revolutionary organizations; there was always friction between the authorities and the students. I was a sympathizer of an organization called Revolutionary Path which went underground after the military coup. Although I never joined it, it was the biggest youth revolutionary organization in the country and was very active in my university and other universities. They were revolutionary socialists in the Leninist tradition. During that period I had two gay friends and both of them had been abroad. One spent some time in London and the other went to the United States for a year and, of course, they both came across other gay men and so they had some idea about what it is like to be gay in the context that we understand the word in this country. I had never been abroad so I didn't know anything about it, but I worked it out for myself. I used to say to them, 'Look, we are living and studying in the most radical university there is, run by a socialist students' union, and these people often declare they're on the side of the oppressed, so why do we have to hide our sexuality from these people? We must tell them that we are an oppressed group and they have to do something about it.' They got so frightened and they didn't want to know. I tried to talk them into it by saying, 'Look, if you don't want to talk about it openly in a meeting, why don't we print a leaflet and distribute it so that people see that there is a thing called men loving men and people shouldn't be treated differently because of that.' But the two friends just thought I was a dangerously radical person. They said that this can't possibly happen in Turkey and so nothing came of it. That was the only serious moment of theory regarding sexual politics that I had in Turkey.

The Turkish language used to have two words for homosexuals, like many other Mediterranean countries. One word describes a passive homosexual and the other the active one. If you ask a person what is a passive homosexual then the answer will be that it is the homosexual who plays the role of a woman in a relationship, so the relationships between two men are always perceived as a reflection of a heterosexual relationship. People just think that they live like a heterosexual couple and they have very defined roles. It is very much a culture like certain Latin American cultures. Therefore, to be *kulampara* – which is the word describing

147

the active homosexual – is perfectly OK; it can even be a flattering word, meaning that you are such a man that, not only are you capable of screwing a woman, but also a man. You can hear fathers complimenting their sons as 'my *kulampara* son'. But to be the other, *ibne* – the only translation which I can think of is 'catamite' – is a terrible thing. It's the biggest insult in the language. At a football match, if the referee decides something and the people are unhappy about it, they all get up and shout that he is an '*ibne* referee'. It is very much linked with the fact that to be a woman is to be seen as a second-class human being. To pretend that you are a woman is even worse – you become a third-class person. I often tease people when I go back to Turkey because I have friends who freely admit that they screw a man and I say, 'Where are these men who are supposed to be screwed? You all say you are this category of gay men who are screwing other men, so for every screwing there must be somebody who is being screwed.' It really confused them!

Q: *Did you have lovers and relationships in Turkey?*

I had sex with men. I didn't have relationships, that is why I consider myself to have been a closeted gay man during that period. The conditions are such that you can have sex with men very easily – easier than in some other places – but to have a relationship, in the sense that one does with a lover, is just not on the cards as far as two men are concerned. Of course, I fell in love and that's also easy to handle in Turkey. The system is very good like that because male friendships and the physicality between men is continuously encouraged. You hold the hand of a friend, your brother; you kiss your father and male members of your family, and you kiss your male friends. It is an insult if you don't kiss a friend after not seeing him for a week or two. Men sleep together in the same bed, not necessarily having sex, and that is expected and, to a certain extent, encouraged. Therefore when I had soft spots for other men, it was confusing. I never had the clarity in my mind that this was something other than what other people were feeling. I just thought it was what I was supposed to feel about men. The system accommodates it perfectly. That is why it is not possible to speak in the context of what coming out means in this country or the West, because in a country like Turkey you can go through your life having a wife and children, and still have lots of men that you have sexual relations with.

I came out properly for the first time in Amsterdam in '74 and it happened like this. Although I was studying engineering I was more interested in social sciences and I used to spend a lot of time in the social sciences library at my university. It was full of American books. One day in the psychology section I saw a book which had 'homosexuality' on the cover in capital letters. It was a really shocking thing for me because I didn't realize you could write books about homosexuality which will be on the library bookshelves. It was obvious that the book was very well used, but there were no date stamps on it. I realized people smuggled it out of the library to read, which is exactly what I did. It was a collection of many case studies – a bit like this interview, I suppose [laughs] – selected interviews, a blunt book saying that Jack meets John and what Jack prefers sexually and how does John respond to that. I was absolutely amazed that you could write about these things and that there were people who made a serious academic study out of something like that. That made up my mind. I decided that I must go abroad and see this for myself, because to see it in print was an amazing experience.

It wasn't easy to go but, eventually, there was an opportunity as a placement student in Cologne. While I was there I discovered a sex shop which I was very interested in because I had never seen one before in my life. They had a corner selling gay books and I found something called the *Spartacus Gay Guide*, and I realized that there were lots of places in Cologne where gay people met. But the thickest part of the book was about Amsterdam, saying wonderful things about it, so I took the train there. I met and fell in love with this Dutch man who took me to an Indonesian restaurant and held my hand under the table. I had this brief romance for a week or two and I went to all the places one goes to in Amsterdam. It was very revealing for me because I realized that it was not just sexual attraction – which I considered to be all there was at the time – but that I could be emotionally attached and want to live and share a house and a life with another man. That was my coming out as a gay man and it was wonderful.

While I was in Amsterdam a friend of mine from Turkey was studying banking in London and he kept saying, 'You must come to London.' But I was so madly in love with Amsterdam that I

Aged 8, Turkey 1959

In Turkey

Kursad (front row, third from left with hat) on a demonstration against Clause 28, Manchester, 20 February 1988

didn't have time for anywhere else. He was insistent, so I travelled to London through the Hook of Holland. When I arrived at Harwich the immigration officers gave me such a hassle. I hated it. They asked me all sorts of personal questions, 'Where are you going? How long will you stay? What do you do? Have you got a job?' The final question was, 'And how much money do you have?' As it happens, I had quite a lot on me but they didn't believe me so I had to produce the money, which was absolutely degrading. I thought it was a terrible thing to do to a visitor. They eventually gave me a visa. That put me off England so much – in fact, I only stayed for one day because, compared to Amsterdam, it was an awful place. Especially after that experience. Funnily enough, the same guy was on duty on the way back. I said to him that because he gave me so much hassle, he can have his country. When I got back I complained about it to some English friends and they said that I was being unfair and that I couldn't make up my mind about London after twenty-four hours. I replied that I could, because I hadn't been treated like that anywhere else. Then in '77 I was on my way to study at a university in Vancouver. Since you can't fly direct to Canada from Turkey I decided to stop off in Amsterdam for a week or two, but friends said that I must stop off in London and really see it. So I did, with the intention of staying a week. But one thing led to another – basically, I met Prince Charming and I always thought that if you meet Prince Charming you do everything possible to make that work.

I met him on Hampstead Heath one afternoon. I didn't know it was a cruising ground, I just went for a walk since I was staying nearby. And he was there. I was very naïve, I didn't even realize he was gay immediately. We saw each other a few times and then he took me to a party he was invited to. I had a relationship with him for two-and-a-half years, but he was married and had two young kids. To start with, the relationship was all right and I was really amazed because his wife was very civilized about it. The problem was that although my lover was gay and his wife knew this and accepted that he had flings with other men, he had never had a lover that he really wanted to spend a lot of time with. He was working in Manchester and I moved there as well. He used to go home at weekends and he really used to be torn apart, because on the one hand he had the responsibilities to these really

152

young kids which he thought he should share with his wife, and on the other hand he wanted to stay with me. I think his wife was really threatened by this as well. Although she accepted the fact that her husband was gay, I don't think at that stage of her life she was prepared to lose him altogether and be lumbered with the responsibility of the kids all by herself. So it didn't work, unfortunately, and it was a kind of heartbreaking separation.

I was upset but I thought that if that had happened in Turkey it would have been more upsetting, because you wouldn't find many other gay men who would be prepared to set up a life with you. But I was young and I was in England with all these thousands of gay men and it wasn't long before I found another person, who I've been living with now for eight years.

Before I came to this country my view of England was that it had economic and unemployment problems. When I arrived I stayed with friends in Hampstead and, of course, none of these problems were visible there. Someone suggested that I took a look at Brixton, so I did, and stayed with the Brixton Fairies in Railton Road. This was quite an eye-opener for me. It was a very hostile environment, with constant raids and harassment by the police on a lot of the Black people in the area. The Brixton Fairies shared a communal, openly gay lifestyle. They were very courageous, politically active – most of them were involved in the Gay Activists' Alliance – and very social. They had a lot of parties and I remember one of them, Lotte Cash, used to play the piano.

When I moved to Manchester I studied at Bolton Institute of Technology. I had a really good philosophy course and I have never enjoyed myself more, academically, than I did in my three years there. One of the first political meetings I went to in Manchester was the Gay Activists' Alliance and I made a lot of friends there, including Bob Crossman. I wanted to set up a gay soc., which was a bit difficult because it was such an engineering-based college. The president of the Students' Union told me that there was a national gay committee of the NUS, so I went to their conferences which was a very interesting eye-opener for me. Then I got involved in the Students' Union. This was '78–'80 and the most important campaign in the student movement was the overseas-student issue. For the first time the government started to put up the fees for overseas students. As an overseas student, I was very much involved with that. When that was finished I got involved with other political issues. I was the convener of Manchester NUS for two years but then, in '82, I had to go back to Turkey to do my military service.

I was lucky because they had just passed a law in Turkey saying that if you had a degree, then you only had to do four months – just the basic training. I couldn't take it seriously. The whole thing was such an alien thing to me that I took part in all this training for four months and I just felt that it wasn't happening to me. I met lots of people that I would never have met otherwise – people from different walks of life, working-class Turkish people. There were also people like me who had been living abroad and they were so lost and so much out of it, but I felt much more at home. It was unhappy to a certain extent because it was terribly restrictive and the army mentality was different to anything that I had been used to. You become part of the machinery and stop thinking for yourself because if you start thinking about whether there is any logic behind an order, then you can't survive the army. You just go into automatic gear when the order comes; you just do it. But it was an experience I wouldn't have missed, although I wouldn't like to repeat it.

When I returned to Manchester I was unemployed for about a year. Then I started to do some teaching at Manchester University which, in my opinion, is full of very objectionable students. It is the redbrick university where all the Oxbridge rejects go and they resent the fact that they have to settle for that. They were basically middle-class Southerners in the middle of Manchester and resenting it. At the same time I got a job with Manchester City Council and recently I've been seconded to help set up the Greater Manchester Immigration Unit.

Q: *What's been your personal experience of racism in this country?*

It's actually an infuriating kind, in the sense that I was never confronted on the street by anybody telling me that I was a stupid wog or something; it only comes across when I start speaking, because of my accent and because of the way I use the English language. My experience of racism has actually been on two levels. Number one has been through the Home Office because of the kind of difficulties and hassles that I've been through – even to this day, when I now have a British Passport. Whenever I travel in and out of the country I am always the person stopped and searched. To a certain extent I expect that, because this is a racist state. The other racism which I experience is the one which frustrates me the most. When I first came to this country and started to get involved in politics I was welcomed by political middle-class lesbians and gay men. They were very wonderful and I was really very happy with them because I thought that these people really had an understanding of the issues. Here I was as a sort of Black person welcome to all these political meetings and I got lots of encouragement. Then the problems started. When I started to become equals with these people in the sense that I started to develop my own political ideas and initiatives and started to articulate these ideas, the same 'right on' people who welcomed me like an exotic flower started to resent me. I had become more assertive and articulate about my political views. I really resent the fact that you are all right as long as you're a decoration so that these political queens and femocrats can have the credibility of being part of a mixed Black and white organization. Now, this is a generalization: I'm not saying everyone of them is like that, but that kind of racism is absolutely unbearable because they are the people who can't afford to be racist in that way.

I'm one of the founder members of the Manchester Black Lesbian and Gay Group. The founding of the group coincided with the left wing of the Labour Party taking control of Manchester City Council. They were very sympathetic to organizations of ethnic minorities and lesbians and gay men. We applied for a very small starter grant – about 200 quid, to publicize the group – and we had our first meeting on 6 January '86. And it just went from there.

One of the things I like best about the group is that there has never been any problem with lesbians and gay men working together, whereas in other lesbian and gay organizations that I am involved in this is a constant problem. We've discussed this within the group and one of the conclusions we came to was that our identification of being Black is so strong and important to us that we can't afford the luxury of dividing as lesbians and gay men.

We have a very clear definition as to what we mean by the term 'Black'. It includes all the people from the Middle East, Asia, Africa, the West Indies and the original inhabitants of Australia and North America, the Aborigines and Red Indians. It is a political definition rather than a purely descriptive one. People are discriminated against because of the colour of their skin and their ethnic origins. British imperialism almost certainly created a hierarchy of Blacks and, if you look at the literature of that period, even the concept of beauty was very much linked to the lightness of the skin of a person. Even some Black communities were conditioned by this, so that if you were brownish rather than Black then you were more beautiful: it's just dilly-dallying to say 'Black and ethnic minorities' – it's just trying to make it more acceptable. Why should we play their game, with their rule? I'm proud to be called Black and if some people don't want to identify me as being Black, then it is their problem – not mine.

Q: *Can I ask you about your sexual life?*

Well, it depends how intimate you will get [laughs]. My first relationship was with Peter and when I finished with him I found another Peter – my life is full of Peters. He's an English person and he's very Yorkshire pudding. He's a lecturer in textile design. I live with him and we own a house together.

Q: *Is it a monogamous relationship?*

Certainly not. I have never been monogamous and that was clear right from the beginning. I object to monogamy on all sorts of levels. I see no reason why I should exclude the human race in favour of one person. After all, the human heart is a very large place.

Q: *What was your response to AIDS?*

For a long time I was very bad about it, in the sense that I am a very healthy person and always react badly to illness. I'm very unsympathetic when my lover has flu – I'm awful like that. Secondly, it was very difficult for me to come to terms with safe sex. Because of my background, it had a very liberating experience for me to practise some of the sexual acts without feeling guilty about it; then I was told that I must reduce everything to more or less mutual masturbation, which I've never been a fan of. So for a very long time I was very bad about it because I didn't want to think about it and I didn't want to do anything about it, but there were lots of good friends around me who forced me to think and face things. And, of course, like many gay men, my sexual practices have changed quite a lot.

I'm almost a continuous fixture of many gay clubs and pubs in Manchester and I enjoy it. But I also think that any person who is serious about the politics of sexuality should not ignore those known as the 'scene queens' – the gay men who go to the bars and the clubs. I'm not just saying that on a theoretical level, because I was one of the organizers of the biggest demonstration of lesbians and gay men ever seen in this country, held in Manchester on 20 February '88, against Clause 28. We made it very clear right from the start that we were not going to exclude those people who are on the scene. It was our priority to bring them in and, in the process, to politicize them if possible. Of course it was difficult. There were all sorts of 'right on' people moaning and complaining, saying, 'How can we have these people? They are this, they are that.' Nevertheless, it was such a successful demonstration and I think it is definitely an historical occasion – not only for Manchester, but also for the lesbian and gay movement in this country – because we actually made it possible to have a dialogue with those people who are on the scene.

I have been involved in the politics of sexuality in this country for eleven years now and my biggest disappointment is that, as a lesbian and gay movement, we haven't managed to become the political force I expected us to become.

Q: *What do you think will be the future for lesbians and gay men in this political climate, with Section 28?*

I don't think in the long run it will make a hoot of difference. We've been here from day one of history and there will always be new generations coming up: but it does not mean that life will not get worse for us. I was talking to these Dutch friends and was telling them about the Clause and they really find it difficult to believe that it is happening in England in 1988.

I think this conservative backlash will go even further. I wouldn't be surprised if the next time they try to ban our books and magazines – but I'm not afraid of that, either. Twenty years after the partial decriminalization of homosexuality, a whole generation of us are around who know what it is like to be ourselves and not to feel bad or guilty about it. They will not be able to take that away. I think they have taken on more than they bargained for. It will be much more difficult to drive us underground now and, to a certain extent, it might even have a positive point, in the sense that it will make most of us realize that enough is enough; we can no longer sit in our closets and carry on as if we are not being attacked. In the short run things may get tougher; but in the long run I'm not pessimistic. How can we lose? That means not only them, but we ourselves have to deny our existence – and we can't do that.

I've just returned from a holiday in Turkey. I've told my parents three times that I'm gay and I once even took my lover to visit them. They were very pleasant, but they still talk about grandchildren. They know I'm gay but they don't like to acknowledge it, so it's a bit frustrating, really. I stayed with some gay friends in Turkey who live with their lovers, which is quite rare. Unfortunately, at the moment it's only a small minority of intellectuals who can live like that. They are strong enough in society, so they can actually set up homes with lovers and face up to sneers and criticisms. A few writers and artists are open about their sexuality now. Recently, there was a hunger strike by a group of transvestites protesting against continual police harassment. It was reported in the Turkish press as a 'gay hunger strike'. Unfortunately, this has created a confusion in many people's minds, so that when the word 'gay' is used, they take it to mean a transvestite. Nevertheless, the gay movement is on the agenda more than ever before and people are prepared to be more forthcoming about it. It also coincides with the feminist movement in Turkey becoming stronger and there is a clear alliance between feminists and a handful of gay men. The debates are very much about the kind of issues I was involved in ten years ago in Britain and I felt a little guilty, thinking that perhaps I should be living there at this time. But I have too many commitments in Manchester to make a big move anywhere else.

I feel myself to be more Mancunian than anything else – in fact, I've chosen to be one. I like the city – in order to understand and appreciate Manchester, one has to appreciate the colour grey – and I like the people. I still think England is an awful country. It's conservative and, in spite of all the lip-service to liberalism, it is racist. But there are still a large number of people that I like so much, and identify with, and am in solidarity with. That is why I'm still here.

Eduardo Pereira, 1988

EDUARDO PEREIRA

INTERVIEWED IN DECEMBER 1987 BY GLEN EVANS

I was born in Santos in 1953, about 60 kilometres from São Paulo, which is the largest city in Brazil and where I was actually brought up. My mother's family used to be part of the coffee aristocracy in Santos. In the fifties there were several coffee crises in Brazil, so they were losing a lot of money and were not so well-off as they used to be. My father used to work in coffee as well. He had a processing plant in the interior of the state and he would buy the coffee from the farmers, process it and send it to Santos to be exported. He came from a Spanish immigrant family. They were very poor and his mother and father died when he was young, leaving him at the age of thirteen to take care of five younger brothers and sisters. So he worked very hard since a very early age to support all his family. He actually worked very hard until he died of a heart attack, when he was about fifty or so. The legend goes that my father was actually making business while he was dressing himself for the wedding.

We lived in a little house near the centre of São Paulo and I remember I was quite close to my nanny. I was quite alone, in a way, because all my brothers were so much older. My younger sister was five years older, and my other sister had always been very ill. So I couldn't really play much with them.

The nanny was not really a nanny as English people have them. She was a maid who used to take care of me. And I used to play a bit with three female cousins who lived around. So I was with females, basically. Also, there was a Black cook who was very old and nearly part of the family; I was quite close to her.

I never got on much with my father since for ever – ever. He saw his duty as providing security and money for the family, because he was quite traumatized by my mother's family losing their money. He was terrified that the same could happen to our family and all of us would be unprovided for. This terror of losing financial status is very meaningful because it runs through the life of our family. In Brazil we don't have Social Security, so if you lose the money, you starve. My uncle was also in the coffee business; in a coffee crisis he lost all his money and had an attack and became a schizophrenic. Since then, my aunt has always been very sick. So my father was terrified of that and he was economical all his life.

Q: *Did religion play a major part in your family's life?*

Well, it was a centre of controversy because my mother has always been incredibly religious. Very Catholic. Catholicism is not the same as it is here. It is the majority religion, so people are not as fanatical as the Catholics here are. But she was exceptionally religious. My father didn't go to church and was quite annoyed with my mother's fanaticism. So we had this choice in the family: mother religious; father not religious. Eventually, all my brothers and sisters gave up church. When I was twelve I gave up church as well.

When I started school, age five, we moved to an enormous house just next to the school where we were all going. The house was very good to us because we made friends in school and my parents were very open to having our friends at home. Our house was always full of friends of my sisters, brothers and, later on, mine. After my uncle died, his daughters came to live with us. It was quite a fun house, with lots of people always coming and going.

I spent all my days in the same school. Everybody who left that school could normally get places in universities. But it was also a very mediocre school. It was very traditional, so we were trained to pass exams. I can pass any exam you put in front of me. You simply learn the techniques of passing exams, but you don't actually learn much. It didn't really teach us to develop any creativity. I specialized in sciences and then I went to study business administration in university.

I was sort of a wimpish person while at school, and was mocked as effeminate since a very early age. I never had a proper sexual education so I tried to find out everything by myself. I once asked my sister to explain it to me, and she told me in very crude terms, using a fork and a cup. I was so disgusted. I couldn't believe it. She was really amazed that I was so shocked, and told, me, 'You must talk to our father or our mother.' But my father was too busy gaining money and had left all the education to my mother, who gave me a book written by a priest which was so full of metaphors that I didn't understand it at all. My whole sexual upbringing was really a mess. By eleven, I had my first awareness in sexual things. In Brazil this is an incredibly late age. People develop sexually there very early.

I had a terrible experience when I first moved to high school. In primary school we went to physical education classes and we never changed; we went with shorts under the trousers. In high school, people started actually changing in front of each other, and the very idea terrified me. There was this medical examination, in a group, with lots of boys. I had never been naked in front of other boys before, not even my brothers. There was this over-whelming feeling that came to me and I had an erection. I couldn't understand what an erection was. Also, I had pubic hair. Nobody else did. They were the same age but nobody else did. I was fascinated by what was happening and horrified at the same time. As soon as the medical examination was over, everybody fell on me, teasing me because I had an erection. And people started joking, saying, 'He's got a big T in his willie.' A 'big T' means erection in Portuguese. But I didn't know what it meant and I thought I was sick. Literally, I thought I had a disease. They spread the word, so the whole school was mocking me and it was a huge school. I was terrified and for many years after, at every medical examination, I became so famous that the doctor would actually recognize me and he wouldn't do the test. He didn't want to put me through that situation again.

The high school was so stupidly puritanical. The boys were separated from the girls until the last three years, so the whole thing about sex was really emphasized – and Brazilian kids are not like English kids, they talk about sex all the time. So there was this enormous thing about sex and, at the same time, there was an enormous taboo. It was really, really difficult.

163

Q: *How did you come to an awareness that you might be gay?*

I didn't think in these terms, 'I am a homosexual.' I remember when I was five, once I was playing in the living-room and my brother was there wearing shorts, reading the paper. I remember very clearly stepping on his foot, and he had hairy legs and I started grabbing his legs and moving around. And I could actually feel something in – this strange feeling – I didn't know what it was, but it was there. I used to sleep with my sisters and the two brothers had a different room. I used to find something very special about that room – the boys' room.

Also, whenever my sisters used to say, 'Oh, he's a beautiful man,' I used to identify with my sisters. I find it very strange when people here say that women don't treat men as sexual objects. In Brazil they certainly do. It was *Dr Kildare* time and I used to find him absolutely wonderful [laughs], and my sisters kept talking about him. I was always aware that I used to find men prettier than women. Besides, I was always called effeminate and *marica* [cissy] – you've probably heard that name.

Oh, yes. There were also the summer holidays which were really hot. Heat has a very strong sexual effect on me. And in Santos, with all these people on the beach with very brief swimming trunks and tanned bodies and water and – really! It almost drove me wild.

Our house and the school were just across the road from this park, which is a cruising ground in São Paulo. There was all these incredibly effeminate prostitutes standing around at night, and the cars running around them, around and around. Male prostitutes – most of them looked absolutely awful. These are the images I had. Once, I was walking home and I was cruised by this man, who was actually quite good-looking. I just got into the car and – we had this experience – then I went home. I felt absolutely guilty and dirty for months. Then it happened again. So until I left Brazil, when I was twenty-two, after university, I had an awful idea of homosexuality. Except for one thing. In university I fell in love with a professor. I didn't tell him, but he realized and was very tactful with me. It was very important because, for the first time, I realized that a man could actually fall in love with another man. I thought that I would fall in love with a woman, and I would be sexually attracted to men; that there would be this incredible split in my personality which would haunt me all my life.

I used to identify better with the mentality of girls than with the boys. I think they were a lot more mature. I never had any sexual feeling or emotional things for them, but I had fantasies about falling in love with women. I always had daydreams about incredibly beautiful talented women. Obviously projections of what I wanted to be. Not that I wanted to be a woman, but I wanted to be beautiful and talented – with men falling in love with me.

There was something else which I think is important and which I was teased for as well. I never could cope with the hypocrisy that boys and girls had with each other. I would see my sisters always swearing with the other girls, and the boys talking about women as really awful objects. I couldn't understand how they could talk in such bad terms about women. And whenever they were together, they would be polite and terribly flattering towards each other. It was all hypocrisy.

As a reaction, I never swore and I acquired a puritanical reputation, which I wasn't, but people misunderstood me. In the last year of high school there was a play on called *Angelicus Prostitute*, and they used to call me 'Angelicus' – which I didn't like very much, but I didn't care because I was a bit more mature then.

Also there was an interview in a magazine then, with Ingrid Thulin [a Swedish film actress], and she was describing free love. Reading it, the whole myth of marriage and heterosexuality and conventionality collapsed for me and I realized it doesn't make sense. I was fifteen – it was '68. I started losing respect for my family. I realized that they were very reactionary and right wing and we were living through a terrible dictatorship in Brazil. I used to hear awful stories which were never printed because of censorship. And my family would bluntly deny it. My brother was at the time the president of the union of the most reactionary university in Brazil, and I had the idea everything was lies.

After I started hearing the first accounts of free love, I started going to the theatre, and I started reading. Theatre is still a very important thing in my life. It taught me some real truths. I saw *Hair*, which was the idea of liberation. I was sitting in the auditorium and they invited the audience to dance. I was crazy to go, absolutely! The impulses were there, but still my body didn't respond – my body couldn't do what my mind wanted. It was terribly frustrating. I couldn't dance. This feeling of being torn apart happened to me all the time.

There was political repression, but the language in theatres started changing with the whole free love mentality. I was a bit too young to become a hippie, but I admired them a lot. The hippie movement was turned into a fashion. So ideas didn't reach very deep, but they were there, and I needed those ideas at the time.

Q: *Did these ideas represent a threat to the political system?*

Oh, no. No, no. I mean, during the whole military dictatorship homosexuality was never repressed. Gay clubs could go on as usual. They never tried to repress them, because they know it's like giving a circus to the people and so they could repress what really mattered. That's something else I didn't like in Brazil at that time – the whole free-and-easy mentality, which is very superficial and very tolerant, in a way. People don't take anything seriously there. And I am a serious person.

Q: *Why did you decide to study business administration?*

It was one of those terrible splits in my teenage times. I am the most uncreative person in the world, and at the same time I absolutely love creative things. When I had to choose in senior high school between the classics and sciences, I chose sciences because I could do that easily – even though I didn't respect it very much. The respectable professions to go into were medicine, civil engineering and law. I couldn't stand law. I didn't want to be a doctor and I despised civil engineering. Then business administration started being acceptable and I thought, 'Well, that's something which deals with numbers, statistics and so on. Things I can do. And at the same time it has a human element to it.' So I went to university and then I developed the idea of what capitalism is, and I was horrified. I didn't want to be a part of it.

I made wonderful friends at university and I fell in love with this professor – maybe *the* experience of my life so far. I think I stayed in university, not because of inertia, but also because that man was there. I used to do crazy things, like in summer holidays I would go back there just to sit by a window, waiting for him to come out. I just wanted to look at him walking towards the car. I never told him. I was totally closeted and I didn't know anything about him – whether he was gay or not.

My life and the situation in the family was terrible. My father had died then of a heart attack and my brothers and one sister were married, so my mother, my other sister and me were living 'alone in a flat where we had moved. It was terrible, because my sister had lots of problems and she used to revolt against my mother – for no reason at all, just because she's very disturbed about her physical situation. She has a rare disease caused by an excess of calcium in the bone – there is no cure. She had developed an incredible relationship with my father, and when he died she probably felt totally abandoned and she turned against my mother, who was actually very good with her. The atmosphere at home was awful.

In a way, I had always taken refuge with my mother. I hadn't been close to my father at all. I always felt despised by him. I could see that he liked my elder brothers and my three male cousins a lot, and I felt very jealous and very despised. I remember feeling an overwhelming sense of responsibility when my father died, and at the funeral I cried more for myself than for him. My brothers and a sister were married. In Brazil people only leave their families when they marry. I knew I wasn't going to marry, so I had to make a point of one day setting off. I had to do it. When he died, I thought, 'So was it going to be up to me now to support and live with my mother and sister? I won't be able to get out. I'll have to stay the rest of my life taking care of these two women – one is very neurotic, and the other is very religious.' I felt that I couldn't really support myself, let alone them. I was terrified.

After one year in university, I decided it was pointless. So I came to Europe for six months, thinking that I must find another solution. I was hoping that I was going to meet some marvellous people and I would find hidden talents in me which I could develop into something worthwhile. It didn't happen. But it was very important to have come, because later on it opened the possibility for me to come again. I went back to Brazil. I decided that one of the things I had to do was to start psychoanalysis. It was quite good, but I was so closeted that I had about one year without telling the analyst I was gay. Obviously he knew, but it was never stated by me.

167

Professionally, I was graduating and I knew I was going to be a terrible administrator – it simply wasn't me. Actually, I applied for a job as a trainee in a firm. I went for an interview and the man was quite impressed by my credentials. But there is this formality you have to go through, a psychological evaluation for the firm, and I failed. I didn't get the job, he never rang me back. I was absolutely traumatized. Because I studied psychology, I knew it would always show – I mean, my gayness, my insecurity, my lack of desire to become an administrator. It would all show. I would be a total failure. All of my life. I started to become aware of all that suddenly, and of my private life. I hated being gay. I didn't understand what homosexuality really meant, that it could have positive aspects. Everything about my life was negative – family situation, professional prospects, sexuality, relationships. I thought there was no solution. I gave up psychoanalysis and a few months later tried to commit suicide.

It was very well planned. It was a summer holiday and I waited one month for my brother, who lived in the countryside, to come over and spend one night with us. I wanted him to find me, not my mother or sister. The day he came over I burnt everything I didn't want anyone to find. I wrote down a message and I took the pills. But there was not enough time for me to die. He found me too soon and took me to the hospital. I stayed there for three days in a coma, and then a week in a psychiatric hospital.

My family visited me every day in hospital, and they tried to talk to me, they tried really hard. We can't talk the same language, in terms of mentality, but we trust each other totally and they gave me as much support as they could. But they couldn't give me what I needed.

A few months later, I decided again that I was going to kill myself. At the last minute I didn't have the courage. I just thought if I go to Europe again, I could just spend some time there, have a good time. If it works – a miracle happens – great. If it doesn't, I'd just throw myself in the river there and it would be easier for everybody. I put it in these blunt terms to my brother and said, 'Listen, I'll need support. I want to go without a return ticket and never come back. If I stay here, I won't be able to survive.' He helped me. And my mother was quite understanding as well. She was shocked, but understanding. They realized it was a desperate solution, but there was no alternative.

So I came to London. I knew this American woman who had been living here for ten years. I met her on the ship going back to Brazil, the first trip. So I arrived here and I rang her and she said, 'Oh, come over for dinner, I'm living in this community.' It was a house with six, seven people living together, in Brixton, sharing everything – income, shopping, cooking, house duties, and so on. The people there were the sort of alternative Londoners of the mid-seventies. It was the first time I ate a vegetarian meal, and I couldn't believe it because I always wanted to be vegetarian, but I couldn't be with my mother and family. Whenever I'd mention the subject people thought, 'He's mad.' But I always found it fundamentally wrong to kill animals to eat. I always felt I was crazy for thinking like that, but there I was with eight people who all thought like me. And it was the first night in London. So from then on, lots of things started changing.

I moved to a squat with that woman, her boyfriend and some English people. That squat was a dream. It was a row of Victorian houses in Kennington Park which were about to be demolished by the council. So these people just took them over and there was a huge battle against the council to keep the houses. They are still there, ten years after. There was an incredible feeling of community in that house. Most people in that street were vegetarian, and we organized communal trips to the market and sold the produce at cost to everybody in the street. Anybody who needed repairs and so on would call a neighbour who could do it. So everybody interacted. It was like a small socialistic dream.

I mean, the freedom that existed in this country at that time was absolutely wonderful. In total contrast to the political repression that I was coming from, right? Nobody had heard of Mrs Thatcher at that time – at least, I hadn't. It was paradise. And the last thing which I found incredible is what happened on probably my first visit to a gay pub.

The gay codes here are so different that I never recognized Earls Court as being a gay ghetto. I saw all these leather people coming into the Kentucky Fried Chicken, where I worked briefly, and I wouldn't recognize them as gay. I thought they were motorcyclists. I had no idea. Some of them were extremely friendly and I wonder how many opportunities I missed [laughs]. I don't know how I heard that the Coleherne was gay, but I went there and I met this man. He was a student in University College and a member of the gay soc. there. He introduced me to gay liberation and he gave me this book to read, *Society and the Healthy Homosexual*. I was ready for that at that time – just reading this book totally transformed my life. I started enjoying myself, enjoying sex, seeing that there was a positive side. Before, I used to despise everybody I had sex with and I never slept with them. Now I could sleep with people and feel all right about them.

I actually wrote to all my friends in Brazil and I came out to them. It was wonderful because all reactions were very positive, from everybody. I have only good memories of coming out. Our friendships grew so much deeper because there was a whole part of me which was concealed from them before. And, reciprocally, they hid things too. From then on, everybody started talking very openly about very intimate things. I was quite moved by how positive it was.

I started giving more and more hints to my family. The less guilty I felt, the more outrageous I became, but I didn't force it. When my mother came over in '78 for one month, I tried to come out to her. We were staying in the flat of a gay couple – my friends – who were on holiday. There were piles of *Gay News* and lots of books on homosexuality on the shelves, so it was quite evident. But as soon as I started mentioning the subject, she would steer away from it. She didn't want to hear. I also had a big shock – after three years away from her – to see how much she had got involved with this fanatical Catholic sect called the Opus Dei, which is horrendous. You can't talk to her anymore. She can't discuss things intelligently. She just recites what the Pope says.

After a couple of years I began to feel nothing was happening in my life again. I was now a vegetarian and 'out' as gay and active on demonstrations, but it wasn't enough. I needed to go further – or go back – into psychoanalysis. The only way I could finance it was to ask for the money from my father's inheritance. I felt incredibly guilty about this, because I couldn't be proud of myself anymore for supporting myself. Besides, I had promised myself not to use this money from my father, given to me instead of love. I invented an 'excuse' for myself – that I needed psychoanalysis to sort out some problems that my father caused me. Every day for a year-and-a-half I had psychoanalysis with a Kleinian. It cost me a fortune, and I had to move to Hampstead because most of the analysts live in that area.

I had interviews with several. The gay literature at the time was very much against psychoanalysis, so I used to put each one I had an interview with to the test. One of them, quite famous, nearly fell off his chair when I told him I was gay, and then he asked me stupid questions like, 'Do you prefer to be like a girl or like a boy?' I said, 'I always feel that I am a man.' He said, 'You misunderstand me. When you have sex.' He actually meant whether I was passive or active. At that time, it was the most unfashionable thing to ask or to be categorized by these roles.

I rang Gay Switchboard about it and they put me off immediately, saying, 'Oh, no! Freudian analysts just make you jump out the window.' It was a stupid thing to say. It's totally wrong. Psychoanalysis itself is not anti-gay. I then tried to see a trainee from the Society of Psychoanalysts, which is cheaper. They were totally ruthless about letting me know that my case wasn't desperate enough to justify being one of their patients. I was absolutely shocked. It just happened at that time that a psychoanalyst recommended by my former analyst in Brazil rang me. I decided to give him a try. He reacted well when I told him I was gay, and I liked him. He didn't make any derogatory remarks, and I made it clear that I didn't want to change to heterosexuality.

I went back into analysis because I felt my life was very limited. I wanted to do something worthwhile with my life, to justify my life. It was a very big thing for me at that time. Also, I had never managed to sustain a proper relationship and I started to think that I never would. I used to pick up someone, sometimes for just one night, sometimes it would be for a few weeks, or a bit more. But I never managed to sustain a very long relationship. Then I met this guy who is still a friend now. He was everything I liked. He was attractive, very intelligent, and English. To be able to get someone English was important to me, it was a form of adaptation to the country. I wanted an English lover, to have a flat together, to live a bit more normally. I explained to him that I was keen on him, that I wanted a strong relationship, but he didn't love me so much. Then he found a job in Germany, and as soon as he decided to go, he decided to fall in love with me. As soon as it was impossible, he really got keen on me. By then I had crossed him out of my mind. I wasn't in love. So. he became a good friend. It's difficult. Whenever I like someone, this person normally doesn't like me, and people who like me, I normally don't want. The obvious conclusion is that I don't really want a relationship.

When I realized that a relationship wasn't going to happen, curiously enough, I found that my circle of friendships was growing. Ex-affairs could actually become friends, and it has worked very well. Because of one-night stands, my group of friends has grown a lot. Also, I realized that I had to start taking care of myself a bit more. I thought, 'If I cannot have this "English lover" with whom I can share a flat, then I must have a flat by myself.' Buying a flat was a very important development. I have the two things I like and need: my individuality and independence, made possible by my flat and my work as an administrative clerk, and a community, represented by my friends and the few things I do in the gay community.

For three years I was involved in a consciousness-raising support group. We met every Sunday and talked very openly about all our problems. We didn't discuss politics much; it was more about ourselves and politics got included in that. And it wasn't therapy because it didn't have a specific therapeutic style and we did things not compatible with therapy – it was a very incestuous group. Many of us had relationships within the group, including me. From that group we branched out into different things. For instance, some of us went to Laurieston Hall, an alternative community centre in Scotland where they hold 'gay weeks' each year. It is for people interested in living in the country or in the idea of supportive communities. We shared lots of things, like different sorts of therapies, and games and music and dance. From this a group in London started to form a similar community project for gay people.

I use the commercial scene, too. It's very important, but I depend on it less. Before, I needed to go to a pub to be with people, or pick up someone. Now I don't need to. I ring a friend to go out, or invite people to dinner. We go to the Gay Centre, we meet at the YMCA – things like this. Also, before AIDS, it was part of gay culture to pick people up. Now you have to be so careful, sometimes it's simply not worth it. A shame, because I had always wanted to be a total sexual being, according to the Gay Liberation ideology.

Complications came during a relationship I had with someone

who was getting involved in the leather scene. At the beginning I thought it was a joke, then I realized he was quite serious about it and, to me, it had horrendous connotations. Not only the vegetarian aspect – that you didn't eat meat because you didn't want to have animals killed, and to wear leather is just as bad – but also the fascist connotations of wearing leather, especially for someone coming from Brazil. We started having lots of quarrels about it – I couldn't accept it at all. But it got more complicated. I was so attracted to him, obsessed by him, that I thought perhaps I had a secret obsession about leather. It was a terrible dilemma to me, a total contradiction to everything I am. But it does not seem so important now.

Q: *How do you see the future?*

I don't see the future [laughs]. I think my problem as a teenager and in university was that I was too obsessed by the future and I could see no future. I couldn't cope with that. I've learnt to cope with the present. I mean, there's no point in thinking of the future, it would just worry me to death. I intend to stay here as long as I can. There's nothing brilliant about my life, but it's comfortable. I enjoy my friends, and going out to the theatres, the ballets, the operas. I enjoy going home and watching television, going to Highgate Pond, going to the YMCA. And if I can keep on like this, I'm sure the future will take care of itself.

1988. Portrait by Sunil Gupta

ZAHID DAR

INTERVIEWED IN OCTOBER 1985 BY WILL TODD

Both my parents were born in East Africa; their parents had migrated there early this century from India. My mother's father was a tailor and my father's father used to work on the railways and then, when he retired, he started tailoring as well. I was born in Nairobi, Kenya, in 1956. When I was about five we moved to Tanzania for a couple of years and then we moved back to Nairobi till I was eight.

I went to school in East Africa, starting when I was five, for about three years. When we were in Tanzania, my father worked in a goldmine, and one of his workmates used to teach me arithmetic. I remember our house and travelling to and from Tanzania to visit my grandmother. I remember my grandmother's house had a rocking-horse in the garden. Up to when I was eight, I just used to enjoy going out, playing in the garden. In Tanzania, I used to have a pet monkey, which we tied to the outside of the house and it could run on the roof and all round the garden. And we had a duck and chickens.

I remember I was afraid to go to school in Kenya because the teacher was frightening, very strict. I remember getting my knuckles rapped for getting the answer wrong. I had a woman teacher who I liked, who wasn't as strict. It was a boys' school and there was an Islamic girls' school nearby. The majority of pupils and teachers were Asian, and the areas we lived in were always populated by Asians. I used to have to go to the mosque to say my prayers and was taught to read the Koran in Arabic. My mother's very pious, but my father's not very religious – he follows, but he's a hypocrite. I thought about it when I was at college and decided I didn't believe in a God, so I don't follow a religion.

175

My parents came to Britain in '63. Trouble had just started over the fact that Asians owned a lot of the shops and had Asian-only schools and Blacks wanted more control over the economy. It seemed that Asians had a lot of property and owned a lot of the businesses. So there was animosity between Blacks and Asians. My parents felt that there was going to be a backlash towards Asians and so they left the country before they were expelled, before the real trouble started. One of my uncles had left and he told my parents, 'Yes, it's a good life in Britain. You can get work,' etc. So they left Kenya and came here. My father was a motor mechanic; his first job was in Walls, working in their garage, fixing trucks. My mother worked in a sweet factory in Hayes.

My secondary school was a boys' secondary modern in Hayes in Middlesex. I started in '69. I hated it; well, I was scared to go at first, but then I got used to it. I found it quite strange that you had different teachers for different classes; at primary school you had one teacher. But I started to enjoy it. I've got three younger brothers and a younger sister. We used to beat the shit out of each other, I recall. [Laughs.] I used to get angry very quickly. We never used to get on. When my parents bought a house in Hayes, there were five children, so there were seven of us in a three-bedroomed house. We always had other families living with us, so every room was a bedroom. And so I'm not surprised we used to get angry at each other. The visitors were my dad's brothers' or sisters' families. As people were coming over, they were staying with us first before they found their own accommodation. We had people staying with us for months and months at a time, before they settled down. All in all, about five or six families went through our house. I can remember it was quite nice having my cousins around because there were more of us to go out and play.

But I know there was always something going on between my parents. They wouldn't fight openly in front of us, but you could see there were tensions. There was always something in the air.

Q: *Did you have any sex education in school or at home?*

No, none at all. The only sex education we had in school was when we did the rabbit in biology and the teacher just threw in at the end of the lesson [laughs], 'And that's how we have babies.'

It was really peculiar. I remember when I was at primary school, somebody told me babies are born and I wouldn't believe them. [Laughs.] I said, 'No, you're lying.'

Q: *What about your own sexual feelings? Were you aware of having any?*

I always fancied boys. I always got attached to someone in the class. I had a very good friend while I was at primary school, a boy who used to live near our house. We used to come back from school together. He was from a family of nine children. But he went to a different secondary school. We stayed friends because we lived close, but we didn't see each other as much as we used to. And he got a girlfriend at secondary school and I just made other friends, but I didn't have any sexual experiences at all. I was intrigued by other boys talking about their sexual experiences with girls, but I knew I didn't want to investigate sex like that – not with women – and I was frightened to do it with boys.

I remember I heard people talking about homosexuality when I was in the second or third year. I looked it up in the dictionary and I thought about it. And I thought, 'Yes, that's me.' It described my feelings. I remember doing this for two or three years, because I wouldn't believe it at first. Then I remember looking up 'homosexuality' in sociology or psychology books and all I could find was that it was a disease. So I was convinced that I had a disease, and that I mustn't ever tell anyone. It was just something that I didn't want to mention. I also read that it was just a phase that you go through. So I just thought, 'I'll grow out of it, like everyone else.' Like I was supposed to. So I forgot about it. I didn't want to do anything about it. And I repressed all my sexual feelings to the extent that when heterosexual porn was passed round the class, I used to say, 'Yeah, yeah; it's really good.'

It wasn't until I got to college in Manchester, in '76, that I decided I was going to buy gay porn because I didn't want to go out and have sex with someone. That was going too far. I hadn't accepted my sexuality. I remember near the coach station there used to be a gay bookshop called Gaze. I just happened to look in through the window and there was a calendar of a naked man. I'd never seen anything like it before. From then on, I always

177

used to take that route into the town centre. Then one Saturday I put on a long coat and a muffler so that nobody would recognize me, because the shop was near the poly campus. I walked into the shop and I bought a magazine and left with it hidden in my bag. From then on, for three years while I was at college, I never mentioned it to anyone. But that's how I released my sexual frustration and I'd buy one magazine for a year. I'd get my grant, buy the magazine and keep it for a year. Then I'd throw it away when I used to have to go home for the summer vacation. If anybody ever found it, I would have just gone to pieces.

I played on the fact that I knew lots of women. In my final year I had an affair with a woman. Because we were always together, most people thought it was sexual, but it wasn't. I'd miss lectures for her. We tried to see each other at weekends and it was really wonderful. It was a relationship – without sex. I mean, I'd get annoyed if I saw her with someone else. She used to talk to me about gay characters in films, so I think she'd guessed, because I hadn't made any sexual advances towards her. I just changed the topic of conversation. I'd say, 'It wouldn't matter to me if someone was gay; I think it's immaterial.' It never came to me that I should accept it and say, 'Yes; I am gay.' I didn't want to. Other people were gay; I wasn't.

When I'd finished college I came back from Manchester and was staying with my parents. While I was a student, living away from home, I had independence so I could go out, see films, go to discos, cope with myself. But when I got back home my parents expected me to be like I was before I left, to have no friends outside the family. Because none of my brothers had been to college, I couldn't talk to them about the things I wanted to talk about. At college I'd been politicized to an extent because I'd joined the Students' Union and I was on the exec. I thought it was great being a student councillor, being on the Board of Governors as a student rep. There was more to life than just watching telly. And life got really boring when I got home because I couldn't talk to anyone. My father reads the *Sun* and my mother likes the *Daily Mirror*.

Having left college, my parents expected me to get married. And because I had this girlfriend in Manchester, I decided that, as they wanted me to get married, I'd like to marry her. From that time onwards, when they were saying, 'Yes, we'll go and ask her parents,' I got really worried because I had to think about having sex with a woman. It dawned on me that I couldn't go through with it. How on earth was I going to do it? I started having sleepless nights and I couldn't eat, but her parents didn't agree to it. They wanted her to marry an accountant cousin of hers. When that fell through I breathed a sigh of relief and I just thought, 'I've got to do something because I can't go through this again.'

My father kept saying to me, 'Look, you can't just die over a woman like this. It's not right, son.'

After that, I used to read *Time Out* and they carried an ad for Gay Icebreakers. For weeks and weeks I used to turn to this ad. Eventually, I was alone one Saturday night and I phoned and I couldn't say a word. Whoever it was who answered said, 'You don't have to say anything.' And he just talked and talked and talked. He knew exactly what I was going through. Eventually, I came out with it. I said, 'Oh, I think I might be bisexual.' I could only ring when everyone was out and I'd also said to this person that I'm going to have to put the phone down if someone comes through the door. Icebreakers invited me to their disco at the Hemingford Arms on a Friday night. I had to get home for eleven, and even that was late for my parents. This was when I was about twenty-two, twenty-three. After that, going to Icebreakers discos and their tea parties on Sunday afternoon, I became more politicized. I met another gay Asian at an Icebreakers tea party, and we became very good friends. I've known him ever since, and I haven't looked back since [laughs].

When I first phoned Icebreakers in '80, I was working as a research assistant in Wembley for a tobacco company. I did that for two years and then the company folded and I took the redundancy. While I was doing that job I told my parents that I couldn't travel all that way every day and that my company wanted me to do an evening class, which was a lie, but I had to make something up. And so I rented a flat with a gay man, lived in Northolt, and it was near enough for work and I could still visit my family. So I moved out soon after I came out to myself.

I wanted to go on the scene. I'd learnt to drive and my brothers had got me a little Ford Escort, so I was able to drive to meetings and to clubs and pubs. Chatan, my gay Asian friend, and I used to go out nearly every night – Harpoon Louis, Wags. We used to

Zahid at a family wedding

Zahid (right) and his family in Kenya

meet at Bunjie's coffee bar and then go on to a gay bar. We used to go to Heaven, Scandals, Spats and Bangs on a Monday night. There were a couple of discos in Tottenham that don't exist anymore. So we used to travel around.

After Icebreakers, Chatan wanted to start a group with gay Asians. We talked about it and I agreed with him that there was a need for a group. He wrote an article in the first issue of *Gay Noise*; I was very critical, but agreed with the gist of it. We asked Gay's the Word if we could meet at the shop and we advertised the Gay Black Group. Two or three people turned up, then four or five at the weekend. When it first started it was amazing the way people said, 'Yeah, I felt like that.' And talking about their family and how they felt about being gay, the pressures to get married. Explaining to their parents, if they had come out to them, what 'gay' meant because such a term doesn't exist in Pakistani or Hindi. There was a lot of empathy in the group. We all understood and that made us feel really good. I'd talked in gay groups before about being Black and gay, with white people just nodding their heads and saying, 'Yes, yes.' There were also occasions where people would talk about the racist door policies of some clubs and none of the white gay groups would take that up as an issue.

I remember an incident in the Bell pub in King's Cross sometime in '83. On a Friday night there used to be a disco run jointly by the Icebreakers collective and the Nightworkers DJs. The Lesbian and Gay Black Group, as it had then become, used to go after the Friday evening meetings. Over a period of a few weeks, there was a marked rise in the attendance of skinheads wearing Union Jack T-shirts and British bulldog tattoos and some fascist regalia. The disco organizers were asked to refuse entry to these people as they offended most members of the LGBG. We were met with rhetoric about choice of one's dress, which had nothing to do with politics. The Lesbian and Gay Black Group continued to attend – as did the skinheads. Then on one occasion I overheard one of the skinheads saying, 'I don't like coloured.' This was not going to go unchallenged. I insisted he leave, but the incident went unchallenged by the organizers. The plugs had to be pulled to get the Nightworkers to make an announcement. This incident sparked off a series of letters in *Capital Gay*. The core of the debate was that Icebreakers could not impose a ban on 'members of the gay community' because of their dress, whereas the LGBG – myself, in particular – felt that the ban was against gay racists and fascists. I should point out that not all members of the LGBG supported my views.

From '81, the Gay Black Group [later the Lesbian and Gay Black Group] just went on from strength to strength. We had lots of consciousness-raising sessions and lots of heated debates about various things: a recurrent one was about the cultural differences between Afro-Caribbeans and Asians and the fact that we called the group 'Black'. We would get Afro-Caribbeans coming to the group, saying, 'You can't call yourself "Black" – "Black" means Afro-Caribbean'; and Malaysians saying, 'I'm brown; I'm not black.' But the political argument for calling the group 'Black' was that it wasn't the colour of your skin that mattered – it was the experience of imperialism and racism; people who had experienced that historical background.

Then there was always the debate about whether gay was more important than being Black. Or, as an identity, was being Black more important than being gay? Personally, I felt that you couldn't hide the fact that you were Black, but you could hide the fact that you were gay. All right, some of us couldn't [laughs], but we felt that our being Black was probably a larger part of our identity than being gay. And that, politically, we should try working within the Black community, strengthening our ties politically with Black activists and raising issues of sexuality within those circles, rather than the issue of racism within gay politics.

We got involved in campaigning for the Bradford Twelve and we used to take our Gay Black Group Banner with us on the marches. This campaign was defending twelve Asian youths in Bradford against charges of 'conspiracy to riot', after buried petrol bombs had been found in a students' residential area. There had been warnings that fascists were going to be marching in Bradford like they had in Southall. In particular, I remember the March '82 demo in Leeds. We used to go along to the Bradford Twelve's London Support Group meetings. I remember marching through the streets of Bradford and holding up the Gay Black Group banner, and people laughing and the crowds watching and saying, 'Oh, look at that.' [Laughs.] It wasn't terrifying, you know. Whereas the thought of doing it was terrifying. I thought people would react violently against us, but they didn't. Most of the people on the demo were quite supportive of us.

I left the group after two-and-a-half years. Towards the end of '82, I began to attend less and less and only key meetings, such as the one in September with Paul Boateng about GLC grant funding for the Gay Black Group. People drifted in and out and I got to the point where I wasn't developing. I felt that whatever I was putting in was just out of guilt. I thought, 'I don't need to do this. There are enough people in the group to carry on.' So I left. After the Gay Black Group, I wanted to try working for Black campaigns. I did quite a lot with the Newham Eight campaign as a volunteer between August '83 and December '83. The Newham Eight had been charged with many things, including a conspiracy charge. The eight men charged had been variously involved in defending their brothers and sisters from racist attacks in school and on their way home. The police provoked an attack against these men and then arrested and charged them. A few were acquitted and a few convicted and sentenced to do community service. I went to most of the police-accountability meetings and distributed leaflets.

Straight after I left the Gay Black Group I worked on the '82 Gay Pride Week committee for a year. Since coming out, I've always been involved in something politically.

In mid-'82, I went to a weekend of gay workshops at South Bank poly where people were saying that what the gay community needed was a centre as a focus point for the community; a while after that there was talk that the GLC were willing to fund one. When I went to my first meeting, I couldn't believe my ears. You know, at County Hall in November '82, people talking about a gay centre. Somebody had drawn up a report about the feasibility and aims of a centre; I agreed, and I was elected on to the steering committee. I worked on that for three years as a volunteer, from '82 to '85. I've also worked for PDC, Publications Distribution Co-op, and after that at Gay's the Word, doing the mail order.

I still see my family quite regularly, but I'm finding it difficult at the moment because I'm nearly thirty and my parents are drawing the line – if I don't get married at thirty, nobody is going to look at me and people are going to talk. I'm finding it quite a strain at the moment, and I've decided not to see my parents as often as I used to because I can't cope with the pressure of constantly being reminded that I have to get married.

184

I've just started to live together with a group of Asians and Afro-Caribbean: two gay men, including myself; one straight man; and two straight women. There's five of us. I like living communally. I think that's because of having lived in a large family and that's what I'm used to.

When I came out, Chatan and I went to all these gay places and I saw it as part of a gay lifestyle. But I don't see the need at the moment. I don't want to be politically active, either. When I was very politically active, going to night-clubs was like a release. That was my way of coping with the stress of working – for example within the Newham Eight campaign. I'd rather use the gay commercial scene than go to a straight place, but it's just there for people to make money. That's why I believed in the gay centre. The commercial scene is a meat market. Of course, I've met people on the scene and had really nice discussions but, the majority of times, I've gone on the scene to pick people up and found it quite depressing because usually you don't pick people up. And I think now, with the AIDS scare, that even on the commercial scene people are beginning to drop the defence and actually talk to people other than for sexual reasons.

I've had a few sexual relationships, but not many. The very first one was important to me, when I first came out. I was very upset when it broke up. I also had a relationship with a bisexual man and that was really traumatic. It meant a lot to me and it still does.

I've recently been to India and, having come back from India, going on the gay scene is not so important to me anymore. In India there aren't any night-clubs. I was away three-and-a-half months and I saw that just because there were all these gay pubs and clubs, I didn't have to use them just because I was gay. This visit was a 'soul-searching and discovering my roots' journey.

POSTSCRIPT BY ZAHID DAR, AUGUST 1988

Since my interview I have moved from the communal house in the Elephant and Castle, have been a part-time and then full-time worker at Gay's the Word, and am now a bookseller in a community in Hackney. I have also been to India again and am now living with my lover, Nick, in a flat we have bought together in Hackney. This list is what I would call the high points of the last three years.

There have been low points, too, the most painful of which was the break-up with my closest friend, Chatan, the Gujarati man I talk about in the interview who I met in '80. We came out to our families during the same time. The communal house just wasn't the same for me after that break-up. I stayed on for two-and-a-half years.

I visited India with Nick at the beginning of this year, which was a totally different experience than the first. We stayed with a gay friend's family in Bombay. We met many gay men. The network of gay men is getting larger, but there is still no political will to form any group or forum other than parties for socializing. There was, however, the first signs of a gay bar. We were taken there but no one had told us it was a gay bar. It was almost like they didn't want to say it. As most bars are frequented by men in India, this one didn't stand out. But the reason why clients came here wasn't because all the men were homosexuals, but because their friends came here.

Some of the Indian gay men believe that AIDS isn't going to come to India and have frequent casual sex. This is despite the fact that some prostitutes HIV-tested in venereal disease clinics are positive. I acquired this information from a gay doctor and AIDS researcher on a visit from Australia. We met in the gay bar.

When I returned to India, I had to deal with my parents' renewed constant nagging about getting married. I then made a decision about not visiting even as regularly as three years ago. Now my mother has stopped asking me about marriage and asks about Nick. The family knows that we live together and one of my aunts commented to my parents that what I was doing was not right, in particular that I was living with a heathen. To my surprise, my mother told her that I had many good points, for all my faults. I couldn't believe she had said that.

When we moved into the flat I asked the family to give me the equivalent of my wedding presents, as I wouldn't be getting married the traditional way. I received money from my brothers and my brother-in-law has helped with the mortgage. All these events have made me feel I made the right decision about marriage. I know of Asian gay men who get married due to pressure from their parents and then regret it later.

My work at Gay's the Word's bookshop branch at the London Lesbian and Gay Centre was important to me because of my involvement in the centre's development. I feel disappointed at the lack of support the gay community has shown the centre. In the present political climate the centre should be used to the community's advantage. Moving on from the development work with the centre to full-time work with Gay's the Word was a pleasant change because I came into direct contact with people. Gay's the Word is an excellent source of lesbian and gay literature and I feel it will remain so.

The interview and this postscript are important to me because I feel that it contributes towards recording Black people's gay history in Britain. I remember hearing Audre Lorde speak at the Shaw. She said how important it was for all Black people to write about our lives and struggles; the more people did so, the more others may be encouraged to do the same.

1988. Portrait by Sunil Gupta

GLENN McKEE

INTERVIEWED IN JANUARY 1988 BY MARGOT FARNHAM

I was born in February 1958. My parents are very traditional Northern Ireland people, quite religious. One of them has a farming background. I have a brother and a sister. I was brought up in Downpatrick, a backwater of a place, a provincial Irish small town, before the present troubles started. It's really only since the Second World War that it was getting over the Great Famine in the middle of the nineteenth century.

It has a rather surprising religious division in that the town itself is 90 per cent Roman Catholic. I was brought up a Presbyterian, which is a variant of Protestantism. The surrounding countryside is largely Protestant because Protestants own the farms, so there was a division between the people in the town. Most Protestant children at that time and still today tend not to mix with Catholic children.

I suppose my childhood was fairly happy, with a few drawbacks, a few limitations. Particularly, it was a very sexually inhibiting place – even of heterosexuality. I can remember being puzzled by naked people when I occasionally got a glimpse of someone, and I wondered why they were like that and what it meant. As I grew older I became more aware of sexual things. By the age of eight, nine, my peer groups were talking about these things and making a great joke of it.

In Northern Ireland, the education system is split along religious lines: the state schools are Protestant and Catholics have a separate system. I went to a state school. I failed the 11-Plus, which was quite a trauma at the time, and my parents were very determined that I should not go to a secondary modern school, where the emphasis was on practical/manual skills and little else.

189

My parents realized that, because of my disability, the only way for me to make good was to have the best education possible so that I could use my mind rather than my body. The local state grammar school at first wouldn't take me. They were full up. In the end I did get in because my mother was in the local Unionist Association and used her influence through the party.

I realized I was different physically by the age of eight, nine: I couldn't run as fast as the other children and I was developing differently because of my disability, which affects the bone structure. As I grew up, my height fell behind everyone else's. At the time I tried to ignore this and tended to perceive my body as basically 'normal', but sometimes it would hit me. I did come up against things that I just couldn't do that other people could do. Certainly, when I was at school people sometimes would push me around a bit. But then that stopped and it grew into a stage where nobody would mention it. I was the only disabled person in the secondary school and it was hard-going. I was excused games but, other than that, I had to do everything myself in the same way as everyone else did – which meant at times great physical pain keeping up with them. But I think I was lucky because the equivalent special schools would have been a disaster: you would not have been able to get any O- or A-levels through those.

My parents tended to drag us, sometimes kicking and screaming, to church until the age of sixteen. Then they gave up because I used to make such a fuss. We used to walk to and from church, which added to my hatred of it. My father tended to overcompensate for my disability and tried to make me more able than I really was. But that had its good sides. For example, he got me to join the Cubs and Scouts. Again, I was the only disabled person and at times they just had to carry me, literally, on somebody's back because I couldn't keep up. Although it was killing, at least I met people; it was fun.

My one reaction to religion has always been intense boredom. First of all, the Presbyterian service is very Scottish and dour. At least in Anglicanism and Roman Catholicism there's stained-glass windows, rather camp churches, ministers in robes of all colours and a lot of to-ing and fro-ing and participation by the congregation. In the Presbyterian service it's much more restrained. You just sit there. The main part of the service is an interminable sermon.

I can remember Sunday School lessons where you sat down and the leaders held up this illustrated Bible. One picture was of a man with his legs exposed. I remember thinking, 'Gosh, those thighs are rather nice.' They held my attention. As an eight- or nine-year-old I'd always been much more interested in doing things with boys of my own age. Gradually, the awareness grew on me that I was gay. By thirteen, I had been masturbating for some years and then began to realize that it was men or boys that I thought about.

There was a fair amount on television, particularly from America, about what 'gay' meant – usually ridiculing it. At that time I remember creeping into the school library early in the morning and I remember getting the *Encyclopaedia Britannica* down and looking up 'homosexuality' because I knew that's what it was. I read it subsequently to see what it said and it's pretty negative stuff, but at least it gives you some factual information.

There was a little group of us at school of rather aesthetic types who didn't play football and we would go to the library or sit around gossiping. We were called the cissies. I was very attracted to one or two of the boys who played football. I was besotted by one boy for about a year or two who was absolutely gorgeous.

The school was very strait-laced. As I reached fifteen or sixteen I became quite frightened of sex, in a way, and very reactionary. Knowing I was gay, I think I tended to shy away from anything sexual, because by then the heterosexual boys and girls I knew were beginning to develop and have adventures. I became disapproving and quite prim about these things. Knowing I was gay, I wanted to get out of Northern Ireland. I didn't know any gay people, except I'd heard of one very effeminate man who everyone laughed at. At school there were a couple of very camp people, two or three years older than me, who the rest of the school ridiculed. And they gave the impression of wanting to be straight as well. There wasn't any open or positive group of gay people.

I can remember watching *Whicker's World* on TV in '73, '74. He used to visit exotic types all over the world and one programme was in San Francisco and it opened with two men getting married. I remember watching this and thinking, 'Gosh, isn't that nice.' I think television opened up and discussed topics like that then, whereas now it's almost going back to what it was like in the fifties. Also, the school library used to get *New Musical Express*. In the early seventies there used to be quite a lot of gay stuff in that. Sometimes I actually cut out pieces for a scrapbook I kept. I knew by that age what I was and that it was men I was physically interested in, but I had no real sense of how you would go about gay sex.

I was aware that there were openly gay people in London. You tend to have this exaggerated view of London as Sin City before you come to it. I wanted to come to London, to come out as gay, and I deliberately planned it that way.

In '76 I was accepted for a course in the University of London. Coming to London to come out as gay, however, was a complete failure. I did find things like sex shops where you could buy magazines. For someone coming from a provincial town, that was quite amazing.

When I came to college I expected everyone would be terribly laid-back and there would be lots of open sexual relationships going on all over the place. Of course, there wasn't. In October I attempted to join the college gay soc. but it didn't really work. I was very nervous and they obviously didn't know how to treat me. I got the feeling that they just couldn't cope with a disabled person. The person who ran it tried to be nice to me but the others were a bit off-hand. I frightened myself back into my shell for two years and I threw myself into my work. That took me to the summer of '78, when I went to Dublin for a month on a course. It shook me up quite a lot, meeting people from another part of Ireland, and it started a process of thinking: where was I going and what was I going to do with my life? That would be the last summer before I took my finals, so I thought, 'You're going to have to sort yourself out. At the end of finals, do you want to come back to Northern Ireland and go into the closet forever?'

When I was in Ireland during the holidays I had seen an interview on TV with a man who'd worked at London Gay Switchboard. I thought he was ever so nice and what he said seemed to make a lot of sense, so I thought, 'You're going to have to do something now.' So when I came back to London in October '78 I made a second attempt to come out, which was more successful.

I phoned Gay Switchboard, who said, 'Here's Friend; here's Icebreakers, but Icebreakers sleep with everyone, you know'! And I thought, 'Oh, good, I'll try that!' (It isn't the case.) I went to

Friend and it didn't work terribly well. I arrived at Friend, entered the building, got lost and walked straight into the rooms downstairs where the transvestite group was meeting! I went upstairs and found the man from Friend but I didn't feel much warmth from him and his counselling techniques were a bit obvious.

I went to Icebreakers meetings which were in people's flats and houses and very enlightening and stimulating. You were made to feel welcome. They were highly political and certainly made you think again, with a vengeance. They wanted full gay rights, everything, no compromises. They ridiculed the family. Nowadays, that's out of the window quite a bit and people have moved away from it, but there are quite a lot of good things in it. It was a GLF attitude.

They had discussion groups and a disco at the Prince Albert, in Wharfdale Road in King's Cross. It was downstairs in a smelly basement, but it was great fun and they sang 'Glad to be Gay' at the end. It was wonderful and friendly. I went regularly to Icebreakers Sunday afternoon tea parties for a year.

I had my first sexual contact with people I met through Icebreakers. That was in the summer of '79. I thought it was wonderful; it blew my mind completely because it opened up a new range of sensations. You tend to want more immediately. I think at that time, when people were quite free, there were open relationships and if you weren't participating or you just had a minor role, you felt a bit out of things; but from then on I began to meet people at discos and things fairly steadily.

One of the problems I had dealing with Icebreakers was that, although there was all this theory, they only went to bed with the pretty ones. If you didn't fit that category, then you felt a bit out of it. I accepted the theory but the practice didn't follow. Human nature didn't work the way it was being set out. I could agree with a lot of the views and still do, although I've moved from some of them, as most people do. Once the mega-commercial discos like Heaven started up, which they did in '79, '80, everyone switched to going to them, even in Icebreakers. I did as well.

After Icebreakers I wanted to do political things. Gay's the Word bookshop, which was an offshoot from Icebreakers, was in quite a bad state at the end of '79. They were looking for new people and some people to put in money. I put in a small amount because I was just a student then, but got involved and from August/September '80 started to edit the bookshop's newsletter, which I continued to do until January '87. I was also involved with various things connected with running the shop. Then, in August '80, I joined the board of Gay's the Word as a director and I stayed as a director until I resigned in July '87.

I had found something to do, people to meet and I felt I was doing something positive. Having an openly gay bookshop in the centre of London is quite a major achievement, and lasting nine years is a hell of an achievement. It was good seeing the way gay literature grew in the early eighties, particularly as we started importing American material. Publishers like Gay Men's Press and Brilliance were getting going and the number of titles increased.

Also in the early eighties I went along to Irish Gays in London and rapidly made friends with people there. Most people were from the Irish Republic and so had a very different background to me, but everyone was very friendly. The group was a bit split on political grounds. It started off an ultra-Republican group. There were a few attempts to support the Northern Ireland hunger strikers and I think people assumed we must support the IRA or Sinn Fein, but Sinn Fein gave us little concrete acknowledgement. My experience of both sides in Northern Ireland was that both Catholics and Protestants were fundamentally rooted in very reactionary traditions. Having said that, though, I think there's not quite the hostility to gays that perhaps you can get in this country.

More than anything, the group was a social group, establishing links with other Irish groups in Ireland. We went on a wonderful trip to Dublin in September/October '81 and had a great time drinking and disco-ing and going to the Irish gay things. Earlier that year we'd gone to the Irish Gay Conference in Cork and I met loads of people there. Irish groups were much more internationalist than British groups then, and the National Gay Federation in Ireland held the secretariat of the International Gay Association at that time. I think a lot of the Irish people here want to keep links with back home, which I wasn't terribly keen to, but we had a lot in common still. There was lots of sex happening, quite a bit of which I got involved with as well. My first sort of long-term relationship was arising from that group. This man was in his early thirties when I was about twenty-three. It was quite warm at the start and after a while he moved in with me. Having a relationship did a lot for me as a person. Sometimes people assume if you're disabled you don't have any sex drive, or you will never have a relationship. This man gave me a lot: it was very good sharing things and having someone to come back to in the evening. He was my main boyfriend and vice versa, although we did have sex with other people. I made quite a lot of the relationship but it didn't work out; there were problems and it came abruptly to an end. He was in the Irish group and that made the ending a bit more difficult.

The group fell apart in '82/'83, but an awful lot of energy was about in '81. I think this is the way a lot of gay groups go. Initially, a burst of energy because people click in a way and form a group which works; it then becomes a bit of a clique; then they don't have the energy to renew things and the group falls apart. You can't maintain the energy, but it was very good.

In '82 – this was a very active period in my life – Elsa Beckett from GEMMA [an organization for lesbians with or without disabilities] organized a meeting for lesbians and gays, with or without disabilities, who were interested in disability. I went to that meeting and met two men, Julian and Angus, and we set up the Gay Men's Disabled Group. Elsa said, 'Come on, you men, it's about time you got yourselves a group going.' We made excuses but then we formed a self-help group for gay men with or without disabilities, but concentrating on men with disabilities to get them organized and thinking. But I think, because gay men with disabilities start with much greater oppression, the group has always been more low key than the others I've been involved with. Quite a few people are dependent on other people. For example, if you're in an institution where people have done things for you, it's very difficult to come out as gay, to start doing things and to relate to people in a different way. I've come across people who expect Gay Men's Disabled Group to provide them with Mr Right. Because their physical needs are supplied, they somehow think emotional needs can be supplied in the same way. That's an extreme example. Also, a lot of things are held in inaccessible venues and that means that some gay people don't bother or can't go. Being physically fit and pretty is very important.

I can remember years ago walking into the Salisbury on my own and being looked over by all the men. You could see rejection

Glenn in the garden, Downpatrick, Northern Ireland, 1960

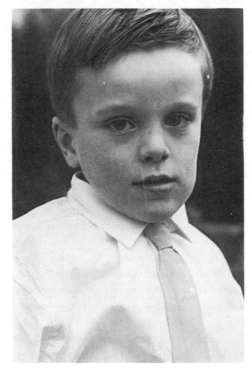

Glenn, Downpatrick, Christmas 1963

on everyone's face. You have to be able to take that and it's not easy if you're a little nervous, a bit screwed up about the way you look. I know my coming out as gay also involved coming to terms with my body and what it was like, what it could do and what it couldn't do. That was traumatic. It didn't come to me in one go, but it slowly dawned on me during the period I was coming out – '79. You have to sort out where you are with your body, I think. There's no use pretending you're something you're not when you're now in the business of meeting other people and having sex. Before I came out I used to go in for baggy clothes that hid my chest. I also had a temptation to sit with my shoulders forward to hide my chest. I think if you're nervous about your body you convey those vibes to other people.

I'm quite willing to talk about my disability. It's funny, though: people at work were discussing something and they were mentioning the name of some disability and I said, 'Oh, by the way, mine's called Morquio's Syndrome' – and there was a deadly hush, as if I'd been very rude. It's named after a Montevidean doctor who put together all the symptoms and gave it a name. I didn't know the name of it, actually, until I started coming to terms with it as well. That took a lot of doing. I have my off-days when I get fed up with it and I feel very decrepit, but generally I try and make the best of it. It's all you can do.

I think a lot of things that gay disabled people can be screwed up about are just more extreme variants of other things other people are worried about, like rejection. You know, every scene queen will be rejected at some stage. It's human nature to be worried about getting old or putting on weight. To some extent, disability is just a more concentrated form of it. But I've had marvellous times with people who've no inhibitions about my body or me about theirs.

In the early eighties I met quite a few people through contact ads. I always said I was disabled and I had quite nice experiences. Another relationship arose out of the Gay Men's Disabled Group. He was an able-bodied man who lighted on me, for some reason. He was quite sweet but I think he was looking for a 100 per cent commitment and he was much more involved with his family. We went on holiday – which is a bit like living together, a trial run – and I knew at one point it wouldn't last. Politically, we were so different. There really wasn't much mileage pursuing it. We broke up in autumn '83.

During this time the bookshop had been growing very rapidly, but that growth came to a halt with the Customs action. In '84 things started to go wrong. We should have realized something funny was happening, in that imports weren't coming through for a couple of months. And then, bang wallop, on 10 April 1984 Customs and Excise raided us. Normally, I go to work about eight o'clock but I had a training course that day and consequently I was at home at about twenty-five past nine when there was a knock at the door of my flat. It was two Customs Officers and they produced some special writ, which I'd never heard of or seen, which gave them powers to enter and they entered. They were investigating Gay's the Word's importing of gay books and they held me in my flat for over six hours, searching, questioning. They started with me and then at midday they did the bookshop.

They took three plastic bin-liners of stuff from my flat, which included gay books like the *Joy of Gay Sex*. They took my personal magazines, videos and letters. All the Gay's the Word papers were filed methodically in a cabinet and they searched through and took it all. One of the Customs Officers shouted at me and made it clear that he didn't approve of me, my attitudes or what I was about. 'This is filth,' he would say. The officer who was the side-kick took notes during the interrogation in my flat. They read them back to me and I thought they were going to put things in. But in fact it was the things they left out which were important: the way they shouted, the way they used abusive language. They didn't hit me, though they did stand over me at one stage and I thought I was for it. These are warden sheltered flats and so I sat beside the emergency cord pull the whole time in case they turned nasty. By three-thirty I'd had enough of them in my flat.

I said I'd like to ring a friend or a solicitor. They kept saying, 'We'd prefer you didn't at the moment.' None of that was in the notes, so when I said, 'You wouldn't let me,' they said, 'You never made any request.' They implied I could phone in, say, half an hour but it was a complete sham and a lead-on and I knew if I made one move for the phone, they'd cut my fingers off me. I kept saying, 'I want to exercise my right to remain silent,' but that broke down several times. The one in charge said, 'Well, a night in clink will loosen your tongue.' For the first couple of hours I tried to take notes, but by about eleven my resolve gave in.

They would also shuffle their papers and put them away. They would build up your hope and you'd be thinking, 'He's going to go soon.' In fact, he wasn't; it was a trick to knock you around psychologically. They then got the papers out and asked more questions. They also interviewed my neighbours about what parcels they'd received for me through the post because I was at work. They were a pensioner couple who didn't understand what was going on, but it terminated our relationship. I think to go through that experience shows you what the real power of the state can be like. In many ways, you see the power of the state in a benign or incompetent form. To realize how little toleration they can really have of you because you are gay is frightening.

Customs only have power over imported material, yet they took the shop apart. They brought in extra officers and carted off loads of books to see if they were indecent or obscene, which is the test that the 1876 Customs Consolidation Act applies. They took the manager off to the Customs branch; she knew if she said no, they would have arrested her.

Immediately after the raid there was a great groundswell of anger against Customs. A defence campaign got going and, after a shakyish start, became very efficient. In November '84 myself and the other directors were charged with contravening the Customs Consolidation Act of 1876 with seventy titles. Customs prevented the shop's expansion during '84 until the middle of '86. The bookshop couldn't get imports during that period and imports were quite an important part of its turnover. Also, a lot of action and thinking starts in the US and then comes over here and so imports are important in building a gay identity. There were no books produced by English publishers on AIDS until several years after the first American books came out. In the early part of '85 all the shop's energies went into fighting the case.

We went to the magistrates' court in June '85, which was an experience I shall never forget. For five days we argued over the books and Customs actions. It was obvious that the Customs officers weren't really prepared for the fight we put up and we gave them quite a good run for their money. In August '85 the magistrate ruled that this case should go to court and we were set to go to the Old Bailey for the autumn of '86. However, in a separate case, nothing to do with us, the EEC court held that Great Britain was acting in a discriminatory fashion because it had two sets of obscenity laws – one for 'home-grown' books and one for imports – and they should be brought into line. As a result of that, a lot of charges against our books were dropped. I think they're still dragging through the courts on six books.

During that time I felt all my energy was drained and that all my social life centred on the bookshop. May '84 to July '86 saw all the battles, but I think we ran a good campaign. Having so much support from outside people made quite a difference. It was also a watershed for me, in a way, because within two months of the case ending I was told I would have to go to hospital for a big operation. I went into hospital in February '87 and stayed for five months, until July '87. Every night I was there I had a visitor and lots of days there were two or three. My friends had organized a rota of visitors because my family only came on a couple of occasions. They were nearly all gay people who came every night from February to July.

I was in a metal halo for most of the time. It was fairly frightening and I know other patients were very freaked by it. My mother has always been very funny about my disability; she won't quite accept it and she couldn't face the halo. I expect it's the old view, that it's a reflection on her. She won't talk about it. I remember when I took my first car back to Northern Ireland, which was in '81, I had one of those orange 'Disabled Driver' stickers. That upset her terribly. It was a label. 'I suppose they won't let you have the car except if you've got that on it,' she said. She took to her bed sick for an evening after it. That was also the occasion I went back with my hair dyed, which upset her even more. It was peroxide blond with a green streak in it and I had an earring. That was my more extravagant days in the early eighties!

When I came out of hospital I was still fairly weak because if you're like that, you can't use your muscles properly. I've been building myself up since then. I went back to work in August. With the bookshop case, then my operation, this has been a chunk now of nearly four years and I think the gay scene has changed very much in that time. Before '84 I was having a good time. During the bookshop case I didn't have a boyfriend, and many social relationships just fell apart. Then AIDS came along. I find it difficult to imagine living with someone again. If I have someone staying, I find they get in the way of my petty little routines. As I've got my strength back since I came out of hospital, I've been to a few discos.

I've always had an interest in leather. Being disabled, I find leather and mild SM fit quite well. There's also a safety aspect to a lot of SM practices. A lot of the scene is about fucking someone or it's very genital orientated. I find difficulty in performing certain sexual acts because of my disability. I can't get into some positions or stay in them for more than about two seconds without it being excruciating, but a lot of SM things stimulate the whole body: fantasy, ritual, images; using different sensations, using different parts of the body. It's not so related to pretty boys or squeezing into your jeans and standing at the Copacabana, which I can't do because I can't stand for very long.

There are people, and I've met several, who want to have it off with a disabled person and some people say, 'Oh, how shocking, you shouldn't indulge them.' I think I go into it with my eyes open and it's no more exploitative than pretty people at the Copacabana having it off and never meeting again. Sometimes it's difficult to meet people if you're disabled. If you meet someone who wants a disabled person and who isn't going to do you harm, they may, at worst, be a bit patronizing, but I don't think it's for anyone else to tell the disabled person, 'You can't do this because they haven't got the right attitude to you.' Not everyone from the group would agree with me on that. We regularly get men who write to the group, wanting one-legged guys. I think it's because they had boyfriends who lost legs in the war. I think it's pathetic that they're trying to capture the past, but I think it's for the person with the amputation to make their decision.

Q: *You've said you've had experiences with your body that have involved pain, like being in hospital. Does it have resonances for you to have pain brought explicitly into a sexual relationship?*

When I've engaged in this ritual I tend to be the one who doles out the pain. When things have been done to me, they've tended to be more about humiliation than pain.

Q: *How do you settle that with the process you described earlier, of accepting yourself?*

It's just a game of exploration. The fear that someone might say something is in many ways worse that it actually happening. When I was splitting up with one of my boyfriends, he called me 'a poisoned dwarf' and threw a beer over me in the middle of the pub. It's pretty upsetting, but in a way it's happened, it's over, you've dealt with it and it's not the end of the world. Able-bodied people call each other abusive names and cope with it.

I'm not very good at coping with pain itself, like at the dentist or in hospital. Those two long-term partners I had were physically much stronger than me. I don't like any form of physical domination at all. That really brings it home, actually, thinking about it: for a joke, one of them used to regularly hold me down and I used to resent that very much. I don't like an able-bodied person doing that to me. I feel very vulnerable in that situation.

Q: *One last thing. You were saying you've come out to your family?*

Ten years ago now. I told my father in person. I told my mother over the phone and she didn't react very well. She took some time to get over it. She's terrified of any relatives finding out. It had two stages: I came out to them about my sexuality and then I came out to my father, but not my mother, about the bookshop trial. My father's reaction was that he didn't understand how someone as clever as me could be as stupid as to get involved with something like that. My brother and sister knew about the trial but offered no support at all.

I think my mother views it all as a phase: 'He'll get over it and come back to Northern Ireland.' When I was in hospital, I was talking to my sister seriously for the first time about relationships. She's known I was gay since '79 and she believes that really I was doing it to wind my parents up! For nine years! She has the preconceived notion about limp wrists and screaming Nellies, a very warped way of looking at it. What I try and do when they visit me is to get them to meet other gay people. I've seen with other people's parents that you can take quite hopeless people a very long way if you make the effort. That's difficult, though, when my parents are in Northern Ireland.

Generally, I'd say my attitudes have changed quite a bit over the last ten years. But society's attitudes have moved on as well and I'm apprehensive about the future for gay people. Having seen the authority of the state brought against you once, it's just so easy to imagine, if they decide to put the boot in, how bad that would be. I want to start up where I left off in '84, though things have moved on, and I want to get involved in new things.

It's a different world that I'm emerging into.

Mark, Gay Pride 1981, Huddersfield

MARK ASHTON
(19 May 1960 – 11 February 1987)
FIVE FRIENDS REMEMBER

INTRODUCTORY NOTE BY MARGOT FARNHAM

After Mark's death some of his friends asked if Mark's life could be recognized by the Hall Carpenter Archives. I suggested some of Mark's friends talking about his life and their involvement with him. I talked with a handful of Mark's friends who knew him at different times in his life. Those recorded interviews form the basis of this tribute. I was given much help by one of Mark's oldest friends Monty Montgomery.

I

It waved above our infant might
When all ahead seemed dark as night
It witnessed many a deed and vow
We must not change its colour now

'The Red Flag'

The strongest memory I have of Mark is of my birthday, 13 September '86. We – Mike Jackson and Mark and Paul McHue – went out to Blenheim Palace. Mike had just got this car and he said, 'Go on, we'll go out for a drive.' Mark and Paul were in the back. Mark had just bought a little suit from Oxfam and had his head shaved with just this tuft on the front. Paul had his hair cut the same. It was the two of them in the back having this frantic conversation. And just being like mad, mad babies. These two little chattering babies in the back. It was crazy. It was something I'll never forget.

Monty Montgomery, friend

Monty Montgomery: The first time I met Mark was at catering college, '76, and it was instant, 'My God, who is this person?' He dressed completely different than anybody else. Very daring. He was going for a fifties look and he had his hair greased up and tight jeans. Nobody wore things like that then. For a lot of us, to go to Portrush was getting away completely from what was going on in Northern Ireland then. The people seem to mix there. There was a club called Kelly's we all went to. Mark was certainly a real mover on the dance-floor. He was a natural. He did Irish dancing when he was at primary school.

One night we'd been out somewhere and a whole crowd of us were in the flat and the discussion got on to sexuality. Mark didn't say he was gay; he said, 'Oh, I'm bi-sexual.' I was in the closet at that stage but a short time after that we came out to each other and said, 'Well, that's the way I am.'

We were both into the music and punk thing. We started dying our hair and wearing all the outrageous clothes; if we couldn't get them, we made them. I'd been to Liverpool for a shopping trip, so one day we said, 'Oh, yes, we'll go to Liverpool. We'll get a job and we'll be set up for life then.' [Laughs.] The first thing we did was go to the job centre and we spoke to someone and they just said, 'What are you doing here? There's no jobs here!' [Laughs.]

We got in touch with an employment agency who said there was a job for us in Tunbridge Wells, so we started work at the Calvery hotel. At the end of the second week we went into the wrong pub and a couple of leather bikers got us. We each bought ourselves a pair of brothel-creepers with the proceeds of our employment and the next morning were off to see a friend of Mark's, Biddy, in London in Museum Street.

I got very homesick and went home. Mark fell for it immediately; it was him. The hustle and bustle, the music, the fashion, the drugs. Later he went to live in Clapham with a few punks from Northern Ireland. They were squatting next door to a group of skinheads. I was still working at home, but would come across for a couple of weeks. I finally made the move in September '81. I started to go to Hell and the Blitz clubs. They were very outrageous because the underground fashion thing was developing. People like Marilyn and George O'Dowd, who Mark knew. Mark would spend three hours in an evening getting his outfits together and his make-up on. And staying out all night and getting home at ten in the morning. He didn't need much persuasion to start deciding he would go out dressed as a woman, not just the Blitz fashionable dress. There was a time when Mark wouldn't go outside the door unless he was in full drag. I think it was the fact that he could pass himself off completely as a woman. He had no aspirations to be a woman. He just lived it for that period.

Around '82, Mark decided he would go out for a holiday to Bangladesh to visit his parents. His dad took redundant textile machinery out there and helped to oversee the installation. Mark went out for about three months and it really did change his whole attitude to life. He became very politically aware. He saw the dreadful poverty. It really upset him to walk out on the street and find these sick kids and people coming up and begging from him. I gradually saw the changes coming on. He started taking a much more serious look at what was going on around him. He got involved in Switchboard in a big way and he joined the Young Communist League. I'm not sure why, but when he did get involved he went in a 100 per cent and devoted nearly all his time to going to meetings. It was Pride '83 when Mark hung a huge red flag out of his window on Ladbroke Grove, where he'd moved, and the police came knocking on the door to find out who it was: 'Take that down, you can't fly that.' Also before he went away we'd be going to the Carved Red Lion, which was Movements disco then, and it was run by a group called Gay Noise who used to produce a pamphlet. It wasn't just that we were gay. We saw a way of getting back at the people who were having a go at us. We felt that we could get together and begin to organize and get involved. We felt we had a common identity – that's how we got to know Jimmy.

Jimmy Somerville: I first met Mark at a party. And Mark really liked my boyfriend and was determined to let me know, so it was queeny looks from one end of the room to the other. I was trying my hardest to be cool, but at the same time I was getting more and more annoyed. After that I saw him at Movements. Everybody was just dancing and having a good time. And then we more or less got into a fight. It was that territorial thing again: this was my boyfriend and how dare you? I suppose I was looking so aggressive at him I think he asked me did I have a problem. This was one of his big phrases. I remember he pushed me; then I pushed him. Then he pushed me so hard that I fell over this table. And then we just started laughing.

With a lot of gay men, friendships are always based on having a sexual encounter. That never happened with us. At that time I was so loud and boisterous. I think that was the thing about the two of us – we were just strongly indignant queens. It was an indignant period. At Movements you could have cheap drinks and pay something like 50p. to get in. It was a breakaway from disco because people were dancing to things like the B52s and Talking Heads and Simple Minds – all the early eighties music. Movements seemed to attract people who were dabbling with the gay thing because it was trendy. It was a club where you'd be dancing to some mad record and then suddenly you'd decide to confront somebody about their sexuality [laughs]. A lot of lesbians used to go as well, which was really good because I just used to go to clubs which were all-male because they didn't let women in. It was such a relief to meet people that you could talk to – and not just about hairdos. You could actually talk politics. At that time the National Front had a real visibility and the Anti-Nazi League still felt strong. I suppose it was, like, the first term of Thatcher and people realized that what she was doing was going to lead to severer things. A lot of people were becoming aware that, with Reagan, there was a real political change in the Western World.

Before I met him, Mark used to go to Blitz and there were still a lot of people who used to call him 'Evil'. 'Evil' was, like, the punk name. After that we used to call him 'Mary Trashton'. Mark's drag period hadn't completely died because we used to go to parties completely done up in drag and Mark used to have a part-time job in the British Legion bar and he worked behind the bar in drag. It was so fab because he would always dress up in fifties drag. It wasn't a very positive image [laughs] but we thought it was good fun. Our misspent youth. Sometimes we would do it out of the blue, just for a laugh. I think like a lot of young gay men we wanted to do the ultimate taboo thing that a man can do, and that's to dress up as a woman – but we were never doing it in a derogatory way. To an extent, people would get taken in by the pair of us but then, oh, forget it, because we'd just be such monsters. When we were drunk was the worst period to ever encounter us. Our mouths used to get us into so much trouble.

I must tell you about another period during our politicization. All the time we were dabbling more and more in politics, but we just used to go on demonstrations because it was a good chance to scream and make a noise and squeal. Then Mark went to Bangladesh and he used to write me letters and say it was bad, there was so much poverty. Then he came back and came to my door and he had a shaved head and an orange robe! That was one of the big things about Mark – if he really got into something, he'd become really passionate about it. I couldn't believe it. Oh, my God! He was dabbling with Buddhism as well. You would go into his flat and all you could smell was incense.

Then Mark joined the Young Communist League. For a period we saw less of each other and I wouldn't see him for a while, but then he'd decide that he needed some trash and we'd go out somewhere and wreck the town. Once Mark got into the YCL and calmed down, we saw more of each other and became even closer than before for a short period. I started working on the *Framed Youth* video and, just before that, Mark met Johnny and had become completely engrossed in this relationship. Mark did some interviews for the video but I was working on it all the time and then formed Bronski Beat and all Mark's energies were taken up with the Communist Party. A month or so would pass and then we would just go out. The best thing was sometimes some of the pubs would play really old records at the end, fifties records. We used to practise jiving in each other's house and he used to swing me up and I'd go under his legs. I was never into fifties stuff before I met Mark, and then we used to play nothing but Connie Francis and Brenda Lee.

Johnny Orr: When I first met Mark he'd just been to Bangladesh and he was really brown. He was this wee Portrush man, and really loud. Gorgeous. I was fascinated by him. Both of us just clicked, both of us fancied each other. He was keeping court at Coptic Street one afternoon and it was time for me to go home and I hung about on the stairs and he says, 'Oh, you know, you can stop the night if you want to, if you really want to.'

He talked about Bangladesh. He had got involved with a mission who helped children who had lost their parents. He was really shocked that his parents had a 'boy' around the house and they called him a 'boy', even though he was older than Mark. I was back and forth from France at this time. We sent long letters to each other. By the beginning of '83 I came back to this country and I decided to stop.

I worked in operating theatres in a hospital. Mark was doing as much work as I was, only he was doing it voluntary through Lesbian and Gay Switchboard. It was real love because I used to sit there all night with him through his shift.

Eventually, we got offered a place by the council, down in Deptford, which was the back end of nowhere. But this was our new flat! All we were seeing was each other and all we had was the dole coming in. Well, Deptford didn't last very long. I got offered this flat here at the Elephant and Castle and we jumped at that. It was near everybody we knew. It was near the pubs downtown because we both did go clubbing at that time. Heaven occasionally, Vauxhall Tavern for the tacky drag nights.

We used to go out walking a lot. Just looking at houses and buildings. And we used to go to a lot of jumble sales. That's how we furnished the flat and ourselves.

Mark was always interested in politics. I couldn't understand this when I met him at first because that didn't involve me. I mean, I didn't even vote. What did I want to vote for? It was Mark that got me interested in finding out that politics involved everybody. Politics was how you thought. That was political. Mark was in the YCL at the time. If there was a cause to be fought, Mark was there in the middle of it. And he knew so much about what was going on. What was so great about him was, when he was having an argument with some of the wallies, he had a store of facts up in his head that he could access really easily. Brilliant to watch. He read a hell of a lot. When he was in the CP he found out about jumble sales that they did. Mark used to buy these really heavy-going books and he would get through them. And remember a lot. Books from the thirties that would talk about the rise of Fascism. He was able to argue the case by pulling all these facts out of this storage system he had in his head.

He used to confront all the time, Mark. He managed to get a lot of motions through the YCL, lesbian and gay rights. He put a lot of energy into the YCL and into unpaid work. For about three years Mark didn't have a job with money at the end of the week and he was worried that it would never happen. Then he managed to get this post as secretary of the YCL.

Monty Montgomery: Mark was the first gay man to become general secretary of the YCL and hopefully not the last. It's through his work in those days that certainly the YCL and, to some extent, the Communist Party now have broadened their outlook on sexual politics. He said there were certain people there who thought, 'Damn the sexuality, let's get on with the revolution.' He would never accept that attitude. He just persevered. And he got the amount of respect that he deserved.

II

Lesbians and Gays Support the Miners

You have worn our badge, 'Coal not Dole', and you know what harassment means, as we do. Now we will pin your badge on us, we will support you. It won't change overnight, but now 140,000 miners know that there are other causes and other problems. We know about Blacks, and gays, and nuclear disarmament. And we will never be the same.

David Donovan of the Dulais mining community,
December 1984

Johnny Orr: The miners' strike had been going about three months before Lesbian and Gay Pride '84. Mark and myself and a lot of our mates were out on the march. We picked flags that Mark made us. He was always doing wee things like that. Like when the election was on! The flats we live in are like a big Soviet block that goes the length of the street and it's got a big glass balcony along the edge of it. Well, half-way up this balcony Mark stuck a big V-O-T-E and then LABOUR. He used to go out on the balcony and all the commuters at the Elephant and Castle would all be looking at this huge advertisement in the sky. He used to make all these wee flags when we had demos, and buy whistles and rattles. He was a showman in the middle of it. At Pride that year we all had these pink-triangle flags stuck on the end of bamboo.

Mark brought along a couple of buckets with him. He said he was going to collect for the miners and I said, 'Come on, you're not going to get much money out of this bunch of Heavenites.' Anyway, he was undeterred, grabbed Mike Jackson, said, 'C'mon, chuck, off we go,' and they shook these boxes up and

211

down the march. Lesbians and Gays Support the Miners had started from the time the first 10p. went into the bucket.

Mike Jackson: I first met Mark when I applied to be a volunteer for Lesbian and Gay Switchboard. I was interviewed by Mark and another man. Mark starts asking me what knowledge I have of the London gay scene and I realize after a while that there's a bit of flirting going on here. At one point I just leaned forward and said, 'Is that question relevant to the interview?' at which point he giggled. Mark resigned from Switchboard about two weeks before I started. He'd written this amazing three-page critique in the internal log of some of the more liberal-bourgeois approaches Switchboard had. He also totally graffitied the religious file – it was covered in hammers and sickles and 'Religion is the opium of the masses.' [Laughs.] That was typical Mark. Although at the same time this dear man would occasionally go to church. He himself had lots of contradictions.

About a week or two before Lesbian and Gay Pride '84 Mark said, 'Do you want to take a bucket for the miners?' So we met and the two of us collected something like 150 quid. The '84 Pride March was still when we were having very small marches. I imagine there were no more than 4,000 people on it. In the evening, independent of Mark and myself, Labour Campaign for Lesbian and Gay Rights had organized a rally at University of London Union and invited a miner to speak. There was standing-room only. I remember we were all a bit staggered by how much this man had thought about things, identifying the two struggles. We didn't realize people did think about us that much.

On the strength of the money we collected, the verbal support we got off the marchers and the number of people who attended this rally, Mark said, 'Why don't we organize a meeting?' We put a very small ad in *Capital Gay* asking people to come to his flat and the meeting was a week later, on 15 July. Eleven people turned up. We decided to produce a leaflet that would go out to the lesbian and gay community about the miners and the reason for making a linking with the two struggles. Looking at the minutes here, Mark had already drafted a leaflet, which was accepted with the amendment of the 'one in ten miners is gay' bit [laughs]. Lesbians and Gays Support the Miners was launched. Take it from there. Right at the beginning we'd no idea what our association would be

Mark, January 1981

Mark with the Young Communist League

213

Demonstrating in London, 24 February 1984

with the miners. For me, I'd been very frustrated politically and just got fed up of having to compromise my sexuality for the sake of comradeship with people who wouldn't accept it. Somehow, this clicked in my head. Let's show the miners we support them, which we do anyway, but let's do it as lesbians and gays. I put my heart and soul into it, as did other people.

At the second meeting we decided to support Dulais because one of the people, Hugh Williams, actually came from near there. It was random. We reasoned that we didn't want to send the money to the national fund because we knew we'd have much greater impact concentrating our efforts on a small community. We contacted Dulais, said, 'We have some money for you.' They wrote back: 'Don't send it, we have someone in London, we'll arrange for him to meet you.' This was David Donovan and we met him in the September.

It's quite comical because we actually had to meet him by the zebra crossing outside Paddington station. [Laughs.] We even forgot to ask him what he looked like. Of course Paddington, because that's the way to Wales. I don't know how it works but you just do know who you're looking for. He said, 'Are you Mark Ashton, Mike Jackson, Robert Kincaid? Nice to meet you, boys.' Gave us a great strong handshake and we were nervous as fuck. He just said, 'Shall we go and have a coffee?' And, oh, tears did come to my eyes. This man had really thought it through again. Told us what a desperate plight they were in, how determined they were, though, to win their fight. He must have spent two hours with us and we came away determined to do anything we could. We wanted the world to know. That evening as well we talked David into coming to the Bell to hand over this 200 quid. Mark said, 'We need a camera,' so I took some photographs. We did a press release and it looked good in *Capital Gay*. In fact, Dai wasn't in the NUM – he worked in a coal washery. But he went and spoke on behalf of the miners eloquently and with their complete blessing.

Before we went down to Dulais a month later we had tremendous anxieties about it. It was a bit, like [laughs], this marriage was taking place. The journey took hours and hours. We got lost. We arrived in Dulais in the pitch black at one o'clock in the morning. That particular valley is on the extreme western edge of the South Wales coalfield. We couldn't have picked a more isolated and more settled community. Eventually, we went past this little sign in the road. Dai and his wife had been waiting up. There was Dai and his wife and two kids, four sheepdogs and twenty-seven lesbians and gay men – mostly gay men – all staying under this roof. The next day we all got farmed out to our respective hosts around the valley and met up again in the evening at the Miners' Welfare Hall, otherwise known as the Palace of Culture. It was a little bit tense. We didn't know what people were thinking of us. We didn't know what we thought about them, but a few drinks, a bit of merriment, and people started to loosen up. Andy Den gave a nice little speech. Andy's working class and from Liverpool and he was nervous up there. I do think in situations like that people much more avidly listen to someone who's obviously not a public speaker. Andy hesitated and fumbled, but his speech was short and it was good and the audience just really clapped him. We were just beaming with pride and confidence.

Johnny Orr: The people that we'd stayed with, there was a young brother, nine years old: 'Ooh, you're the gay men!' When we got to the miners' do we couldn't have been treated better. There was one guy who came up and said something quite heavy and these other two guys came up and said, 'What did that guy say, because we'll have him outside if he said anything to upset yous.' Dead protective towards us. I think the most shocking thing for the miners, for the women up there, was that there was some people who wouldn't eat meat. That was more shocking than being a lesbian or a gay man. Vegetarians were the ones who were taken last.

Mike Jackson: We had lots of laughs at home because some people would ask funny questions, but nobody had been offended because it was a genuine human curiosity: 'We have never understood you before. Let us now try to understand you.' There'd be one or two miners and their wives who just couldn't ask questions. They were a bit embarrassed. But we were very much protected from any bad feeling. We only know now, really, after the BBC *Open Space* programme that they interviewed the people we stayed with. Because they have got a confidence in our friendship, and we in theirs, they're now actually saying, 'Of course there was hostility from some quarters and we had to fight that out amongst ourselves.'

Apparently, there were titters and giggles the very first time it was suggested we go down. They had discussions about us and our politics and sexuality before we met them. That was it, and it went on from strength to strength and we had loads of visits and people made personal friends.

Monty Montgomery: The warmth and friendship and solidarity were something I'd never experienced before. They would talk about being gay mostly to do with the way they were being treated by the police: 'Well, we know what you people have been facing for a long time now. When the strike's over, you can rely on us because we will be there when you need us.' That trip certainly made Mark more committed, as it did for everyone who went down on that journey.

Mike Jackson: We obviously had a lot of political fighting to do within our own community. One cry which was always a bit hurtful was, 'Why are you doing all this for the miners? There's people dying of AIDS and the lesbian and gay community needs support.' For a start, a lot of people in LGSM did lots of things for the community anyway. We didn't support the miners with regard to whether they supported us or not. We supported them because we were socialists, but we were wanting to be 'out' to them and we hoped there would be a dialogue. By the time '85 Pride came, we wanted to show to people that the miners did care about us. Real links were made. So we asked the miners to come and march and they did. And they brought the lodge banner and people started gathering around us. I could hear the whispering, 'It's the miners!' There were so many people gathered around the miners' and our banner, that one of the organizers came running up and said, 'We have to have you at the front.' And we'd asked the Big Red Band to join our section. The pride and that was just wonderful. We'd made 100 red flags to carry with us.

Johnny Orr: Lesbians and Gays Support the Miners was written up in the *Sun*: 'There's a group of perverts now supporting the pits.' So we had a big do called Pits and Perverts. This was held in the Electric ballroom to which Bronski Beat were our big pull. We raised thousands at that. It was brilliant and through that we managed to get a mini bus for the mining community of Dulais

Valley. This wee mini bus. I mean, four years later they were talking about this mini bus. It got really battered. A white bus with a big pink triangle on the side saying 'Lesbians and Gays Support the Miners'. You can imagine this wee bus running through all these tiny towns in Wales. Lesbians and gay men. It was outrageous.

III

Ashtar Alkhirsan: I first met Mark in the reception area at the Labour Party headquarters. I'd started work at Red Wedge and, on my second day, someone called up that there was a chap that had come to deliver something. I'd never really come into contact with any 'out' lesbians and gays, and I'm straight. He was standing in the foyer and I thought to myself, 'He won't want everyone to know he's gay.' So I said, 'Are you the chap that's come about the [whispers] Gay Rights leaflet?' And he just looked at me and it was ridiculous because he had a pair of little pink socks on and a skimpy pair of cut-off denims. I got on with him really well and managed to persuade him to do some voluntary work for Red Wedge. After that, I'd see him practically every day. After a while, I started living with him. From the first day I met Mark he was ill.

There were lots of things he wanted to do, he'd liked to have stood for local council. He was very involved in the Tenants' Association. I remember at Christmas they brought round five turkeys that Mark carved up. It took him about four hours to do it, and then he served it all up for them. That was the politics he believed in – social action. His politics did spill over into every minute of the day. Quite often I'd come home and Mark would be on the phone to the *Sun*, screaming at the news desk. Three days before he went into hospital he was at Wapping on the picket line. He would always talk to people and he would be able to spot a communist a mile off. On our way to Sheffield once, Mark managed to get involved in a conversation with a guy from the Indian Communist Party – we spent the entire journey talking to this bloke.

Johnny Orr: Mark never told me he was ill, that he was HIV-positive, until I went up to Guy's and then he told me that he'd got full-blown AIDS. Fucking hell, that was mega-shock. He'd had a chesty cough, although he'd given up cigarettes and was trying to lead a healthy, well-balanced lifestyle. Mark was always a hypochondriac! I didn't think he was really ill. What, what, what, what? I think he didn't tell anyone who was close to him that he was HIV-positive. With me, that was probably one of his ways of not putting pressure on me to make a choice between him and Kevin. Me and Mark was dead close. We were no longer having a sexual relationship but we had our own bedrooms and when I was up here Mark used to sleep with me. I think he used to sleep in my room even when I wasn't here. We had all the emotional bit, all the chat. I had said to Mark that I was going to be monogamous from now on with Kevin. When me and Mark were lovers, in those years, people used to have non-monogamous relationships. That was the done thing. I've changed since then. I realized that you don't just go home with somebody. You do that once, but the second time it's not somebody unknown. It gets a bit more and that's what happened with me and Kevin.

When Mark told me in the hospital that they'd come back with the tests and he had AIDS, I cracked up. I stayed with him from then on. I used to stay overnight on a couch, so I was lying right up against the bed. We used to lie there holding hands and chatting and watching the bloody box. We both used to stay awake through the night, because he had night sweats. The nurses let me do all Mark's nursing. The first day he was in hospital, I went out to demand a television. The room was wallpapered with cards and by the day all these bloody bunches of flowers arrived. I asked Mark, 'Is there anything I can bring you? A nice blanket off your bed or something?' I didn't understand why he was worried because I was convinced he was going to get better. After the third day he asked me to ring his mum and dad and tell them he was ill but that he was going to be fine. He wanted to keep her and his father away from the hospital because he thought he would feel guilt-ridden about having this horrible disease. It has a stigma attached to it. A few days later his mother appeared on the scene: 'Johnny, I'm here.' She was brilliant. So good. She understood everything.

He was only in hospital a week before he died.

Jimmy Somerville: I still haven't really reacted to Mark's death.

That's fine if you're like that for a couple of months, but it's still the same. It's almost as if it never happened. I think it's got a lot to do with the situation I was in. We were in Spain doing some promotional TV. I'd seen him in hospital before I went away and we were under the impression that he was getting better. I was in the middle of a rehearsal when someone telephoned to tell us that he'd died. I was actually singing [pause], we were doing, 'Don't Leave Me This Way'. There were all these Spanish kids laughing and jumping around. I couldn't react really because it was such a surreal situation. I wasn't there. I just felt so lost because I was nae there.

Johnny Orr: Mark wanted the red flag over his coffin. This wasn't to be, although we managed to get it in through the back door. I bought a huge big bunch of flowers and tied a red flag round them that he had up in his bedroom. The funeral was over so quick. You know, it was, like, three minutes. Three minutes. This young man had made so much noise in his life and in three minutes it was finished.

Afterwards, we had a wake in the house. This was wall to wall with people who knew Mark getting together with a lot of drink, a lot of wailing and crying and reminiscing. We also had a memorial event at the Tabernacle. It wasn't dour, it wasn't sad or solemn. If it had been any one of us that had died, Mark would have had a nationwide fund-raising thing and consciousness-raising about AIDS, so after the memorial we started the Mark Ashton Trust.

Ashtar Alkhirsan: The original idea behind the trust was to provide people with basic amenities, to make sure they didn't have to worry about paying their bills if they were ill. Or if they were ill at home and didn't have a washing-machine. Ours is a drop in the ocean. Some of the cases we have received are really dreadful. One bloke's flat was so cold he had to sleep in the kitchen on a makeshift bed. Another bloke, he was incontinent and he didn't have any money to buy new sheets. He needed a new bed and the local authority wouldn't give him any money. They actually wrote and asked us for the money. People shouldn't have to go through this. Straight opposite our balcony here they had one of those AIDS posters and I remember both of us seeing it every morning.

But even if safe sex or condoms are a feature of people's lives now, the fact that so many people have died so far isn't. People are still dying and there's little sympathy for them. Obviously it's because they are gay men.

Jimmy Somerville: We talk about Mark, but at the same time we don't. I don't think anybody's said this, but I think it's because we all know that one of our friends are going next. When, who, how, we don't know. I think we are secretly privately saying, 'Keep something for the next one.' Your approach to death becomes completely different to what it would have been before, if there hadn't been AIDS. This probably sounds ridiculous, but you incorporate death into your life like waking up in the morning and washing your face.

I was really angry when Mark died because you were so scared about expressing your grief, you were so scared about what people thought, 'Oh, just another queer who's got AIDS and died.' That's why we done 'For a Friend', because it's just so awful the way the gutter press deal with AIDS. They don't see these people as having friends, as having family. They just see them as another scandal, another shock story. Nobody wanted to do anything about the sad side of it, the emotional side of it. One review in the *Record Mirror* was, 'Oh, here we have another AIDS record.' The record industry won't deal with AIDS. Most people who appeared on the Nelson Mandela Birthday Party were all asked to do International AIDS Day and most of them were saying, 'Too busy.'

IV

Ashtar Alkhirsan: Mark reached a really wide section of people. There's one thing he did which was so brilliant. My sister [long pause] came up to London to stay. She and Mark had never met. Of course, as soon as he saw her – she's a seventeen-year-old hairdresser from Weymouth and she turned up in a pair of slingbacks and a knitted two-piece – they got on incredibly well. My sister just adored him. They talked and talked and he taught her how to play the Marxist version of Monopoly. She went back to Weymouth with such a positive image of what a gay person is! [Weeps.]

He made me realize that being active politically was important. For a long time I didn't really think it was. I've done a lot of work on Clause 28 and I follow it very closely. It's become a big part of my life. It's, like, because Mark's dead, there's one less voice. There's one less person on the marches now, so I go along there because I think I can take that one place. I find it a great comfort being here in the flat. All I've got is good memories. I've changed the flat but we haven't been able to bring ourselves to get rid of his clothes and everything.

Jimmy Somerville: When Mark and I met it was almost like we needed each other to grow and expand and discover everything. At that time I think we were too much for other people to cope with. Both of us bit our nails, we would just chew them to bits [laughs]. Both of us sat at a table and everything would shake, we had so much hyperactivity between the two of us.

When Mark died I didn't want to be sad about him because there were so many things about him which were so wonderful. And he could be a nasty, selfish queen sometimes. That's a good way of dealing with it. The other thing is I like to think is that when Mark died he was just going to sleep one night and he says, 'I think I won't wake up. I can just imagine them, they'll all be running around screaming and squealing. Because it won't be the same twice round or three times round.' Because he was the first it was such a shock to us. And you just feel, another first! He had to do it first. I always think that. I makes me deal with it a bit better.

Monty Montgomery: Mark was certainly someone that anybody whose life he touched will never, ever forget him. The world is a sadder place because he's not here. I don't know, it's hard to explain it. He gave me the encouragement to pull myself out of the seventies and get myself going. That if you'd just go out and have a go – something would come of it.

Mike Jackson: I'll never forget Mark. He has made a tremendous impression on my life. That passion and that belief. He was always such a big person, involved in so many people's lives. At his memorial there were banners all round: Caribbean groups, Anti-Apartheid, anti-nuclear, community groups, the Communist

Party, LGSM . . . I'm sure he would have been immensely proud to have seen them, because he loved razzmatazz.

When I was trying to get a relationship together with my lover, Steve, Mark said to me, 'It all depends on material circumstances.' I think what he meant was, 'If you love the guy, don't just tell him; don't show him symbols; show him it; do it.' That's Mark's politics, isn't it? You don't sloganize, you do things.

Johnny Orr: Mark was a stable; something that was always there. [Weeps.] We used to say we'd go down and collect our pensions together, still arguing the point all the way, because we used to argue like cat and dog. I've got used to coming home now. It's mine and Ashtar's; it's not mine and Mark's. Mark made a hell of an impression in my life. The good thing for me, what I've learned from Mark, is that politics involves us all. That what goes on in the news is important and does involve us. [Laughs.] It is important to vote, and to use anybody else's vote you can as well. I used Mark's vote after he died.

Jimmy Somerville: I remember Mark running round at Pits and Perverts, organizing everyone. I used to love it when Mark got excited about something – he just used to glow, you could just see the passion radiate. I felt so chuffed with him. LGSM, I think that was the greatest thing any of my friends could have done. He really achieved something really fab.

This chapter was edited by Margot Farnham.

1988. Portrait by William Pierce

KYRIACOS SPYROU

INTERVIEWED IN MARCH 1988 BY PAUL MARSHALL

My parents are both from Cyprus. My mother is from a farming family and until she left home, that was all she knew. She can't read or write. Her family consisted of six daughters and one son. My grandfather couldn't afford dowries for all the daughters, so he sent my mum and two of her sisters over to England to find their fortune. My father is quite well educated, by Cypriot standards. They both came over here in the fifties, but not together – they hadn't met by then. My dad became a postman and my mum learnt how to use the sewing-machine and became a seamstress. For years she lived in a house with three families. Money was really short but by scrimping and saving she built up a dowry. My parents met in 1960. It was an arranged marriage. They had my sister about a year later and, after a five year gap, I was born in Plaistow, London, on 3 July 1966.

My parents were led to believe that the streets of London were paved with gold. In Cyprus you would either become a farmer or, if you were rich enough to have a good education, you'd become a doctor; there was nothing in between the two. They came over here expecting to earn lots of money, but they didn't. I think that they were quite shocked at the discrimination they faced – especially my father, because he could understand English and knew what people were calling him. After independence from the British in '56, there was still a feeling that they were our allies and my parents thought they would come over here and be looked after. Over the years there grew to be quite a bit of resentment amongst my family towards the British people because of the way they were treated.

My mum and dad lived in Haringey for some years; in the late fifties and early sixties it was very much a Greek ghetto. My mother's always mixed with Greek people and that's partly why she's never picked up the English language. Until I went to school I couldn't speak English because I wasn't allowed out to play with the other kids and my parents only spoke Greek to me. My parents had to go into the school and were told off for not teaching me the language, since it meant I was very much behind. But I picked it up.

From what I can remember, my infants and junior school years were great. There were kids from all different backgrounds – a lot of Black people, Asians and lots of Cypriots. This was in Plaistow. Once I'd gone to school I was allowed to play out in the street and have my own friends. By this time my parents had a fish and chip shop in Upton Park, so I was looked after by a childminder most of the time and I liked that because I was mixing with other kids. My aunts lived with us and when they came home from work they'd look after me and my sister whilst my parents were at the 'chippie'.

Ever since I can remember, I've always been attracted to boys in a really nice, innocent way. At junior school I never thought there was anything wrong in it. It was only when we moved to Essex and I went to secondary school and people started saying things that I realized that other people thought it was really bad. It was then that I started feeling depressed and isolated. I started to feel very paranoid about getting too close to the boys in my school in case they sussed that I had these feelings, so most of my friends were girls.

Also at about this time, I realized that there were certain aspects of my culture that I didn't like, so I totally rejected it. I refused to be called by my proper name and chose an English name; I refused to speak Greek at home or listen to any Greek music and just caused a general stink about it all. A lot of it was seeing my dad's outlook on life. My dad sat me down at the age of eleven to tell me the facts of life and basically said, 'If a woman's got a hole, you cork it up.' That was his sex lesson and it wasn't at all what had been going on in my head. Seeing the way he treated my mother, and the way women were generally treated in our community, gradually made me think that this wasn't how I felt. Also the men in our community were very, very macho and I knew I couldn't live up to that. If people ever discovered what I

226

really was then I'd get rejected anyway by the community, so I felt I should reject it before they had the chance to reject me.

When I was fourteen I was looking through a magazine in the newsagents and there were things in it about gay men and I gathered that this was what I was supposed to be. I was confused because the impression I had been given of gay men were the archetypal stereotypes, like John Inman and Larry Grayson, and I couldn't relate to them so I wasn't sure if I was gay or not. I knew what my feelings were saying but I couldn't identify with those images I'd been given. There were contact numbers in this magazine so I rang up Gay Switchboard and they gave me a number of the Gay Teenage Group. They told me that I was too young to join – you had to be over sixteen – but I looked old enough, so I lied about my age and went along and that's how I began coming to terms with myself. I was petrified when I first went. I didn't know what to expect but they offered me a lot of support. Yet there were a lot of things going round in my head about my family which I felt they wouldn't necessarily understand, being from different communities; but it was nice meeting people my own age. Also around this time I went to a pub in Euston. I remember it was Hallowe'en night and it was my first pub and I was totally bowled over, actually seeing a room full of men dancing together and holding hands and knowing that I could actually look at someone and not be frightened of being beaten up. For the first time I was seeing something that explained exactly how I felt. It wasn't all stereotypes and there were people there from all different walks of life. It was an amazing night, it really was, knowing that there were places I could go and meet people the same as me.

I was still very rebellious around my community and I'd also got involved in punk music and dressing like it. It was a way of saying to my family that I was different from other Greek boys, but I didn't feel articulate or strong enough to say that I was gay, so I was trying to express myself through a style, a fashion. It was rare for Greek boys to have their ears pierced but I did and I had my nose pierced as well – so they were more worried about how embarrassing I looked than wondering about whether I was gay or not.

I'd met another young bloke at the Gay Teenage Group and we began having a relationship. He stupidly left a diary lying around with my name and phone number in it and his mother read it. Not realizing that we were both new to the whole thing, she thought I was corrupting him and I got the blame. She rang my father and he hit the roof, for two reasons. My father's an incredible racist and the bloke was from Trinidad, so not only was I having an affair with a man, but with a Black man – and that made it totally unacceptable.

When this happened we were due to go to Cyprus for a holiday to visit my relatives, so my dad took the opportunity to try and marry me off in Cyprus. I was sixteen. It frightened me because he was adamant that I wasn't going to leave Cyprus until I'd at least got engaged. The only way I found to get out the situation was to be totally embarrassing to him. Whenever he brought a young woman and her family to meet me I'd say, 'Look, you're very nice but, I'm sorry, I'm not interested in women.' He was so embarrassed he brought me back to London. He thought that the only other alternative was to sell up and move to a different part of the country because he was sure that my being gay was the influence of the people around me. He gave me an ultimatum that if I didn't prove to him that I was heterosexual within three months, then I'd have to leave home. I wasn't going to backtrack and I wasn't going to lie to him. I said to him, 'Look, I'm gay and I'm not going to change.' He thought it was a choice I'd made and I hadn't tried to be heterosexual. So when I was seventeen I left home.

I went and lived in a squat in Battersea with a man I was having a relationship with and then we rented a flat in Leyton. He was also seventeen, an ex-rent boy and a drug addict. He was on heroin and it was a very traumatic, difficult time for me because not only had I to become independent myself, but I also had to help him. I was totally in love with him but it was hell for about a year. He was prostituting himself to pay for his habit and I had to look after him when he was sick. He left one day and went back to Newcastle. I'm now very grateful that he did leave because I felt I was getting dragged down with him. That period made me grow up a hell of a lot.

I would ring my parents and tell them I was all right but I wouldn't tell them where I was, because it was important for me to gain independence. Maria, my sister, was very supportive because she'd had her own battles with them. My mother knew that me and my dad had rowed but she wasn't sure why, no one ever told her. She's been mentally ill for quite a few years. She'd always wonder what had happened but she'd been too frightened of my father to ask. Nearly three years ago my parents split up and are now divorced. When she was on her own I felt I could tell her and she's been incredibly understanding and supportive. She didn't have an education and she can't understand English, so she doesn't acknowledge that there is prejudice against me and so has never taken on that prejudice herself. She doesn't see anything nasty about it because she's never been told any bad things about being gay. She just sees it as love – as long as it's love, that's nice: as long as he loves someone and someone loves him.

I was on the dole for quite a while after I left home, then some people from ILEA got in touch with me through the Gay Teenage Group. They wanted to do a lesbian and gay youth video called *First Feelings*, in which two lesbians and two gay men talk about coming out. I worked with them for about a year-and-a-half, going round schools and colleges talking to sixth formers about what it's like being gay.

I got a lot of negative response from the school kids but also some really positive reactions. Some really stuck their necks out when their friends were saying that they didn't like 'poofs'. They'd say, 'Hold on, he's OK, give him a chance.' Just by walking into a room in a jacket and jeans and a pair of boots I broke the stereotype instantly, because a lot of them still thought I'd walk in with stilettos and a handbag. Once, I sat in the common room with them and they kept saying, ''Ere, we've got a poof coming to give us a talk today.' They assumed I was just a new pupil and then the teacher came in and introduced me and they were shocked, so it was an instant breakdown of the stereotype. It was good to work like that and I really enjoyed it.

I was going out a lot at this time and drinking quite heavily. I went to lots of pubs and clubs, the Asylum at Heaven on Thursday nights, the Bell at King's Cross, the Black Cap in Camden Town – you name it, I went there. I was out every night of the week because I didn't want to be in the flat on my own, there were too many memories of the bloke from Newcastle. I'd go out with friends sometimes, but mostly on my own; I'd get totally wrecked and go home again. I had quite a lot of casual sex but

Aged 3

Kyriacos and his sister on a demonstration in Haringey organized by
'Positive Images'

I was also very cautious and careful about who I went home with, because when I was younger I'd met someone who turned nasty on me half-way through the night. He was a punk and he had handcuffs and chains and stuff and I thought it was all part of the get-up, but when we got home it wasn't. He forced me to have anal intercourse. He was very rough with me and I had to go to hospital. That made me very wary of going with just anyone. So I'd have casual sex but only up to a point. I'd only do certain things with men because of that past experience and I never wanted to take part in anal sex.

I met someone who moved in with me and who was in love with me but I didn't love him. We were together for a year and it was quite stormy. One morning I woke up and said that I wanted out, but with no explanation. I treated him badly but it was unintentional; it was just that I'd met him at the wrong time and was with him for the wrong reasons. I was feeling very low and lonely when I met him and I was still screwed up over the bloke from Newcastle, so I ended up hurting him which I never really wanted to do.

I became very conscious of AIDS when I was having a relationship with a bloke that I wasn't in love with. I was monogamous out of respect for him, really, but when we split up I actually thought about being careful about who I slept with and I've practised safe sex ever since. I feel quite good about that and I've also been vaccinated against hepatitis.

I got involved with another ILEA project, a photography course for young lesbians and gays. The end result was like a photo love story but with coming out as the theme. I really enjoyed doing that. Then I enrolled at Walthamstow Tech. to do fashion, but I found the people really homophobic. Just because they were into fashion it didn't mean to say they were broadminded and, because I was used to being 'out' at this stage, I couldn't tolerate going back into the closet again. So I left and went back on the dole.

I started working with a friend of mine doing 'one-nighters' at the Scala cinema and arranging warehouse parties around London Bridge and in a disused bus station at King's Cross. I used to help with the publicity and guest lists and sort out the PA system and decorations. I enjoyed it because it was a nice crowd of people and the money was good.

In '86 I got a job with Haringey Youth Service as a lesbian and

231

gay youth development worker. Basically, the job required looking into the needs of young lesbians and gays in the borough by building up a network of young people and holding events and discussion groups. The aim was to get enough support and to compile enough reports to stress to the council the need for a centre for young lesbians and gays. Unfortunately, the project was shut down through lack of funds when the council got into a financial crisis, but straight after that I got a job with Haringey Lesbian and Gay Unit.

The Parents' Rights Group was very strong in Haringey at that time and still are. They're made up of a lot of right-wing English people who play on the naïvety of parents from different communities and whip all this hatred and anger against us with the help of the media. Some of them are councillors and some are well-known ex-members of the National Front who are also involved in the hate campaign against Broadwater Farm estate. They will latch on to anything that seems a bit dodgy in their eyes. They used to attack anti-racist awareness campaigns and now they attack the Positive Images campaign for lesbians and gay men.

We held an event for young lesbians and gays who were under twenty-five and a woman from the Parents' Rights Group wanted to come in and see what was showing. We asked her to leave the premises, since she was neither lesbian nor under twenty-five. She said she was concerned about a video we were showing called *How to be a lesbian in thirty-five minutes*, which was badly titled since it was about young lesbians talking about their experiences and coming to terms with their sexuality and their families' reactions. It was a totally innocent video. We told the woman to ring us on the following Monday if she wanted to discuss the matter and we would even arrange a showing of the video for her to prove that nothing underhand had gone on.

She left peacefully, but on Monday we got a phone call from her, wanting to know my full name because she claimed that I had punched and kicked her. I then got a summons to appear in court on an assault charge. In court she claimed that she had been pregnant and miscarried because I'd attacked her. When they asked me to stand up and be identified as the accused, she mumbled, 'I can't go through with this.' The Reverend Rushworth Smith was with her. (Rushworth Smith went on a hunger strike in an attempt to force Haringey council to drop the Positive Images campaign. He was unsuccessful.) There was no evidence that she had been beaten up nor that she had been pregnant, so the case was thrown out of court. The whole thing had been a total set-up. Even though I was innocent, my name was still printed all over the gutter press. I was angry that I was never able to make a statement to clear my name because, as council employees, we're not allowed to talk to the press but the council made no attempt to clear my name either.

The whole thing made me very paranoid and very frightened of walking out alone. I've been threatened with physical violence. They tried to get a photograph of me as we left the court but, luckily, we left through a back entrance. We've had a lot of hate mail at work. The council have destroyed all evidence of our home addresses to protect us. It was the Parents' Rights Group that got in touch with David Wilshire and Dame Jill Knight which helped along Clause 28 [now Section 28].

With help from the Committee for Free Britain, the group are now targeting their anger at Reading Matters bookshop, which is partly council funded and sells anti-racist, anti-sexist and lesbian and gay books. The shop has also received anonymous hate letters and bomb threats. It's part of the backlash against lesbians and gays and with Section 28 they're taking away from us what little freedom we have. It frightens me that Britain is turning so right wing.

We had a march in Haringey, organized by Positive Images in conjunction with the Broadwater Farm Youth Association. Smash the Backlash was very big, very proud and very successful, with over 3,500 people walking through the streets of Wood Green Shopping City and down Lordship Lane, protesting about the backlash against lesbians, gays and Black people. We were shouted at and called perverts and AIDS-carriers but it didn't turn nasty until we reached the park, where the police arrested some people for obstruction.

I was a steward on the Clause 28 march in London in January and 12,000 people turned up. It got really nasty at Downing Street and there was quite a bit of violence. From then onwards the police were very aggressive and when we reached the park for the rally they totally lost their temper. They were swearing at stewards and there were police on horseback with riot shields not allowing people to leave the park. By contrast, the police kept a very low profile on the Manchester anti-Clause 28 demonstration [20 February 1988] so there was no trouble and no arrests. It was the biggest lesbian and gay march we've ever had in this country and it completely took Manchester by storm, the place was at a standstill.

I moved from the flat in Leyton to where I'm living now because it had too many memories. The lover I had from Newcastle came down to see me for the first time in three years, then he went back to Newcastle, where he died. I realized then that I had to forget the past and that included moving out of the place where we had lived together. Ever since leaving home I've always wanted a place of my own. I've got a partner now and we spend a lot of time together, but he's got his place and I've got mine. I now really value my own space and my own time.

I got a phone call from my dad after the court case, and he said, 'How dare you embarrass the family like this?' That caused a bigger rift. I don't see my father now. He wants nothing to do with me and that's because he sees me as being a failure and not being a real man. There's a big fallacy that because homosexuality happens frequently in Cyprus, then it is accepted, but it only occurs because the men are not allowed to touch the women until they marry. If there's someone that's either slightly effeminate or seen to be weak, the men have sex with them; but as long as they're the dominant ones, they're still the men – they never consider themselves to be gay. It's not acceptable at all if you are the passive one.

I go back to Cyprus a lot and now I feel quite positive about it because there are a lot of nice things about the culture, such as the food, drink and the music and also the extended family. If you're in trouble there is always some member of the family to look after you or help you out. That can have negative aspects, though; for instance, when I came out as being gay, my uncle and older cousins all got involved in this big discussion about my life. That sort of thing can be quite suffocating, but the support network can be a very positive thing. Also, people are very open with their affections in Cyprus. The men hug and kiss each other and are very friendly and hospitable so I try and focus on the positive aspects of the culture.

I feel confident about my sexuality, so I've written articles in the Cypriot newspaper about being gay and I've started a Cypriot Lesbian and Gay Group. I feel good about that. In Cyprus homosexuality is still illegal, so I hope they don't find out about my activities because the next time I go there I could be arrested. The reactions here have been varied. Some people are really supportive but, with others, it's sheer hate. I've had a lot of hate mail at work, saying that I have brought shame on my community, that I'm breaking it down after they've spent years building up a respectable community. It saddens me but it also makes me feel stronger, more determined to open up things that they don't want to talk about, because it's something that's happening and something they've got to acknowledge. People are ringing up the Cypriot Lesbian and Gay Group all the time. I don't want people to go through what I went through with my family – that's why we've built up a support network.

Whatever I do, I'll never be able to prove to my father that I'm a man and worthy of his respect. Nothing I do will be valued by him, because I am gay, but it makes me more determined that one day we're going to get somewhere and that it's going to be talked about and begin to be accepted.

POSTSCRIPT BY KYRIACOS SPYROU, OCTOBER 1988

Since this interview, Section 28 has become law. At work we're all waiting for the first court case to be announced. I'm afraid the new law has already begun to affect my work, since I constantly have to stress, in committee reports, that I'm trying to redress the imbalance and discrimination faced by lesbians and gays, not 'promoting' homosexuality. The word 'promotion' has become really contentious.

My personal life has been getting better and better. I'm incredibly happy with my partner. This is mainly due to the type of person he is. We talk a lot and he knows all about me, so realizes why certain things may upset me. I feel very stable within myself, which I feel he's responsible for, and for the first time I've met someone who is interested in my culture and wants to learn more about it.

INDEX